Consuming Confessions

Consuming Confessions

The Quest for
Self-Discovery,
Intimacy,
and Redemption

Sharon Hymer, Ph.D.

Hazelden
Center City, Minnesota 55012-0176
1-800-328-0098 (Toll Free U.S., Canada, and the Virgin Islands)
1-612-257-4010 (Outside the U.S. and Canada)
1-612-257-1331 (24-hour FAX)
http://www.hazelden.org (World Wide Web site on Internet)

00 99 98 97 96   6 5 4 3 2 1

Library of Congress Cataloging-in-Publication Data
Hymer, Sharon.
    Consuming confessions : the quest for self-discovery, intimacy, and
redemption / Sharon Hymer.
        p.   cm.
    Includes bibliographical references.
    ISBN 1–56838–118–2
    1. Self-actualization (Psychology)   2. Confession.   3. Redemption.
I. Title.
BF637.S4H95   1996
155.2′5—dc20
                                                                                96–24985
                                                                                CIP

Book design by Will H. Powers
Typesetting by Stanton Publication Services, Inc.
Cover design by David Spohn

Editor's note
Hazelden offers a variety of information on chemical dependency and related areas. Our publications do not necessarily represent Hazelden's programs, nor do they officially speak for any Twelve Step organization.

All the stories in this book are based on actual experiences. The names and details have been changed to protect the privacy of the people involved. In some cases, composites have been created.

The following publishers have generously given permission to use material from copyrighted works: From *The Complete Poems of Emily Dickinson* by T. H. Johnson. Copyright 1929 by Martha Dickinson Bianchi; copyright © renewed 1957 by Mary L. Hampson. By permission of Little, Brown and Company. "Healing" by D. H. Lawrence, from *The Complete Poems of D. H. Lawrence* by D. H. Lawrence, edited by V. de Sola Pinto and F. W. Roberts. Copyright © 1964, 1971, by Angelo Ravagli and C. M. Weekley, Executors of the Estate of Frieda Lawrence Ravagli. Used by permission of Viking Penguin, a division of Penguin Books USA Inc. From *Who's Afraid of Virginia Woolf?* by Edward Albee. Copyright 1962 by Edward Albee. Reprinted with the permission of Scribner, a Division of Simon & Schuster.

To my best, beloved confidant, Steve

Contents

Acknowledgments

Consuming Confessions took me on a personal and professional odyssey. I am indebted to several people for their expertise, support, and encouragement along the way. John Ratti, my "manuscript mender" and friend, provided advice, a discerning editorial eye, and good humor at just the right moments. I thank Natasha Brightman, Janet Heetner, and Mary Cargill for their helpfulness as resource guides. Father Raymond Daley, Father Arthur Pappas, and Rabbi Dov Lerea made religious confessions come alive through their stimulating presentations. Gilbert Hymer's erudition provided a treasure trove for literary illustrations. Special thanks go to my publisher, Dan Odegard, and to my editor, Betty Christiansen, who have treated this project with tireless dedication and loving care. This book owes its life to the faith and perseverance of my agent, Carol Mann. My patients are an unending source of inspiration. Much of what I have gleaned about confessions I owe to them. Finally, my husband, Steven Goldberg, through his constructive suggestions, wit, friendship, and love, brightened my days and nights.

Consuming Confessions

Prologue

The Changing Face of Confession

ONFESSION FULFILLS a spiritual hunger in us. It allows us to achieve intimacy with others and, thereby, to realize that we are no longer isolated and alone. *Consuming Confessions* examines our need to contact the dark recesses of our souls in order to find redemption.

One of the reasons people like confessional groups, especially programs like Alcoholics Anonymous, is that they can identify with the stories other members tell and can see, dimly at first, a spiritual side to the gritty, familiar, sometimes awful world we all live in. Our own secrets, ordeals, and sufferings gain meaning and dignity when we see that we share them with other people. We can discern that some people have actually begun to find their way out of the spider's web of secrets and deceit we are all capable of weaving.

As a therapist, friend, and family member, I have been privileged to be both the recipient and the discloser of many meaningful secrets during my life. The following pages present what I have learned—that confession is a special gift to ourselves and others that enriches and transforms our lives. *Consuming Confessions* explores our universal need to confess in order to move from isolation to intimacy. It shows how confession is a way for us to express and celebrate our authentic natures.

Part 1—The Confessional Journey—depicts confession as an ongoing process rather than a onetime venture. The journey, beginning with risk, frequently ends in redemption. We become integrated, whole beings in the process. Part 2—Confessions from the Cradle to the Grave—explores how confessions emerge in childhood and change over the life cycle. Ethical dilemmas posed by the issue "to tell or not to tell" force us to look beyond ourselves to determine when disclosure poses a threat to the larger community. Part 3—Healing the Self; Healing Relationships with Others—highlights the healing power of coming to terms with hidden parts of ourselves and sharing our vulnerabilities with others in order to strengthen the bonds of intimacy and trust. It explores how, ultimately, confession empowers us to change our lives and find redemption.

Confessional Consumers

The title *Consuming Confessions* came to me when I realized that we have become a society of confessional consumers. Our need to devour confessions is barely matched by the onslaught of TV programs and media events devoted to baring ever more lurid, eye-popping, ear-stretching secrets.

Many people are "confessional addicts." The more outlandish the secrets they hear, the greater becomes their tolerance of even more dark and bizarre secrets. And the larger the doses of tabloid and TV exposés parading as news, the more the addict craves. The very popularity of talk shows attests to the rapacious appetite for confession.

The crass commercialism, intense competition for guests and ratings, and the sheer "entertainment" aspects of these shows cast serious doubt on the disclosers' sincerity and authenticity. Guests can be motivated by greed, by exhibitionistic needs to achieve Warhol's "fifteen minutes of fame," or even by an overwhelming desire to receive attention at any cost.

Talk shows offer a stripped-down, commercialized caricature of confession. Gone is the vital spiritual aspect, the bond created when only a chosen few hear our secrets, the soul-to-soul communion in which the confidant helps us deal with—not simply spill out—our secrets.

Many media critics and public interest groups resent that the significant social problems of our time—teenage pregnancy, AIDS, racism, addiction, and so on—are not aired unless they have a titillating angle (e.g., "I became pregnant through incest"). These groups, along with Congress, have begun to put pressure on the producers of these programs to tone down their more violent and inciteful programming.

Examples such as this suggest that, as a society, we are experiencing a radical change in how we consume confessions. Rather than being treated as mass-culture commodities, confessions are again becoming precious treasures to be shared selectively and treated with reverence. Spirituality in America has grown steadily, evidenced by increased attendance at conferences and workshops devoted to spiritual concerns, high levels of participation in various spirituality movements, and the soaring sales of books that focus on psychological and spiritual growth. The various spiritual approaches emphasize disclosure as an integral aspect of healing and redemption. In this changing period, traditional confessors—priests and therapists—are and will continue to be even more important. As lay confessors such as self-help groups, teachers, parents, and friends become more prevalent in our society, they will be more knowledgeable and concerned about their roles as both good listeners and discriminating disclosers.

We also do not want to be consumed by our confessions. As we obsessively weigh the dangers of disclosure against the dangers of concealment, we become prisoners of our own secrets. *Consuming Confessions* sets us on a confessional journey that frees us from an endless cycle of worry and indecision.

As confessional consumers, we need to find a level of consumption that is satisfying, but not addictive. Confession—consumed as well as disclosed in balanced fashion—should nourish the spirit and add meaning to our lives.

The Price of Confessing

The range of confessors available to us in the twentieth century has greatly expanded. Ironically, the closer we are to potential confessors such as friends, parents, and lovers, the larger loom the repercussions of disclosure, such as abandonment, blackmail, and loss of love. For those of us who fear that confession will actually alienate us from intimates rather than strengthen an existing bond, we may opt for the quick-fix approach of a one-shot revelation to a cab driver or a stranger on our travels. "Familiar strangers" such as neighborhood hairdressers and bartenders, situated midway between high-risk lovers and no-risk strangers, provide us with a sense of acceptance without obligation or commitment.

Regardless of whom we choose to hear our confession, our secret—whatever it is—loses its obsessive grip on us when we share it. The risk we take in confessing is the price we pay for redemption, but it is not the only price. In confessing, we may also destroy an old aspect of ourselves while simultaneously experiencing a rebirth, the emergence of a new identity.

The historian of religion Mircea Eliade suggests that during initiation rites or other rites of passage, we witness the metaphoric death of an old, inadequate self in order to experience rebirth on a higher level of existence. Traditionally, specific rituals such as all forms of puberty initiation involved the revelation of secrets and sacred knowledge allowing the initiate to become part of the tribal community. Eliade maintains that in contemporary society, we find this spiritual meaning in our lives through the help of small groups. Here, rebirth involves reorganizing our self-image, rather than re-creating it. In AA, for example, the old self that has "hit rock bottom" may be revitalized as it finds a life with purpose and meaning. There can be no major renewal without some kind of psychic death, no new start without letting go of outmoded or self-destructive aspects of ourselves.

Confessing—facing ourselves squarely and sincerely and expressing that truth to others—fulfills our deep need to undergo the heroic task of stripping away layers of self-deception, of coming to terms with our secrets, and of creating a new self for the changing meaning and circumstances of our lives. Psychoanalyst Carl Jung was fascinated with the heroic and religious as well as the demonic in us. Psychotherapy can be seen as a form of psychological as well as spiritual initiation in which the patient embarks on a journey in search of meaning, with the therapist as guide. On this quest, old selves are shed, old relationships are refashioned, and new versions of self are forged.

When psychotherapy is a successful journey, we are transformed both psychologically and spiritually. As in other initiations, we may undergo spiritual crises, but we must pass through those crises in order to achieve more responsible and creative lives.

The Appeal of Confessions

Although the media have made confessions more accessible to a wider audience, our fascination with confessions is hardly new. Early on, mankind came to the conclusion that confession was good for the soul. The person with too many secrets was often seen as flirting with a kind of spiritual death.

In the *Egyptian Book of the Dead*, written thousands of years before the birth of Christ, the soul seeking resurrection enters the hall of truth and appears before the gods. Here the supplicant's heart, symbolic of conscience, is literally weighed on a scale. The supplicant who is found truthful and worthy is led into the presence of Osiris, god of eternity. Unless the heart is free of secrets, the *ka*, or soul, cannot move on to the immortal bliss of the afterworld. A similar insistence on truth can be found in the Christian tradition, where, as in Egyptian theology, a clear conscience is a vital key to redemption.

The word *religion* itself connotes a binding together—a social connection linking us to each other and a spiritual connection linking us to our God. It is no wonder, then, that everyday confessions evolved out of religious traditions. Yet our confessions are not meant for God alone, even in religion. "Confess your faults to one another," it says in the Epistle of James, while Christ's parables frequently demonstrate the role confession plays in achieving redemption and renewal.

When Charles Borromeo (later St. Charles Borromeo) introduced the formula for oracular confession in the sixteenth century, an institutionalized rite took root in Catholic Christianity in which the priest was given the authority to evaluate the seriousness of the penitent's sin and to assign an appropriate penance.

This religious tradition of confession became, at least in principle, a great equalizer. Both the ordinary people and the nobles possessed the same human foibles and were likely to have committed the same or similar sinful acts. In Dante's *Inferno*, all pretensions and class distinctions were to no avail to sinners who were all assigned the same horrendous punishments if they had been found wanting in the sincerity of their confessions and the humility of their penance.

Judaism, Christianity, and Islam all rely heavily on the Word, as contained in the Torah, the Bible, and the Koran, respectively. "In the beginning was the Word, and the Word was with God, and the Word was God" is the familiar expression of this idea in the Gospel of John. Oral-aural communication became the way to relate to God and to each other. Confession dignified the Word and conveyed powerfully how words could bind believers to their faith and individually transform and redeem them. It would be hundreds of years before Sigmund Freud would challenge some of these basic assumptions.

New-Style Confessions

Freud revolutionized the nature of confessions. By emphasizing the benefits of patients "confessing" to a nonjudgmental therapist, he opened the door to a more humane approach to confessions. Notions of sin, preordained morality, and punishment were not part of the therapist's canon. Patients' confessions were neither condemned nor condoned; they were rather viewed as important communications to be explored and worked through. In Freudian therapy, the personal, spontaneous process of free association in which patients were encouraged to tell the therapist whatever was on their minds, along with the ongoing relationship with the analyst, gave rise to a special intimacy. A new, unique arena for confession was born.

Indeed, revealing secrets was at the heart of early psychoanalysis. Anna O., a patient of Freud's colleague Josef Breuer, referred to her treatment as "the talking cure," because when she revealed certain secrets, physical symptoms that had tormented her would disappear. And as she drifted into a deep hypnotic state, she was able to uncover secrets that had never before surfaced in her conscious life. Confession in the nonjudgmental, clinical setting allowed Anna O. to express her innermost thoughts and feelings without fear of anyone's disapproval or retribution.

Close to a hundred years after the landmark cases chronicled in

Freud and Breuer's *Studies on Hysteria,* many of us still feel most secure disclosing our secrets in the safety of the therapist's office. When we do shy away from confessing to a therapist, it is often because we are carrying over feelings from previous intimate relationships into our relationship with the therapist (termed *transference* by psychoanalysts). Sometimes we confess to test the therapist's loyalty and commitment to us. If the therapist responds to our confession in a receptive, empathic way, we often see her as an ally or an alter ego, rather than as an adversary or judge.

Philosopher Friedrich Wilhelm Nietzsche anticipated the dawn of new-style confessions when he exhorted, "Follow not me, but you." In more recent and secular times, subordination to a higher authority, as exemplified in old-style religious confessions, is supplanted by a dynamic in which each of us becomes our own primary decision-maker. When we rely solely on ourselves, confession becomes self-reflective discourse or a meditative exercise of searching within rather than relating to others as a means of resolution.

While sin carries with it a religious connotation, conscious and unconscious secrets exert their influence in our everyday secular lives. Conscious secrets can be positive, making us feel special. Guilt or shame is the result of other conscious secrets we harbor. (See chapter 5 for a more detailed discussion of guilt, shame, and narcissism in confession.) Unconscious secrets—secrets of a primordial, sometimes horrendous nature—are those we keep hidden even from ourselves. Gaining access to the unconscious is one of the primary vehicles for attaining insight and understanding in psychoanalysis.

The new approach to confessions considers each person's unique life story. As children, were we ridiculed, scorned, or belittled for our "dirty deeds," or were we encouraged and praised for telling all? Did we guard our secrets protectively from intrusive or punitive parents, while still confiding in friends or older adult surrogate parents? Or did we grow up so neglected or abused that we opted for "self-sufficiency" even as children, finding ourselves in a world where everyone and everything became suspect?

The leveling of the playing field after the Freudian revolution for those confessing and for those hearing their confessions continues.

This trend has also affected religious confessions. The Catholic, Greek Orthodox, and Episcopal churches, in some parishes, have moved away from the confessional booth toward face-to-face encounters or side-by-side kneeling between priest and penitent.

Nowadays, secular confessors are not likely to provide prescriptions or conditions for repentance, nor are they likely to tell us precisely how to repent should we feel the need to do so. The choice about "what happens next" becomes ours: to move on or to repeat the past; to wallow in inertia or risk revealing ourselves in order to resolve our dilemmas and find a sort of redemption.

Communicating through Confession

Confession is a special communication that is different from all other forms of self-expression. For one thing, confessions are usually made exclusively to one other person, or to just a few select individuals.

How often has one of our good friends prefaced the telling of a secret by saying, "I've never told this to anyone before." Patients often introduce their secrets to me by saying, "This is so disgusting, awful, terrible, and so on, that you're the only person in the world who will probably understand when I tell you . . ."

Most people, across the board, will be much more emotional when confessing. Guilt, shame, or narcissistic bravado generally goes hand-in-hand with the opening remarks of a confession. Inevitably, we try to prepare our listener for what we are going say, and we also try to protect our own sensitive feelings from possible negative reactions. Confessional preludes such as, "This is probably the weirdest thing you've ever heard," underscore the emotional, dramatic quality of our secrets.

An accomplished, sophisticated woman of thirty-six who had been in therapy with me for a year and a half began a session one day with uncharacteristic, feverish intensity. She prefaced what she was going to tell me with the thought that, although she felt she had been honest in therapy for the past year, there was something she had kept secret from me because it was both difficult and embarrassing for her to disclose. Yet the secret was marring her life; so she had no choice but to tell me.

Usually a highly articulate woman, she began to stammer as she repeated, "I'm . . . I'm . . . I'm. . . ." My human, nonprofessional tendency would normally have been to try and help her fill in the blanks. But I knew as a therapist that if I was wrong in my supposition about her secret, I would be doing her a disservice and could even cause her greater anguish. So I patiently waited until she finally blurted out, "I'm a virgin."

As she continued with her story, she lowered her voice, averted her gaze, and began to blush. She also slumped farther down on the couch and her voice became higher in pitch and more childlike — dramatic cues that helped me decode just how emotionally charged a secret it was for her.

This woman's confession demonstrates how important it is for confidants to tolerate ambiguity and be with the discloser empathically throughout the confessional ordeal. Too often we have a tendency to try and "help out" others by completing their thoughts or feelings for them. In life, we all need to develop our own voices and take responsibility for our decisions — including when and how to confess. This woman was given that opportunity.

Changes in self-esteem often follow confession. When we confess to a trusted other who truly listens and cares, we usually experience heightened self-esteem for having taken a risk and won acceptance from someone important to us. For those of us who harbor repressed grandiosity (e.g., "I have to tell you that I have written the greatest great American novel ever"), confession provides the momentous occasion for sharing our grandiosity with others. When these secrets are met with empathy or enthusiasm, instead of the feared reactions of scorn or disbelief, our self-esteem rises dramatically.

Many significant confessions concern self-identity. Whether the secret involves having had silicone breast implants, being gay, or remaining a virgin in a sexually charged world, we see a greater piece of our identity bound up in confessions than in other forms of communication. To confess is to acknowledge our very identity, to reveal an intimate bit of our core self to another person.

Some people confess specifically to proclaim their identities to the world. For instance, in recent years many gay men and lesbians have chosen to bring their hitherto secret identities "out of the closet" to define or even stake out their roles in the community and to claim their self-esteem. "I am what I am/And what I am needs no excuses," a song from *La Cage Aux Folles* exclaims. Needless to say, these confessions are likewise undertaken with the hope of being accepted by confidants.

Confessions are also a way of telling ourselves and the world how special or unique we are. "My secret is lurid, different, exotic, unusual," is a familiar refrain I hear in my practice. Unconsciously, many of us deal with significant secrets in our lives as rare narcissistic treasures split off from our conscious feelings of guilt, shame, or anxiety. When we confess one of these secrets, even in the calm atmosphere of a therapist's office, we often begin our revelation haltingly, nervously, only to build up steam and end in a wave of revelatory enthusiasm. William Blake once wrote, "Pride is shame's cloak." Our need to share gripping stories about our lives can, ultimately, turn the most shame-ridden secret into an exciting adventure worthy of a Broadway production.

The Emergence of Confessions

From the beginning, the experience of being heard, of being listened to by people who matter to us, has been important in the development of our sense of self. We like to feel that the words of the secrets we share can be returned to us in an enriched, illuminated form.

For instance, through being heard, a child learns how to listen. In fact, we learn that throughout our lives we need feedback from empathic others to maintain our stability and a sense of well-being. Communication with other people is not a luxury in our lives, not just the icing on the cake. It is a deep need. Positive confessional experiences from childhood onward provide such a foundation, in stark contrast to lives passed in prolonged loneliness in which there is no interchange or communication with others.

Although we might routinely tell some secrets to our parents or a priest in childhood, fearing punishment in this life or the next, we work very hard to suppress other secrets. Shame, guilt, or merely the need to have something strictly for ourselves in our own private world gives us the discretion and, sometimes, the courage to safeguard such secrets.

There are still other secrets that we may remain unaware of for most of our lives. These unconscious secrets often emerge during therapy. This is fortunate for us because these secrets are often so startling, terrifying, or horrifying that we need to feel the security of the therapist's presence in order to even allow them to emerge.

Joan P.'s story illustrates how a secret buried for decades can affect the entire course of a life. Joan was having her back x-rayed when she found herself being fondled vaginally and on her buttocks by the x-ray technician, who kept suavely saying "excuse me" and smiling blandly.

This incident triggered a terrifying nightmare in which a man threatened to kill Joan by putting a poisonous substance in her mouth. In her dream, Joan asked her attacker to rape her rather than kill her, but he put the thick, poisonous substance in her mouth anyway.

The triggering incident with the technician, compounded by the nightmare, catalyzed Joan's really terrifying secret that heretofore had only been a dim memory. I had heard the first part before. As a child of seven, Joan's cousin had brought her into a dark basement and made her fondle his penis. At this point, her memory always seemed to become blurry and Joan could not go on.

But her nightmare brought to light the truly terrifying secret that her cousin had also forced her to perform fellatio on him. This confession was followed by a stream of insights revolving around Joan's relationship to her own mouth, which she viewed as a "dirty area," and her lifelong bouts with anorexia. In many respects, this secret, while remaining unconscious for many years, had literally ruled her life.

Are Confessions Redemptive?

Webster's New World Dictionary defines *redeem* as "to get back or recover, as by paying a price." In confessions, we frequently recover or rediscover a part of ourselves that had been lost or disavowed. Confession itself is the price we have to pay for living free of self-deception and for giving up the security of our defenses.

Making a true and serious confession really does mean that we can never be exactly the same again. Yet the price is also the gain. Revealing ourselves to a trustworthy, competent other begins to free us from our imprisoning relationships or from our divided selves.

Sometimes the sheer enormity (in our own eyes) of a secret and the possible consequences of it being revealed can render us impotent, unable to act. We wonder, "How can I possibly face my maker, my victim—myself?"

Yet what is our alternative? If we put no effort into confession, we are left with a life scarred by secrecy. When we miss opportunities for telling the truth, we continue to bury, rather than resolve, problems.

Confessing can be a truly redemptive act. Religious confession provides a powerful route to redemption through faith in God and atonement. Therapy also provides fertile soil for this process. The confidentiality, acceptance, empathic receptivity, exploration, and interpretation built into the therapy relationship frees us to take more risks and to experience redemption through our own efforts, with the therapist as guide.

Can we ever truly recover a secret or a lost part of ourselves? When Eliade writes about "eternal return," he emphasizes that what predominates in all cosmic-mythological-lunar conceptions is the cyclic recurrence of what has been before. Yet we can never go back to an unaltered, pristine past. Nietzsche's notion of eternal return does not signify a return to the status quo, but to a past mastered and transformed in the light of present awareness. Thus when we rediscover a lost piece of a past relationship or a lost aspect of ourselves by paying the price of confessing, this "return" is always altered by who we are now and how we choose to understand the past.

We are constantly in the process of becoming. When we return "to the scene of the crime" in attempting to come to terms with a secret, we never actually retrieve, like psychic archaeologists, a secret preserved, a fly in amber, exactly as it was. Rather we mold the secret into a coherent story that fits with our present and future conception of ourselves.

When we acknowledge that there are destructive aspects in us, we can then move on toward the ultimate goal of integration. Transcendence is the vehicle that allows us to make that passage. And one of the most rewarding ways to achieve transcendence is through confession, which empowers us and transforms the hidden aspects of ourselves into creative expression.

Redemption through transformation is nowhere better illustrated than in the paintings of Mexican artist Frida Kahlo—a woman, who at the age of eighteen, was maimed in an accident in which a bus she was riding on was hit by a trolley, causing an iron handrail to rip cruelly through her lower abdomen and vagina. In the biographer Hayden Herrera's words: "Painting herself bleeding, weeping, cracked open, she transmuted her pain into art with remarkable frankness tempered by humor and fantasy. Her art became an extended series of confessions revealing her suffering and her identity. She would over and over again go back to that trauma in her art as a way of recording her suffering, while seeking after redemption." It is even possible that her work literally saved her—helped her stay alive longer—by transforming her trauma into artistry.

All of us are creative artists, painting vivid images that only become accessible to us through our dreams. In our dream life, we can leap barriers and conventions to retrieve secrets that open the door to redemption. My patient John was a thirty-three-year-old buyer who had put aside his more creative pursuits of acting and graphic design. He was now making a major change in his life by giving up the security of his dull job to go back to school.

John presented me with the following dream: "I am on a boat that is angled. There are very large- and small-shaped distorted objects on board. The water around the boat is high and turbulent. Everything seems to be out of control, but the boat is okay."

Together, we began to work on the dream. John acknowledged that he was the boat. He also saw himself as the different shapes. John continued: "Sometimes I feel very large [representing his grandiose creative plans], but other times I feel small, like Alice in Wonderland."

John experienced the water as destructive, and yet felt he was surviving. I reminded John that chaos and feelings of destruction often come before or announce redemption. It was clear to me that in therapy John had recently discovered a lost side of himself (when he was five he enjoyed drawing and arranging rooms) that he wished to develop for the future. He subsequently went to school for more technical training. John's dream illuminated the combination of destructive and constructive principles that together set the stage for his redemption.

When we confess, we face ourselves in communion with others. We move away from self-sufficiency toward joining the world, linking our destiny with others. To experience the emotional release of confession, we need the reassurance of a human ear.

The person we confess to becomes our partner, a kind of surrogate, who absorbs the secret and allows us to see ourselves in a more forgiving light. "For now we see through a glass, darkly," writes Paul in his *Letter to the Corinthians*, "but then face to face: now I know in part, but then I shall know even as I am known." By removing the obscuring glass of secrecy, we see ourselves in one another, and the charity we would extend to another comes back, full circle, to us.

As early as 1895, Freud compared the therapeutic encounter to "the unlocking of a locked door, after which opening it by turning the handle offers no further difficulty." We all have the power to shut ourselves out even from ourselves or to open doors to set our secrets free. The choice is ours, as we proceed to delve into the lives of those who have chosen to risk opening the doors to their very souls.

· I ·

The Confessional Journey

1

Risk

ONFESSION, real confession, significant confession means
change; it means leaving where we are and taking a step into the
unknown; it means moving to a place where we have not been before. It means risk. What do we gain that makes the risk worthwhile?
Sometimes we gain freedom, release from a nagging hurt that has
kept us frozen in place. Sometimes we gain a new world, a new life
that had been hidden all the while behind the false shutters of guilt
and just plain inertia.

All journeys worth taking have an element of risk or danger about
them. If we risk an inward journey, it could lead us into the underworld of our own darker natures—an underworld we may have
spent much time and energy rationalizing or explaining away to
ourselves and others. An outward journey might entail the risk—and
challenge—of being authentic, of presenting ourselves to the world as
we really are, not as whom we would like people to think we are.
The reward of risking the world without disguise is the possibility of a
truly new and exciting life, lived without pretense or excuse.

We can never be the same again after a real confession. Confessing
means we have taken a vital and irrevocable step into the future. Yet
many of us are so wedded to the past and hold so tightly to the old, familiar problems which are part of it that we are afraid to focus on, or
even think about, the future.

Who can forget Miss Havisham in Charles Dickens' *Great Expectations*? Dickens, the great portraitist (some would say caricaturist) of

the human condition, captured in the almost spectral Miss Havisham something that is in us all. Like Miss Havisham, the jilted bride who in decades has never taken off her wedding dress nor left the eerie, darkened rooms (resplendent with mice and the ruins of a never-eaten wedding feast), we are often unwilling to shed either our former selves or our familiar surroundings. We drape them around our shoulders and they become both security blanket and albatross. Yet it is only by risking ourselves—by sharing our secrets with others and weaving them into our present existence—that we can develop the self-confidence to face the future, head on.

To risk confession is to face ourselves and others no matter what the outcome might be. And the repercussions of real confession can be terrible: abandonment, loss of love, censure, and blackmail.

Why, then, do we choose to confess at all? Because in presenting our core selves, stripped clean of the detritus of illusion and evasion, we hope to be accepted as whole persons, with all our foibles, vices, weaknesses, and blind spots.

A confession, to be fruitful, to be genuine, takes the form of a journey of exploration in which I, the listener, the understander, the absolver, agree to be with you as a fellow explorer. Confessions between master and slave, employer and employee, are probably doomed from the beginning. For confessions to heal, I have to see you for who you are—respect you—rather than "over-see" or "super-vise" you; that is to say, be over and above you.

Over sixty years ago, pioneering psychoanalyst Otto Rank linked the emotional well-being of individuals with their ability to combine autonomy and intimacy in a satisfying way. Confession can be very much like Rank's picture of well-being. We, the people "confessing," take responsibility for our confession and live through its consequences with the meaningful people in our lives beside us. When we risk self-disclosure, we let go of safety and comfort. Through real relationships with significant others, the person confessing, letting go, suddenly becomes able to move in new, creative directions using the insights gained from the confession. The confession can be savored, puzzled upon, and even played with in an attempt to stitch together the pieces that fit it into our life stories.

When you confess, it is not enough to gain insight into the origins of one of your most carefully kept secrets and then follow that up with blaming your mother, your father, your dog, or even yourself for the lack of forward movement in your life. Once you have understood your secret and then looked at it with the important people in your life through "new eyes," you have to be prepared to abandon, accept, or transform it. It is no longer "your secret"; it loses its power—its obsessive grip on your life. You have taken the first step on the road to redemption. In the long run, it is the first step that is the most difficult, and the one that probably counts the most.

In life, we all experience a series of ordeals, dark secrets, and nagging doubts about what could happen if we exposed all our secrets. In Dante's journey in *The Divine Comedy*, especially at the start of the cantos that form *The Inferno*, the poet passes through the giant gates into the lower realms of the next world. The inscription on the gate reads: "Abandon Hope Ye Who Enter Here." Yet hope is what we desperately hold on to when we pass through our own personal hells racked with unrequited love, guilt, shame, and any other sicknesses of the mind and soul. Like Dante, who at the start of *The Divine Comedy* finds himself in a dark wood where the straight way is lost, we, too, feel lost until we find our own Virgil to guide us on the confessional journey. Remaining with us is the eternal human hope that redemption will be reached at journey's end.

Taking a risk is the turning point in the confessional journey. We sometimes delay the journey, fearing that our secrets will make us seem foolish, prideful, unworthy, or unlovable to others. For this reason, many confessions are discrete one-time events, involving little or no risk. When I tell my story to the captive passenger sitting next to me on a plane, am I merely looking to pass the time or to appear fascinating to a stranger? The same can be asked of my disclosure to a cab driver or a fellow traveler in another city.

In all these instances of confessions to anonymous or almost anonymous strangers, there is little risk, yet also little gain. True, I may feel temporary relief, but I am making no attempt to understand myself through another person, to challenge myself through another's gaze.

People who choose to confess indiscriminately to everyone are not intimately connected to anyone. The compulsive confession frequently brings no lasting change. It is in the encounter with Martin Buber's "Thou"—the meaningful other—that "my spirit touches yours." Confession to everyone, more often than not, will turn a meaningful encounter into a meaningless discharge.

For riskier confessions, a paradox often appears that could become a roadblock; namely, the greater the intimacy with the listener, the larger the danger of repercussions such as betrayal, abandonment, or loss of love. When it comes to friends, family, and romantic involvements, there are no norms—no clear signposts—to ensure confidentiality and acceptance. It is no wonder that in our day, the therapist, as a trusted low-risk confessor, along with the more traditional priest and the anonymous stranger, often become our preferred confessors.

The therapeutic journey in confession is an extended process rather than a one-shot outpouring. This is especially true when confessions concern serious life issues touching on who we are and who we can become.

Secrets often revolve around turning points in our lives. For those who have spent their lives hiding, confession becomes a special rite of passage signaling a journey out of the darkness and into the light. For those who risk declaring to the world "I am gay," "I am a former mental patient," or "I am a recovering alcoholic," confession conveys a sense of belonging along with the sense of separation each implies. Even if the most feared consequences of confession come to pass— ostracism from the family or loss of friendship—becoming authentic may also place disclosers in the bosom of a like-minded community offering strength and support.

External Journeys

Confessions sometimes involve real risks that can shatter our very existence. Dire repercussions—or wondrous healing—may follow a serious disclosure. Our lives can turn unexpectedly when we dare to be authentic, when we dare to tell the truth. Secure within the family's embrace, we may suddenly find ourselves exiled—or feeling even more loved—as those closest to us pass or fail the test of self-disclosure.

Disclosing incest to the family, "coming out" sexually to friends, or revealing alcoholism to co-workers entails formidable risks. Anyone who has seen a performance of Jean Racine's great tragedy *Phaedra* will recall the momentum that builds toward Phaedra's wrenching confession to her nurse and companion, Oenone, of her incestuous infatuation for Hippolytus, her aloof stepson. In Richard Wilbur's prize-winning English translation, the despairing Alexandrine couplet that sums up the heroine's mood is, "When you have learnt my crime, my fate, my shame/ I'll die no less but with a guiltier name." Phaedra, teetering on the brink of madness brought on by her guilt, has little hope of redemption through her confession. But speaking of her forbidden passion to a close friend takes the sharp edge off her pain, if only for a moment.

We can draw on our inner strengths and resources to push us through our doubts toward the conviction that we have more to gain than lose through revealing our inner selves, our true selves, to another. Knowing the confessional journey can be perilous, fraught with risk of social sanctions, ostracism, job loss, or even legal repercussions of some sort, some would-be travelers turn in their tickets at the dock before they set sail. Others embark on the redemptive journey and face any obstacle in order to truly be themselves and be loved and accepted as themselves. Friends, a community of like-minded peers, and sometimes the divine presence represent a collective spirit that guides us through the stormy waters of this difficult passage and brings us to a new freedom—a freedom from hiding.

The myth of Theseus and the Minotaur embodies the labyrinthine complexities of the confessional journey. The tribute that Minos, King of Crete, exacted from the Athenians consisted of seven young men and seven young women sent each year to be devoured by the Minotaur, a monster with a bull's body and a human head. The Minotaur was kept in a labyrinth built by Daedalus. Against his father's wishes, Theseus volunteered as one of the victims to rescue his countrymen from this tragic fate. Ariadne, the daughter of King Minos, fell in love with Theseus and gave him a sword to fend off the raging Minotaur and some thread to mark his twisting and turning path into the labyrinth in order to find his way back out.

What were the ingredients that went into making Theseus' journey a successful one? Ariadne guided Theseus by providing him with specific physical tools—sword and thread—as well as a vital spiritual tool—love—to complete his heroic task. We also see the redeeming power of love in Ariadne's willingness to incur her father's wrath by helping Theseus.

Confessions often resemble a labyrinth. There are many different paths, some hazardous, some simply dead ends. Much is needed to slay the monsters of prejudice and intolerance we face whenever we bare a secret integral to the core sense of who we are. Virginia Woolf called these kinds of events "moments of being," describing them as shocks that allow us to face reality. Confessions are such shared moments of being. Sometimes armed solely with our resolve to be ourselves at all costs, sometimes with the loving guidance of others, we come prepared to embark on the confessional adventure.

Myths, like confessions, are stories that tell us much about the heroic risks we are willing to undertake in the quest for justice, self-awareness, and authenticity. Because myths occur outside of actual time and history, we can more easily accept their lessons and assimilate their heroic feats in order to take greater risks in our own lives.

The myth of Perseus and Medusa speaks to us in this way. Perseus set out to kill the monster Medusa. Medusa had the sinister ability to turn living things who looked at her into stone. Approaching Medusa while she slept, and taking care not to look directly at her but rather at her image reflected in the bright shield given him by the goddess Athena, Perseus cut off Medusa's head and presented it to Athena.

With divine help, Perseus is guided on a heroic journey in which he faces and overcomes Medusa. When we confess, our task is not so clear-cut. For those of us who seek divine intervention prior to confessing, God's ways and instructions are often mysterious. Our confessional dramas usually include many players (family, friends, co-workers) who inevitably have a variety of motives for being there.

In the myth, Perseus is warned not to look directly at Medusa, but rather at her reflection. We sense here the dangers of transparency and direct contact. Yet confessions often find us gazing directly into our beloved's eyes as a route to intimacy and even to the soul. Our eyes, interlocked in communion, can indeed become the mirror of the soul. Allowing ourselves to become transparent through the affirming reflection of intimates helps us feel loved, understood, and confident enough to risk self-disclosure in the first place. (The issues of transparency and intimacy are expanded upon in chapter 9.)

Internal Journeys

In confession, we make the long, sometimes tortuous journey from darkness into light. The darkness is linked with the unknown; we fear grappling with the dark side of our own natures.

Face-to-face confession eases the transition into the light. Psychologist Michael Argyle demonstrated that eye-to-eye contact is a strong indicator of intimacy and love. People who are able to risk the vulnerability of such nonverbal soulful encounters are more prepared to risk confessing. And partners who can return each other's gaze are more likely to reveal their innermost selves to each other in a secure atmosphere of caring and closeness.

While eye-to-eye contact signals trust and soulful communion, ironically most terms for *seeing* in the English language are related to the more impersonal, cognitive concepts of knowing or understanding. We speak of "the mind's eye," along with "insight," "foresight," "introspection," and "supervision." In view of the critical importance of vision, it is interesting that in many myths (Perseus' slaying of Medusa and Orpheus' fleeting backward glance at his wife, Eurydice, in their ascent from the underworld) direct face-to-face contact is prohibited by the gods. Orpheus, who disobeys the gods and looks, comes to a disastrous end.

These divine injunctions against looking suggest how powerful our looks can be in enhancing trust and building intimacy. The gods knew how powerful a look could be in seducing mortals and bringing them to ruin. Remember Medusa's petrified victims! Looking also can be fraught with the dread of reexperiencing the "evil eyes"—literally the evil eye doubled—of the powerful, toxic mother or father. Yet even in very disturbed persons, the progressive development of the mutual gaze between two trusting intimates can begin to repair the toxic parental glare.

In sayings such as "if looks could kill," the fantasized omnipotent parental eyes of childhood become endowed with magical power and potential use for severe punishment or retribution. When we begin to think about eyes in this way, face-to-face confessions can seem to be rather risky adventures indeed.

We risk more when we make ourselves known face to face. But we also stand to gain more from that added intimacy. Confession becomes a process that removes our blinders and reveals a world of possibilities.

In Plato's famous allegory of the cave, the cave dwellers, who have been chained so that they can only see shadows in front of them, still avoid looking into the light when they are liberated; they prefer staying in the dark instead of facing the uncertainties and possible dangers of the "real" world that is now open to them. Plato equates the journey upward into the light with the intellect. Descartes noted, "Those who become so accustomed to walk in darkness weaken their eyesight so much that afterwards they cannot bear the light of day." Not unlike Plato's cave dwellers, we often remain comfortable in the dark and may unconsciously choose to remain out of sight of insight. For some of us, to be "in sight" of revelations is to defy, and even betray, our parental overseers who still dictate what we are to reveal and what we are to conceal.

Confession is a journey that moves us from the darkness toward the light. When we begin to trust a friend, therapist, or lover, we are better equipped to risk looking at the landscape of our own lives head-on.

The myth of Demeter and Persephone tells us much about the risks and rewards of descending into the underworld and facing our darkness in order to find redemption. Persephone, the maiden of the spring, was the daughter of Demeter, the earth goddess. Pluto, the god of the dark underworld, was so captivated by Persephone that he carried her off to his mysterious kingdom to be his wife. In her grief, Demeter would not allow the land to flower as she searched the earth for her daughter. Zeus intervened by sending his brother Hermes down to the underworld to plead with Pluto to allow his captive bride to go back to Demeter. A compromise was reached. Persephone was to pass the winter with her husband and the summer with her mother.

Confession can be experienced as a descent into the depths of our psyches to retrieve a lost part of ourselves. Persephone's time with Pluto in the underworld, alternating with her stay on earth, can be seen as a comment on the need to lie fallow, to hibernate, to let ourselves "be" with the mystery of our secrets, without rushing into action. The allegorical seed is planted in the darkness of our psyches and needs time to grow before it is ready to break through the fertile soil of our consciousness. Just as Persephone rejoins her mother when she is ready, we risk confession when we are ready to bring our dark inner demons into the light of day.

In taking the interior journey into the psyche, we face our own demons or disavowed selves. Unlike heroic extended journeys based upon real risks of abandonment or censure, interior journeys revolve around feared risks—finding out something about ourselves with which we cannot live. Like the unknowns in the darkness of Hades that Demeter had to face in her quest to recover her daughter, we fear the unknowns, the hidden monsters, in the blackness of our souls.

Confession is a way of acknowledging the split-off or disavowed parts of ourselves. Confession is a first step, a vital first step, in putting all the parts of ourselves into a coherent whole. We may not achieve our goal completely on the first try, but we will at least have moved toward accepting multiple aspects of ourselves. We come to realize that our gray or black "underworld" side is as much a part of our nature as the bright and sunny side, and that we really don't have to go through life trying to turn all our dark shades into pastels. We gain wisdom from tending to our sorrows and griefs as well as from celebrating our triumphs.

Demeter appreciates the time she has with her daughter, knowing that it is limited. We revel even more in the blooms of spring, knowing their time is short but that they will return again next year. The cycle of death and rebirth is one form that redemption takes.

Whenever we risk disclosing a hidden, forbidden aspect of ourselves (lust, envy, or deviousness, for instance), a cherished illusion dies. Unlike Professor Henry Higgins in *My Fair Lady*, we do not "have the milk of human kindness by the quart in every vein." We can be downright mean, greedy, and just plain ornery at times. Revealing and acknowledging those pieces of ourselves releases us from the burden of a false claim. The risk we take in disclosing our dark sides redeems us from a life of deception.

How do we come to terms with the dark undersides of our natures, and even revel in them, as they are creatively transformed to work *for* us? Few of us like to admit, let alone live, with the revelation that we are greedy or envious. But suppose we did play out each scenario differently by seeing where our greed and envy, fully acknowledged and broadened in scope, might take us on a confessional journey.

Here is the first scenario: *I acknowledge that I am greedy. Let me feast at the table of poetry and philosophy and grab hold of life instead of living so much on the sidelines. Let me use my greed to expand my nature toward the light rather than constrict myself further into the darkness of the unknown.*

The second scenario: *I am envious. Let me follow the Latin motto "Pete summa alta" and reach toward the heights in aspiring to be the best person I am capable of being. Let me thus ascend into the realm of enthusiasm and joy rather than descend into the muck of apathy and bitterness.*

In the nineteenth century, when people harbored sexual secrets such as having syphilis, the only confidant they would risk telling was the doctor. Families with children who had congenital diseases worked strenuously to conceal those problems so that future marriage prospects would not be damaged.

Henrik Ibsen's play *Ghosts* speaks to such secrets and the long-departed people many of us carry within us. The widowed Mrs. Alving, the play's sad heroine, has had to cope with the fact that her husband died of syphilis. She says of herself at one point, "I'm anxious and fearful because of the ghosts that haunt me, that I can't get rid of." Mrs. Alving's son Osvald is, in a sense, possessed by the ghost of his father, as he, too, is racked by syphilis. When Osvald reveals his condition to his mother, she is devastated. His confession at once evokes and shatters the cherished beliefs and aspirations she had for her son.

The Victorian taboo against revealing personal secrets, especially sexual ones, is still with us. Many people who die of complications from the AIDS virus are said to have died of something else. People who have been hospitalized for treatment of mental illness often omit that "secret" from their résumés and from the telling or writing of their life story.

Jung saw the shadow as the dark side of the personality—the part we want to hide from ourselves and also from the world. But Jung also noted that we need a dark side in order to be whole. By becoming conscious of our shadow, we remember that we are human.

Confession is the bridge that spans the gulf between our known self and our shadow (as Jung called it)—our secret self. The journey inward in confession forces us to confront our dark side and bring it to consciousness.

We do not become whole by cutting out entire chapters of our lives. Wholeness comes from embracing our inner darkness, from coming to terms with the whole of our nature. Coming out of the closet, whatever the label on the closet door, can be a truly redemptive experience. Redemption comes from acknowledging secrets and bringing them into the light.

In *Modern Man in Search of a Soul,* Jung noted that all the initiation and mystery cults of the ancient world recognized the significance of confession. He quoted the following line from the Greek mysteries: "Give up what thou hast, and then thou wilt receive." Jung goes on to say that full confession involves not merely intellectual acknowledgment of the facts, but also their confirmation in the heart of the person confessing.

When confession comes from a deep, authentic place within us, it is more than an intellectual exercise in which we dredge up an unconscious secret and gain new insight as a result, more than a quick emotional release enabling us to feel better and forget about the secret. Confession in which heart and soul truly work together harmoniously means that we take hold of our secret, claim it, and see how it fits into the fabric of our lives.

Risky Business

When our need to confess conflicts with a perceived loyalty, the business of self-disclosure can seem as dangerous as a game of Russian roulette. Even when the secret does not indict those to whom we owe allegiance, the hazard of consequence remains.

At all phases of our lives, confession begins with an evaluation of risk, with the exception of those confessions that burst forth from the unconscious whole, dramatic, and unplanned—catching us unaware.

In Eugene O'Neill's play *The Iceman Cometh*, Hickey confesses to his barroom cronies that he killed his wife after years of marital bitterness. Remonstrating that by killing her he gave her peace and freed her from the misery of loving him, the confession then takes an unexpected turn when his true feelings rocket out of the unconscious. He recollects standing by her bed and saying, "You know what you can do with your pipedream now, you damned bitch." He stops with horror and stammers, "No, I never . . ." His confession, beginning with a calculated risk, erupts into a highly unexpected disclosure. The second part of Hickey's confession once and for all lifts the veil of self-deception.

The Low-Risk Road

When we wish to test the waters of honesty, we may begin by making confessions to those who do not play a large role in our lives or who are "safe": strangers, clergy, and therapists. The anonymous cab driver and the stranger we meet during our travels are usually safe confessors. We know it is unlikely that we will ever see them again, and we certainly don't have to worry about winning their approval or maintaining a relationship as we would if we were confessing to someone close to us.

Even clergy and therapists are not always viewed as safe ears. For instance, many priests, particularly in smaller parishes, become parental figures or friends to members of their flock. In these situations, the personal, ongoing relationship with the priest or minister can make confession seem risky. If I reveal a really shocking secret about myself, am I going to lose a friend as well as the respect of my spiritual leader?

Confession is an expected and accepted part of therapy. Moreover, the stream-of-consciousness atmosphere of the therapeutic process induces confession. Why, then, do some patients think of therapists as high-risk confessors? Perhaps it is because through transference (the carryover of intense thoughts and feelings from previous relationships with significant others), the therapist comes to assume for the patient the emotionally overladen roles of father, mother, siblings, and lovers. When such transferences consume patients, they may act against their own best interests and conceal the very secrets that brought them into therapy in the first place.

When the word *confession* is brought up, most people think of its religious connotation. Yet confessions to priests among Roman Catholics in the United States has declined precipitously over the past few decades. Acknowledging guilt for one's sins in a therapeutic culture that often considers guilt a disabling emotion and sin an outmoded concept puts the faithful in an awkward bind.

Confessions to priests are still very much with us, however. Many believers find solace, relief, and meaning in the rites and rituals of the church. They look for deeper truths which, they believe, lie beyond them and humanity, and can only be found through God's grace and forgiveness; namely, that sin damages the soul and that seeking God's forgiveness ennobles rather than diminishes the believer.

Alfred Hitchcock—a rather uncomfortable Roman Catholic himself—was a master of the twists and turns of confession. Masterfully inverting the theme of the penitent risking disclosure, Hitchcock makes the priest assume the risk in hearing rather than revealing the secret. In his 1952 film *I Confess*, set in Quebec City, a lawyer named Vilette is robbed and killed by Keller, the caretaker of the local parish church. Keller confesses his act to young Father Michael Logan. Since two children saw a man in priest's clothing leaving Vilette's house, and since the priest has no adequate alibi, the evidence is strongly against him.

The murderer's confession to the priest carries virtually no risk. Bound by his priestly commitment not to reveal the killer's identity, Logan maintains his silence at the trial. He is acquitted when a verdict of reasonable doubt is returned. But the truth is revealed when the killer's wife turns against her husband. It is the spouse—the high-risk confidant most intimately bound up in his life—who betrays him.

Sometimes strangers who are safe because of their anonymity hear far more secrets than they would care to. When we confess to strangers, we are not concerned about information being passed on to our intimates. Strangers who move on give us the illusion of invulnerability and unaccountability.

As mutually captive ears, strangers sitting across from each other in a train can either become more intimate by extending the conversation or, through body language, convey the message that the confessional interlude is over. The travel writer in Anne Tyler's novel *The Accidental Tourist*, who is recognized and pursued by a fellow traveler, starts to read a book. Further opportunity for self-disclosure is thereby aborted.

The sociologist Erving Goffman speaks of "open spaces" as areas that promote social exchanges. Low-risk areas become conducive to sharing secrets, especially for the lonely who have few friends and distrust therapy.

When we want to own our secrets—to take responsibility for their nature and meaning within the context of our lives—we may risk going into therapy. Exploring, gaining insight, and working on a secret in the presence of the therapist as a nurturing, accepting, scrutinizing guide in the ongoing dialogue helps us face ourselves and break free from the hold of the dread secrets—whatever they may be.

The confessional journey is often an adventure of the spirit in which the discovery of the secret helps round out our identity and make us whole. T. S. Eliot, in his "Four Quartets," cogently describes this kind of psychological journey:

> We shall not cease from exploration
> And the end of all our exploring
> Will be to arrive where we started
> And know the place for the first time.

Many people fear the intimacy and familiarity of therapy, yet need ongoing support that is soothing and low-risk. Twenty million Americans prefer to file into church basements and other meeting halls instead of visiting confessionals or therapists' offices to talk about their deepest secrets and strangest cravings in a variety of Twelve Step and other self-help support groups. For these individuals, talking and listening to their fellow sufferers provides a salve to their psyche, with lower risk and less cost in time and money than doing the same thing in the presence of a therapist.

These group meetings, in which confession plays an integral role, are an amazingly effective antidote to loneliness. Members' pain becomes more bearable when shared with others who are very much "in the same boat." Confined to peers with the same problem (overeating, alcoholism, addiction to sex), these groups made up of "familiar strangers" who have "been there" engender a maximum freedom of disclosure without constraint.

What makes support groups of this kind especially potent is that they are based on the ancient concept of community, in which strangers gather to help one another by telling their story. Because strangers are low-risk confessors, nothing is too personal to share — not even cross-dressing or continually falling in love with priests.

A historic meeting between Dr. Robert Smith, a surgeon, and a New York stockbroker named Bill Wilson — both heavy drinkers — led to the founding of AA, the pioneer Twelve Step group. What these two men discovered was that self-disclosure in the presence of peers who were also alcoholics, coupled with acceptance and working on one's addiction "one day at a time," was a healing and redemptive process. Confession is so powerful in AA and its spin-offs because we face ourselves, our God, and our fellow beings in coming to terms with our problem. When drinking, we might curse, steal, lie, abuse family and friends, or even attempt suicide as we prey on ourselves and others. As we confess to others and make amends, we rediscover our humanity.

The Moderate-Risk Road

Some relationships are in-between, difficult to define and thus somewhat risky. Neither friend nor stranger, the hairdresser or bartender who become "regulars" in our lives stand midway between low-risk and high-risk confessors.

Risking confessions with these confidants in some ways places us on dangerous ground because no rules exist that guarantee acceptance and confidentiality. How can I be assured that the hairdresser or bartender who becomes "the ear" to so many regular clients will not betray me by spreading gossip?

Moderate-risk confidants are a part of our lives and yet apart from us. Like Chaucer's stock characters in *The Canterbury Tales*—the Wife of Bath, the Friar, and the Miller—these confessors are types we run into whose roles and personas are more critical than their interiors. The bartender is there as a safe repository for my secret. Yet if I become a regular, he gets to know me more intimately. At some point, we are no longer strangers; we become quasi-friends.

Bars, cafés, and beauty parlors become hangouts—free zones—for uninhibited conversations where confessions are bound to happen. In these "great good places" (sociologist Ray Oldenburg's felicitous phrase), we are more likely to be ourselves than we are at work, where the roles we play define us, or even at home, where family needs shift the focus from "me time" to "we time."

Confession serves the human need for communion. With the decrease in religious confession, there is a quest not just for new confessors but for new shared spaces where we feel comfortable baring our souls to others. The neighborhood bar or coffee shop is a welcome beacon fending off loneliness and alienation. It provides a neutral ground when we need some immunity from family and friends who can get uncomfortably tangled in our lives.

These places are great levelers. Fears involving confessions to authority figures—children to parents, employees to bosses, parishioners to priests—are greatly diminished or absent here. Confessions can flourish in places where unrelated people can relate, but with none of the complications of shared history and potential repercussions.

These third places away from work and home show that "familiarity breeds content." Inhabiting a place over time engenders a kind of fluidity and ease. Confession flows out of this atmosphere, which fosters a no-strings-attached intimacy in which we can relay secrets with little danger of psychic or physical entrapment. I come and I leave at will. And if the confession that comes out during this time is so horrendous that I find it unbearable to face myself or those I confessed to (remember Hickey's confession in *The Iceman Cometh*), I need never return to the scene of the confession.

We sometimes invest special places—cafés, bars, clubs—with loving qualities. Not only people but also places contribute to our sense of intimacy. One of the reasons the TV program *Cheers* became such a permanent fixture in so many people's lives was because it showed a place, an atmosphere, and a cast of characters to which many people could relate. It was a show that dramatized the need to confide in others outside our family in a familiar setting.

We need more intimate spaces in our lives. That is one of the challenges we face in contemporary culture: not so much to develop ever more sophisticated technology, but rather to create intimate spaces that allow us to be ourselves in intimate or not-so-intimate relationships with others. Spouses often become so preoccupied with balancing their careers, children, and household tasks that the home, once a temple of intimacy, becomes an efficiency zone for getting things done—an office away from the office.

The neighborhood coffee bar and small-town diner can again become a welcome transitional space to bare one's secrets about the family away from the family. In bygone days, the pub was a welcome spot for couples to go to reclaim lost intimacy. Sometimes it is safer to risk potentially explosive confessions in a space where breaking objects and breaking bones are more or less off-limits. The convivial, familiar atmosphere of a neighborhood haunt can be more conducive than home ground for couples to at least hear each other out.

Life is lived within boundaries. Boundaries confine, but they also give structure and security. Sharing secrets in coffee bars or at the office puts us at moderate risk because the boundaries are amorphous. These places may be viewed as a home away from home, but they are not our home. Some people, bereft of family and friends, share secrets solely with their co-workers. Although these people may not feel loved, they are at least recognized and appreciated for their contribution on the job, and thus feel more comfortable confessing to co-workers.

Co-workers become surrogate family. But because these relationships do not carry true family allegiance and because gossip is often an office pastime, the risks of sharing secrets are moderately high. Secrets unmask us, making us more vulnerable. The co-worker as confidant may even attempt to gain leverage through being privy to the secret. When personal and public boundaries overlap in this way, the possibility of leakage is heightened.

The workplace has always been a hotbed of secrets. The philosopher Michel Foucault contends that secrets and confessions are the province of the powerful. Sexual harassment cases are a recent phenomenon, since the boss, the feudal lord, or the king as power brokers once owned and controlled secrets. Threats and sanctions were levied against anyone who challenged the power structure. The victim of sexual dalliance was further victimized through ridicule, threat, or job loss, should she try to go public with her secret.

The growth of employee empowerment is helping to turn the tide of sexual harassment and other workplace abuses. Open disclosures about these issues have become more common and are not as frequently relegated to whispered gossip during coffee breaks.

Mythology and religion provide many examples of the dangers inherent in crossing over boundaries. Icarus, the son of Daedalus, was taught how to fly by his father who made wings of feathers secured together with wax. Daedalus warned his son to fly only at a moderate height and to keep nearby. But the exuberant Icarus soared upward, leaving the guidance of his father. The blazing sun softened the wax holding the feathers together, and Icarus plummeted to his death into the sea.

Icarus, in his manic disregard for caution, crossed over the physical as well as psychic boundaries in spurning his loving father's advice and guidance. When we confess, risks must always be weighed against consequences. Bucking the power structure when authorities are instructive and loving, as Icarus did, can be short-sighted and deadly. Just as we seek to overturn unjust power every time we risk revealing experiences with incest or sexual harassment, we also want to listen to the wisdom of loving authority figures whose guidance can be invaluable in evaluating life's risks.

Observing boundaries also plays an important role in Judaism. The Torah describes the twin sacrificial offerings prepared by Aaron, the high priest, in preparation for Yom Kippur, the Day of Atonement, in which the nation collectively confesses its sins. The first was a burnt offering; the second (the scapegoat) was sent out live into the wilderness. The interesting larger context for this ritual involved the death of Aaron's two sons who made an additional unsolicited offering to God, after which a fire emerged from the altar and engulfed them.

Their folly involved coming too close to God, thereby perhaps breaching the separation necessary between the holy and the human. Many might argue that the punishment was too severe. Nevertheless, what we can glean from this parable is that we need to consider psychic boundaries in confession. Just as we can go to extremes by vigilantly holding any confession at bay, zealous, indiscriminate offerings can also be our downfall.

The High-Risk Road

People seek therapists and "lay confessors" precisely because of their reticence to share their secrets with friends who might reject or betray them. Because we risk abandonment, loss of love, inadvertent leakage, and even blackmail when we confess to friends and lovers, the potential costs can outweigh the benefits. The stakes are just too high. Without the protection of anonymity and confidentiality, we may risk everything in confessing.

Since many of us consider friends, parents, and lovers to be our three most vital relationships, an enormous risk is incurred in confessing to these significant others. Children who confess their homosexuality to parents run the risk of being disowned or disinherited. Lovers who confess their infidelities to each other may forfeit their relationship in return for such disclosures.

To risk confession, marital partners must have a sense of commitment—of ongoingness—in the relationship. When security needs override the need for depth, self-disclosure becomes a casualty.

We disclose ourselves and make ourselves vulnerable in friendships and love relationships to validate our self-concept by obtaining support and understanding. In the 1960s, psychologist Sidney Jourard found that married people disclosed most to their spouses. More recent findings indicate that couples disclose the least when their secrets concern each other and most when "cooler" secrets that do not involve each other are in play. Also, research conducted by psychologists Jourard, E. M. Waring and Gordon Chelune, and Judith Wallerstein indicates that happier, more secure couples have higher rates of disclosure than their unhappy, habitually sparring counterparts. Since disclosing "hot" secrets to family members often produces disastrous results, one might again wonder why we would ever disclose to our families at all.

In the classic film *On the Waterfront*, Terry Malloy makes a very risky confession to his brother Charley during a heart-to-heart talk in the backseat of a car. Charley is supposed to kill Terry if he cooperates with the city crime commission. Terry pours out his heart, blaming his brother for ruining his career by making him lose a boxing match ("take a fall") for money: "I coulda had class! I coulda been a contender! I coulda been somebody! Instead of a bum, which is what I am! Let's face it! It was you, Charley!"

Once Terry discloses that there is more to life than being a bum (meaning working for the mob), he takes the greatest risk, knowing his brother must either kill him or face death himself. Confession, first to the priest, then to his girlfriend, and finally to his brother, turns Terry around from being someone with few morals to someone of the highest moral caliber. Terry is shown moving, symbolically, from the devil's abject, self-hating legions to join the ranks of Christ's redeemed. Walking with the dock workers unassisted after he is beaten up, he leads them back to work, thereby defeating Johnny Friendly and the mob.

The way the director films Terry's walk, backed by the film's powerful orchestral score by Leonard Bernstein, leaves little doubt that a redemption has taken place, a Christ-like redemption. Terry is helped on his metaphysical journey from the darkness into the light by his girlfriend and by a priest who help him see the moral decisions he has to make. His confession dramatizes his change of character and his redemption.

Confessions made to spouses can be free of turbulence, bringing the couple even closer together. In Daphne du Maurier's novel *Rebecca*, for example, the story turns on a sequence of revelations. Brought home to the great Cornish house called Manderley, the second Mrs. de Winter (she is never given a first name in the novel) is haunted by the image of her deceased predecessor—the beautiful, sophisticated, accomplished, adored Rebecca. The new bride imagines that her husband's frequent air of brooding preoccupation has to do with his unresolved grief for Rebecca and his inability, even after his remarriage, to forget her.

But when the unhappy bride at last confesses these suspicions, her husband makes a startling confession of his own: "You think I loved Rebecca? I hated her!" He goes on to reveal the cause of his preoccupation—he himself had brought about Rebecca's death.

These twin confessions provide a new and stronger basis for love and alliance. Confessions transport the jubilant couple into the higher realms of redemption and renewal. Freed of the burden of their secrets, the de Winters prepare for a new life.

Successful disclosure to high-risk friends can be one of life's most rewarding experiences. Because we often get a sense of who we are from our friends, confessing to them helps define us to our friends at the same time that we gain insight into ourselves by expressing our secrets out loud.

Cicero defined a friend as a "second self"; Aristotle as "a single soul dwelling in two bodies." If we are so intertwined with our friends, why would confession pose a risk, let alone a high risk? True, when we see our friends as extensions of ourselves, and when the actual secret does not involve the friend, then friends may indeed support us against the strains of discord and conflict. Even when the secret involves the friend, fast friends can weather the storm. Think of the wonderful friendship between d'Artagnan and the three musketeers in Dumas' perennial romance *The Three Musketeers*. With the rallying cry, "All for one, and one for all," even d'Artagnan's disclosure to Athos that he slept with his wife, Milady, (who was believed dead) does not faze Athos. These four friends truly work as a unit—a single soul. Their camaraderie and mutual regard enables them to withstand the most startling disclosures.

Friends who appreciatively mirror each other attract secrets. Yet these same dynamics can be deadly at times. I am reminded of a forty-three-year-old patient I had who bitterly complained about a hitherto close friendship. "I buy a record. She gets the same one. I rush into a store to get an Eskimo sculpture. She has to have the identical one. I cut my hair. She has to have the same style. Sometimes I feel as though she is stealing my identity. She won't let me have anything for myself."

She went on: "I can't confide in her anymore, because she somehow manages to assimilate my private secrets as though they're hers. She'll often use the term *we* when she's talking about herself. She acts as though we're joined at the hip."

Secrets are part of our unique nature. To have a secret is to no longer be the same as Dad, Mom, and brother. Now we have something that is ours alone. When we risk sharing a secret with a friend, our secret may become diluted in the process. As this patient's friend borrowed aspects of the patient to give herself the illusion of wholeness, secrets can also become part of the shared property of friendship. When this patient realized she no longer needed the adulation her friend supplied, she decided to stop confiding in her in order to preserve a separate sense of self.

Friendships, like dreams, are sometimes built on wish-fulfilling illusions. But unlike dreams, these illusions can perpetuate themselves over years. So when a disclosure such as, "I've been angry at you for months for being so self-involved," shakes the cozy assumptions of the friendship, the friends may not be able to withstand the aftershocks of the eruption. Retreat or even dissolution of the friendship could occur. When friendship is based on more solid ground than just a mirroring in which the two stroke each other's egos, or idealization in which one exalts the other as a god, even risky disclosures may strengthen the friendship as the anger and hurts are worked out and a new appreciation for honesty and openness solidifies the relationship.

The risk of self-disclosure greatly diminishes in what I term "narcissistic friendships." In such friendships, each friend may find his lost self in the other. Forever misunderstood by others, each perceives the other as the one who understands and accepts him. This alliance can then be established to fortify the pair against a hostile, unattuned world.

Friends are there to buttress each other's self-esteem and affirm each other's worth. Secrets divulged to such friends are usually met with acceptance and help bolster the teller against parents or other intimates who are seen as judgmental and intolerant.

Confessions are rarely completely risk-free. Yet when the other meets us with understanding and acceptance, we gain the courage to move further along on the confessional journey.

Confession, including religious confession, is never simply a license to get sins or secret misdeeds off our chests with impunity. Christianity teaches us to hate the sin but love the sinner. In our secular lives as confidants, many of us try to find forgiveness in our hearts toward our parents, children, or friends who have wronged us, even as we condemn the wrongful acts themselves. In all forms of confession, we must take responsibility for our disclosures in order to set our own house in order as well as to right wrongs done to others. When we combine accountability with responsibility, confession creates the possibility for us to move forward on the journey that ends in absolution or redemption.

2

Relief

The peace, the end of the quest, the last harbor, the joy of belonging. . . .
For a second you see — and seeing the secret, are the secret.
For a second there is meaning!

RALPH WALDO EMERSON

FOR CONFESSIONS to change our consciousness, even if only
for a moment, the emotional outpouring that ushers in the second phase of the confessional journey—relief—must spur us on to
plumb the secret's impact on our lives. A confession with full emotional release helps us achieve not only the meaning of the experience, but also a meaningful experience. When we only indulge in
emotional release, we are prey to the self-deception Emerson writes
about in his "Illusions" essay: "Then the hand lets the veil fall and you
are alone, lost in the fog again." When confessions bring long-lasting
relief, we no longer sense a mind-body split. Our bodily expression of
emotions—tears, shouts, laughter, anger—accompanies recall of the
secret to heighten the experience.

When we reveal a secret without emotional release, we are often
indulging in an intellectual exercise that brings no lasting change. I
am reminded of my patient Bob who would dutifully divulge that his
mother never loved him, pouring her passion into a charity instead,
and only used him to further her own grandiose ends. It was not until
years later when his mother—by then a bed-ridden invalid—complained that he had never said he loved her, that the normally reticent

patient came into his session straight from the maternal encounter, shaking and sobbing. "She wants my love after spending her whole life caring for her charity—never showing me love. I hate her. . . . Sometimes I wish I could kill her." Body and mind came together after ten years, enabling Bob to finally achieve abiding relief from his long pent-up rage.

On the other hand, getting a secret off our chests through primal screaming or bodily shaking at a workshop or prayer meeting may bring only temporary relief or even increase anxiety. Once the charismatic influence of the leader and ritualized setting have worn off, followers sometimes are left with drained feelings devoid of insight and transformation. Catharsis in the absence of insight does not bring lasting relief.

The mind and body must work together for lasting relief. To heal ourselves, we must *own*—not simply discharge—emotions. By reuniting ourselves with our secret feelings, we can work them out to achieve long-term, lasting relief. When we become aware of previously disowned feelings, our sense of self—of who we are—is fulfilled.

Long-term versus Short-term Relief

Early psychoanalysts likened cathartic relief to the need to cleanse oneself of bodily wastes or undesirable emotions. The psyche was viewed as a repository of energies requiring periodic discharge. Today, with advances in physics as well as psychology in place, we consider both body and psyche as open-ended systems. We are socially and spiritually motivated rather than biologically driven to seek relief in confessing.

When I confess in a heartfelt way to my God, my therapist, or my friend, I want to be understood and unconditionally accepted in all my taboo, demonic, or destructive aspects. Relief does not spring merely from ridding myself of an unwelcomed secret. Long-lasting relief is relational. Relief springs from being accepted and loved for who I am, including my secret. Relief also comes not only from owning my feelings, but also from trying to deal with them in my life.

Again, the old idea of purgation through catharsis implied that relief resulted from getting rid of evil, alien, or unwanted secrets through exorcism or other means. Yet, owning our feelings and achieving spiritual wholeness through confession means coming to terms with these disavowed feelings—not simply releasing them.

Experiencing and letting go of secret fears, resentments, envy, and murderous rage can make us feel lighter as we divest ourselves of secret baggage. The Roman sage who declared, "I count nothing human alien to me," also tapped into a universal truth: namely, that fear, envy, guilt, and shame are all part of our nature. To discover that we can be ourselves, warts and all, in the presence of a confidant or group reminds us that we are all part of a larger social community. It is a relief to discover that not only do our parents truly love us, but that we can also be accepted by our AA group, church, or therapist without fear of reprisal.

We can obtain lasting relief on a confessional journey only by sharing our secrets in an ongoing, trusting relationship with confidants who can help us work out, rather than simply spew forth, the secret. True relief stems from coming to terms with our disavowed emotions—by either discarding them or integrating them into our lives. If my secret involves wronging others, I might atone. If I was sexually abused as a child, I might change the way I see myself from a depressed victim who blames herself to an angry survivor who blames the aggressor. I may then choose to take action by confronting my abuser.

Relief is most likely to last when we seek to solve the dilemmas wrought by the secret. In so doing, we begin to view ourselves in profoundly new and revitalized ways.

The other kind of relief—quick-fix purgation—is short-lived; still, it is often adopted because it does make us feel better in the short run. The release we experience from immersion in a theatrical character's guilt-ridden secret or from the emergence of a painful secret at a religious revival enables us to let out powerful emotions through the safety of ritual. We can temporarily unburden ourselves of the weight of our secret. The secret is seen as an alien or sinful object to be eliminated at all costs. This is in sharp contrast to the long-term relief that comes with fully acknowledging and coming to terms with *all* parts of ourselves, including the demonic. The resolution of our secret comes with understanding and working out the secret—not with release alone.

Yet many of us benefit, if only temporarily, from unburdening ourselves to a cab driver or bartender. The more confession involves a one-shot encounter with an anonymous stranger, the more desperate we are to rid ourselves of our secret. The cab driver or stranger on our travels are substitutable "everypersons" who are simply available at a juncture of great need or loneliness in our lives.

It is easiest revealing secrets to cab drivers, strangers, and priests outside our parish, since they will never be seen again. One cab driver commented: "The physical set-up [in a taxi] promotes confessions. My back is to the passenger. Because I don't see them, they feel freer to talk." Another observed, "Daily pressures build up, and a few minutes in a cab gives riders an emotional outlet."

Because of time constraints, those baring secrets to cab drivers are pressured to get the secret off their chests within the time parameters of the ride. A captive stranger sitting in the adjacent seat on the plane, alas, sometimes wishes that a buzzer would sound signaling the end of the confessional period. There also exists, however, a minority of confessional voyeurs who greedily cherish every morsel of the confessional intake.

My interviews with cab drivers, bartenders, and travelers have revealed some striking patterns. First, many disclosers see their secrets as too risqué, shameful, or unacceptable to reveal to intimates, yet feel compelled to voice them as a way of gaining some relief. For example, a bartender was told by a "nonregular" customer that he was a kept man whose mistress made him leave the apartment on certain nights when she had other people in. The customer revealed that he was in a slave relationship in which he was "like a pet whose owner let him off the leash once in a while."

A second pattern which emerged revealed that some people who lack any intimate relationships at least have the courage to avail themselves of anonymous others. Relief can be achieved, if only for brief moments, when the desperate can temporarily let down their guard. Often bereft of intimate relationships in their new country, for example, illegal aliens frequently reveal their secrets to priests or bartenders outside their neighborhood.

Third, some secrets have an adverse impact on both the teller and the intimates. The *idée fixe* that the repercussions of revelation would be terrible propels the discloser toward the relative safety of the taxi or bar. A seemingly unflappable cab driver told me that only once was he thoroughly shocked by a disclosure, which he then related to me: A customer confessed that on his first day out of the penitentiary, he was meeting his girlfriend—not his wife. His girlfriend was a pen pal who he had started a correspondence with while he was in prison but had never met, while his wife had waited faithfully for him for five years.

While his relationship with his new love quickly evolved, his wife was devastated by the disclosure. Having remained true to him throughout his years of incarceration, she felt especially disillusioned and betrayed by the relationship he had kept secret from her for so many years.

In quick-fix relief, we shy away from ongoing relationships that we perceive as too risky. Anonymity is equated with absolute safety. Those who seek immediate relief often want instant gratification with no risk of repercussions and no strings attached.

Not all confessions produce relief. Risking self-disclosure may initially heighten guilt or shame. But given the right ongoing relationship of trust, understanding, and empathy, confession is more likely to relieve us than to hurt us.

We are not "seething caldrons" seeking biological discharge of our hidden forbidden thoughts, feelings, wishes, and memories. As psychoanalysts Morris Eagle, Roy Schafer, and Leston Havens have noted, we develop a sense of selfhood, in part, precisely by acknowledging these secret parts of ourselves and making them part of us rather than apart from us. We can thus enlarge the sense of who we are instead of trying to split off our unacceptable parts.

Psychiatrist Harry Stack Sullivan noted the "not me" part of ourselves marked by horror, loathing, or dread. Our defenses protect us from secrets we are not equipped to handle. A compelling case can also be made for facing our demons and even welcoming the dark side of our natures. By owning the "not me" secrets, we become geared to feel the full range of our emotions and take responsibility for working out our secrets. When the secret becomes an acceptable part of me, I no longer have to dread my unknown demons.

Relief is not an automatic outcome of sharing secrets. Still, for most of us, the act of revealing ourselves promotes relief, either immediately or in time. Take the case of Ellen, a twenty-six-year-old computer programmer who would relate harrowing events in her life to me in a monotone. I would find my eyes glazing over, and yet I was surprised at my reaction since the dramatic content of Ellen's disclosures more than made up for her impassive way of relating. The secrets, though clearly expressed, were blanched of all emotion or feeling.

One day Ellen came in and started to tell me how she would get angry with her mother on occasion. When I asked her for an example, her habitual demeanor gave way to blushing and hesitant stammering, as she mentioned that she was embarrassed. I responded that she need only tell me if she wanted to.

Ellen slowly began to reveal that when her father died, she began to sleep in her mother's bed in order to console her. Her mother would masturbate in front of her, which mortified Ellen. This confession, while prefaced by embarrassment, gave way to profound relief. Following Ellen's disclosure, I noticed how her facial muscles softened and how her entire body seemed to sink more easily into the couch.

The process of confession often takes place in stages. The same secret, like musical variations on a theme, may be revealed in myriad ways over time. When the secret is finally revealed in all its emotive splendor, replete with vocal, facial, and bodily nuances, the person can most fully experience relief.

At other times, emotions arrive unbidden as precursors to the secret. Haven't we ever woke up sobbing or wracked with free-floating anxiety without any discernible cause? In these instances, we find ourselves in the grip of emotions unmoored from their context. Instead of bringing relief, however, these emotions heighten our distress. Relief arrives only after we are able to attach meaning to our seemingly random emotional outbursts. My tears guide me to the secret I at first could not reveal to myself through ordinary memory—that today is the first anniversary of my father's death. My grief reaction on this anniversary brings relief only after I attach meaning to my tears.

Religious rituals are another means to sustain us through our crises and tribulations. When we sense that God hears our confessions, we experience profound relief. Since the dawn of civilization, we have confessed in one form or another to God or the gods. Religion was the first watershed moment in relief through confession. People sought atonement for their sins by confessing to the gods of nature so that fertility or peace might be restored. As formal religions developed, ritualized forms of confession also came into being. For those who were truly contrite and willing to repent, relief took the form of atonement for sins. The relief that the penitent experienced stemmed from the safety of the ritual, along with the realization that forgiveness was forthcoming if one truly atoned.

By the thirteenth century, Lateran IV declared that the faithful had to confess at least once a year in private to a priest. The Renaissance focus on "man as the measure of all things" even came to penetrate the confessional. Each person's own secret idiosyncrasies and peccadilloes became the subject matter of self-scrutiny.

Religious and Ritualistic Confessions

The emphasis on authenticity—genuinely feeling remorseful for what we have done—has always been a prerequisite for obtaining forgiveness in religious settings. For those who use the confessional as a quick-fix means of obtaining relief for committing adultery or abuse, only to do the same thing next week or next month, the Roman Catholic Church is unforgiving. The church does not dole out fixes to confessional addicts who are compelled to repeat their sins. Only those who are willing to genuinely atone—to be "at-one" with their God in feeling truly sorry and repenting—should experience long-lasting relief following confession, according to religious doctrine.

From a religious perspective, we confess in order to receive God's forgiveness for our sins. It is consoling—and truly relieving—to know that God will forgive anything if we are truly contrite and resolve to do better. Think of the famous story of the woman who was caught in adultery and brought before Christ. Instead of stoning her, as was the traditional—and horrific—punishment for adulterous women in ancient Palestine, Christ said to her punishers, "He who is without sin among you, let him cast the first stone."

Religious confession, of course, does not guarantee relief. I am reminded of a colleague who told me that his most memorable confession involved him passing out. "As a teenager, I experienced so much anxiety for confessing masturbating for the umpteenth time, that I remember developing tics and going into a panic. When the tension became unbearable, I passed out." He went on to describe his deeply entrenched guilt and his sure conviction that he was damned.

Although passing out was an extreme reaction, many have experienced fear, anxiety, and dread in connection with confession. More psychological sophistication on the part of the clergy, along with the greater humanization of confession through face-to-face contact, has done a great deal to dispel these harsh feelings and replace them with love and relief at the prospect of forgiveness.

Many feel a burden lifted following confession, yet lasting self-transformation often occurs only when relief is accompanied by a willingness to examine our sins in the context of our entire life situation. This is because a major element in religious confession is our resolve to change—not to simply go through the motions and obtain short-term relief, but to actually work at transforming ourselves through genuine remorse and a willingness to do better.

It is beyond the scope of this book to systematically go through the history and nature of confession in all religions. Yet certain watershed moments point to how our beliefs regarding sin and confession strongly influence the degree of relief we are likely to experience.

In more recent times, the Oxford Group (a nondenominational spiritual movement) emphasized sharing in a group or with an individual. The confession, referred to as "sharing for witness," involved members disclosing their sins and the ways in which they overcame sin. Relief took place as members would often bear witness with happy hearts rather than heavy hearts, sometimes revealing how they escaped from sexual inhibitions with Christ's help. What a far cry such good-humored confessions were from confessions in some more traditional groups in which penitents might come to equate virtually every sexual thought or act with depravity and sin!

Sharing was a departure from traditional confession. Suddenly the laity—we, the people—became valued confessors. You could share with a friend who would then do the same with you. Confession here became democratized. Mutual sharing practiced by the Oxford Group, as well as Christian Scientists, Baptists, and Quakers, demystified confession, making it more accessible to everyone. People experienced relief as they came to see themselves not merely as sinners but as joyful celebrants offering testimonials on how they overcame sin. Among evangelists, the preacher who approaches his congregation as "sinners saved by grace" has always had better results than the "fire-and-brimstone" preacher who speaks only of the evils of sin.

The dramatic rituals and emotionally charged atmosphere virtually guaranteed relief for celebrants who entered into the spirit of confession. The privacy of the traditional Roman Catholic confessional gave way to public displays of confessional fervor at Protestant revivals. Sinners might jump up and "testify" to their past sins, which the audience could relive together in imagination. An Aristotelian-like catharsis could thus be experienced by audience and confessant alike.

The period of great revivals began on the American frontier around 1797 and, *mutatis mutandis,* continues in various Protestant denominations to the present day. Similar to tribal ritualized confessions, some revivals went on for days, fatigue joining other forces to break down one's ordinary defenses. The idea was to experience a rebirth of the self in which the emotions were summoned to achieve release and renewal. Swooning, "quaking," rolling, and speaking in tongues engendered excitement in the audience, along with individual and sometimes collective audience release. Of course, sometimes the intensity and unpredictability of these bodily emotional displays resulted in uncontrolled eroticism or even psychotic-like brief breakdowns. But, for the most part, confessions coupled with frenzied bodily emotiveness produced joyful relief.

In Judaism, individuals engage in an encounter with God through prayer. We can view this spiritual meeting as a confession. King David provides a powerful example of the range of disclosure we can make to God and still experience the relief that comes with feeling loved and forgiven. True, he disclosed his sins, such as deliberately sending Bathsheba's husband into the frontlines to die so that he could have her, but he also revealed his fears and even his anger at God. David was not afraid to be open with God through prayer. In so doing, he found forgiveness for his sins, along with grace. If David could confess himself so fully to God and find relief, why not us?

On Yom Kippur, the Day of Atonement, Jews appeal to God as a loving God. The Jewish view of confession is that, although we deserve to be punished for our sins, God's forgiveness, tempered with his love, will heal us and bring us abiding relief.

Repentance is a vital aspect of Yom Kippur prayer. The Hebrew word for repentance is *teshuvah*, which means "return." When we repent on Yom Kippur, we return to God. We concentrate on our need to achieve forgiveness for our sins against God, yet first we must ask for our neighbor's forgiveness and make proper restitution. Through individual restitution and the ritualized communal prayers to God, confession accompanied by true repentance brings solace and relief as we chart a new path moving toward renewal and rebirth.

The relief that repentance brings sets us on the road to redemption. Horrifying, secret misdeeds are not catastrophic when we acknowledge our sins and seek repentance. In our attempts to heal our broken relationships with others, nature, and God, we find relief in purifying and revitalizing ourselves.

So pervasive is the idea of sin and catharsis through confession that many tribes use priests, shamans, or chiefs to perform ritualistic confessions to supernatural parent-surrogates or ancestors. Frequently, public confessions are likewise made to the whole society of one's transgressions against society's code. In this latter vein, in 1995 an unprecedented number of political and spiritual leaders, ranging from French President Jacques Chirac to Pope John Paul II, publicly acknowledged national and international wrongdoing against Jews in World War II. Acknowledgment and contrition, regardless of the broader moral issue of whether these declarations are too little and too late, are designed to bring collective relief from guilt for wrongdoing through repentance and openness about hitherto closeted crimes.

The psychoanalytic anthropologist Weston La Barre discovered that, in many Native American religions, confessions were designed to end sickness, difficult labors, bad weather, and poor hunting—all ascribed to the unconfessed sin of someone. Among the Aztecs, for example, sins are confessed in order of occurrence and penances—including fasting and piercing the tongue with a thorn—are given according to the gravity of the offense. Individual confessions of sin not only usher in personal relief, but also allow the group to breathe a collective sigh of relief as the group's misfortunes are now believed to be over.

Again, it is emotional relief coupled with the *belief* that change will take place (e.g., hunting will improve, or childbirth will be eased now that secret sins have emerged) that makes religious and anthropological confessions so powerful. The priest, shaman, chief, or medicine man is the designated purveyor of relief through ritual. The absolute faith in the power of these confessors, along with the conviction in the healing power of prayer, ritual, and group solidarity, guarantees relief following confession.

There are some striking similarities between these tribal rituals and AA or OA meetings in which individuals air their secrets in a group setting. Acceptance, group solidarity, and shared identification with a previously hidden secret—alcoholism or any other addiction—brings relief to the discloser in the safety and embrace of the group. These shared secrets also strengthen group members' resolve to continue on the path of abstinence.

What all cathartic ceremonies do, ranging from revivals to shamanistic drum beating to Catholic rites of exorcism, is provide us with a socially sanctioned ritual that gives permission to express hidden taboo thoughts and feelings. The entire group backs us in our quest to express our secrets and find relief; we are accepted and loved for releasing our secrets.

Confession and Catharsis

The role of religion and ritual in confessions is by no means confined to the theological or anthropological realm. Edward Albee's powerful drama *Who's Afraid of Virginia Woolf?* speaks to the dangers of living with illusions and to the power of confronting our secrets in order to free ourselves from the stranglehold of self-deception. George and Martha's big secret, which George insists they keep from their guests, is that their son, of whom they often speak, does not exist; he is a chimera they have created out of the disappointments and pain of their marriage. Confronting the truth through confession and ritualized exorcism gives George the courage to save himself and Martha from their destructive illusion.

During a visit by George's colleague Nick and his wife, Honey, Martha crosses over the agreed-upon boundaries by revealing the secret of her son to Honey. Act 3, entitled "The Exorcism," introduces the final symbolic and ritualistic "game" that George creates. The traditional Latin prayers of the Requiem Mass that George recites—including the mournful and chilling Dies Irae—symbolize both the death of their imaginary son and the death of their deceptive way of life. The ritual provides relief by formalizing and legitimizing the death of their imaginary son. They can now go on and find rebirth through their own efforts, stripped of illusion.

To get the sense of release through exorcism, here is a sample of the dialogue:

George

Now listen, Martha, listen carefully. We got a telegram;
there was a car accident, and he's dead. POOF! Just
like that! Now, how do you like it?

The catharsis begins with Martha's howl that weakens into a moan.

Martha

NOOOOOOOOOO.
No, no, he is *not* dead; he is not dead.

George now begins the ritual.

George

He is dead. Kyrie, eleison. Christe, eleison. Kyrie, eleison.

Martha is now crying.

Martha

. . . I mentioned him . . . all right . . . but you didn't
have to push it over the EDGE. You didn't have to . . .
kill him.

George

Requiescat in pace.

Psychologist Richard Lazarus has shown how important our beliefs
about our identity and our place in the world are in emotional expression. The exorcism jolts Martha into reality by destroying her illusory
belief about an imaginary son. The guests serve as an audience—as
confidants—to validate the secret illusion as well as its destruction.

In order to experience authentic relief, George and Martha take
the games and rituals seriously (what Lazarus calls *appraisal*) and
thereby acknowledge the meaning of the confessional exorcism in
their lives. Perhaps the final ingredient in offering the hope of lasting
relief is how the couple copes with the confession that their son is
dead. Now that their illusory son is gone and they are free of self-
deception, George and Martha are forced to rely on each other to
create meaning in their lives.

A second watershed moment in relief through confession grew out of
Aristotle's philosophy outlined in *The Poetics,* in which he describes the
expression of inner drama as cathartic. Theater is viewed as having a
cathartic, therapeutic function by allowing the audience members to
purge themselves of fear and pity in tragedy and laughter in comedy.

The basic meaning of the Greek word *catharsis* is "to cleanse or
purify." In a sense, then, Aristotle's conception of tragedy is not
merely to provide an emotional outlet for the audience to experience
pity and fear, but also to purify and clarify these emotions by passing
them through the medium of art. The safety of the darkened theater,
along with our vicarious participation in the characters' dilemmas, is a
secure way to indirectly deal with our own secret flaws. Yet for lasting
relief to occur, we must not merely succumb to passive relief experienced in the safety of the darkened theater, but also actively reclaim
those secrets, risking disclosure in the light of day in our own lives.

If we relate this approach to the previously mentioned patient Bob (see pages 41–42), who experienced a full-blown hatred of his mother, we can see that Bob's expression of rage alone did not enable him to experience lasting relief; it was also his conviction that through the drama enacted with his mother, he was exonerated from guilt.

A third watershed moment in confession and catharsis centers on the psychological revolution. Confession became more humanized as it was stripped of its sinful connotations and removed from the indirect, vicarious participation advocated by Aristotle. Freud and his associate Breuer first used hypnosis and later free association to help patients release unconscious forbidden or bizarre thoughts and feelings in the safety of the analyst's office.

Breuer and Freud initially used the term *catharsis* to mean cleansing (a patient, Anna O., called the same process "chimney sweeping"). They also used catharsis in the medical sense to include the removal of alien or pathogenic matter. Freud wrote about the relief of symptoms by the cathartic method as the removal of a "foreign body," and Breuer compared the "talking away" of symptoms to Roman Catholic confessions.

The idea was to recover repressed memories and emotions in order to discharge them and thereby relieve the patient's symptoms. While the method was successful in releasing hidden thoughts and feelings, the theory was less compelling. As medical men, Freud and Breuer subscribed to the hydraulic model in which, as closed-ended systems, we must release "dammed-up affects" associated with repressed traumatic secrets. The emotion was seen as toxic, requiring a purging akin to an excremental bowel movement.

What this approach did not sufficiently consider was the *meaning* of the emotional release in our broader lives. Take a common example: "Crying our eyes out" after recalling a secret of childhood abuse may only produce short-term relief and actually increase our sadness and rage in the long run. Expressing our repressed rage to deafened ears can make us more rageful than relieved.

In *Studies on Hysteria,* Breuer and Freud asserted that each hysterical symptom disappeared when the memory that provoked it and the accompanying emotion emerged as the patient described the event in the greatest possible detail and put the emotions into words. Freud, in time, came to realize that relief through catharsis was not simply a biological act. He implicitly recognized the importance of the social bond with the therapist, whom he referred to at different times as a midwife, elucidator, teacher, and even, tellingly, father confessor.

The healing power of "abreaction"—the emotional reliving of the traumatic event—was advocated by two of Freud's disciples, Sandor Ferenczi and Otto Rank. They contended that when the therapist as confidant became more relaxed, responsive, and empathic, a safer climate was created for the patient to relive the secret childhood trauma.

We do not meaningfully change by singular abreactions, which are dramatic but short-lived, warned Wilhelm Reich. It is rather through sustained catharsis over a prolonged course of therapy that secret thoughts and feelings can emerge and be worked through. Further, emotional release, to be effective, has to be accompanied by understanding. We are best off gradually letting down our guard—our "character armor," in Reich's words. In this way, we can let out and let go of our secrets without feeling the need to put up more walls.

In contrast to Reich's advocacy of gradually removing the obstacles preventing secrets from emerging, the 1960s became the "let-it-all-hang-out" decade. A variety of emotive therapies became popular, including psychodrama, encounter groups, primal therapy, and bioenergetics. The emphasis was on the release of raw emotions—through screaming, massage, or confronting a stranger in a group and expressing your hate for him—often to the detriment of understanding and taking responsibility for one's actions. Simply releasing these intense emotions without gaining insight into the secret would be a frightening rather than relieving experience for many of us.

In recent times, many therapists favor looking at memories connected with the whole emotional climate of a person's childhood rather than at specific traumatic secrets that must be "archaeologically unearthed." Chroniclers of child abuse, such as Alice Miller and Leonard Shengold, implicate the entire warped childhood atmosphere rather than any one event.

In exploring our secret pasts, if we are obsessed with finding *the one significant secret event,* we are disregarding the multiple secret events that make up the complex collage of our existence. My patient Emily was convinced that once she discovered the one deep, dark secret that mired her life (incest? with whom?), she would experience relief and freedom from her ruminations. Yet this thinking would drive her into a spontaneous frenzy, imagining different friends or relatives as alleged culprits.

Emily gradually began to reveal the gothic climate of her childhood, replete with a retarded aunt whom Emily and her brother forced to perform oral sex on them, a father who spent more time with his mistress than with his children, and a mother who preferred soap operas to child rearing. When she realized that it was the entire toxic family environment rather than a specific dark secret that contributed to her feelings of inadequacy and distrust of men, Emily began to achieve relief.

Acceptance

When I am accepted following disclosure, relief arises from knowing that I am no longer in exile from my fellow beings. I acknowledge "I am a sex addict" or "I went on an eating binge" and discover that I am accepted in the group for being myself. Relief stems not only from being accepted, but also from my conviction that I belong to a network of people who understand me.

We sometimes feel alienated, believing that our secrets and emotional weaknesses render us unacceptable. Complete emotional release occurs when we realize that we are permitted and indeed encouraged to express our secret thoughts and emotions.

One of the great literary portrayals of relief in a climate of acceptance is that of Hetty's confession to Dinah, the Methodist preacher, in George Eliot's *Adam Bede.* In this story set in the eighteenth-century English midlands, the simple carpenter Adam Bede falls in love with the beautiful Hetty, whose precipitous meeting with the squire Arthur Donnithorne eventuates in her pregnancy and downfall.

In a powerful outpouring, Hetty confesses to Dinah as though her life depended upon it. The climate of permission to bare all is established by Dinah's pleas to Christ to love and save Hetty: "Saviour! It is yet time—time to snatch this poor soul from everlasting darkness. . . . Let her see that God encompasses her."

Hetty, emotionally overcome by her deed (leaving her child to die) and by her overwrought feelings catalyzed by Dinah's charismatic pleadings, sobs out, "I will speak . . . I will tell . . . I won't hide it anymore." She whispers: "I did do it, Dinah . . . But I thought perhaps it wouldn't die—there might somebody find it. I didn't kill it—I didn't kill it myself. I put it down there and covered it up, and when I came back it was gone. . . . It was because I was so very miserable, Dinah . . . I didn't know where to go . . . and I tried to kill myself before, and I couldn't."

Hetty goes on to reveal that she could not bear others' scorn, but then the thought occurred that if she got rid of the baby, she could go home again. She continues, "I don't know how I felt about the baby. I seemed to hate it—it was like a heavy weight hanging round my neck."

A silence is followed by a shudder. At last, Hetty bursts out with a sob, "Dinah, do you think God will take away that crying and the place in the wood, now I've told everything?" Hetty feels accepted by Dinah, yet needs reassurance that God will forgive her.

Hetty's feelings of being readmitted into the human community after being morally exiled, according to Jung, is at the heart of relief. To one degree or another, like Hetty, we risk self-disclosure through psychically disrobing in exchange for the relief that comes from being recognized for who we are. We experience relief when we receive for the first time, or retrieve, the unconditional love we were supposed to have gotten as very young children. The recipient of our secret—priest, lover, or friend—often is recast in the role of the parent who accepts us in all our nasty, destructive, or downright horrid guises.

Self-Expression

Far too often, we are a house divided. Secrets separate us from parts of ourselves deemed by us or others to be too risqué to emerge. When we gather the courage to express these disavowed thoughts and feelings, we experience relief. By getting out our repressed thoughts together with the feelings, we experience a new level of integration.

The confessional journey takes a major step forward when we move from relating the story of our secret to viscerally feeling the emotional impact of the secret. Joyce, who was repeatedly raped by her father between the ages of ten and fifteen, related a particular episode to me with unexpected convulsive sobbing. As it dawned on her that she had been robbed of her childhood, the relief she experienced was far more profound than when, earlier on, she had merely recounted the terrible events of her childhood.

Confession along with emotional release can bring greater self-awareness when we risk revealing the parts of ourselves we preferred not to acknowledge in the past. Jamie's confessions in Eugene O'Neill's *Long Day's Journey into Night* remind us in a startling way that meaningful relief sometimes involves knowing ourselves and revealing ourselves to others, regardless of the final outcome.

In his climactic confrontation with his brother Edmund in act 4, Jamie drunkenly confesses that he intentionally lured Edmund into situations that would "make a bum" of him: "Made my mistakes look good. Made getting drunk romantic. Made whores fascinating vampires instead of the poor, stupid, diseased slobs they really are. Made fun of work as a sucker's game. Never wanted you to succeed and make me look even worse by comparison. Wanted you to fail. Always jealous of you. Mama's baby, Papa's pet."

While witnessing these confessions, we, the audience, sense that Jamie is not confessing to rid himself of his troublesome emotions, but rather to widen awareness and sympathies. O'Neill also suggests, more in line with religious and Aristotelian views of catharsis, that the only way to cleanse the family is through the process of confession.

Jamie's purgative confession of his love-hate feelings toward his brother relieves him of the burden of self-deception. Now that he feels cleansed, Jamie believes he is worthy, for the first time, of his brother's trust. All the characters struggle with their ghosts in the dark night of the soul, but Jamie's is the most wrenching confession of all because he acknowledges what he did to his brother and who he is in the present; the others confess as a way only to justify their pasts.

Self-Destruction

Some of us feel so desperate because of our conviction that we are sinful, morally corrupt, or just plain unworthy, that we experience relief only through self-destructive acts. At times, the behavior itself becomes a symbolic, nonverbal confession that needs to be decoded in order to get at the secret. My patient Elaine cut herself with a piece of broken glass as a way of "getting out the poison." It was only after I continually exhorted her to get out the poison in words that she gradually revealed that this was her only way of expelling the "mother/devil" inside her who told her how stupid and bad she was. Elaine felt compelled to enact the cutting ritual over and over again because cutting brought only temporary relief; her internalized toxic mother would appear again to torment her. Putting her behaviorally played-out secret into words offered her more abiding relief when she saw she could trust me not to hurt or taunt her the way her mother had.

Elaine's initial means of gaining relief through self-mutilation mirrored religious rituals in which punishment for wrongdoing or moral imperfections in the form of scourging or self-flagellation brought relief. Since the dawn of time, gods and heroes as well as men, women, and children have undertaken mutilation to purge themselves of evil spirits for high and noble purposes rather than as a form of perverse relief. In several religions and among many preliterate peoples, relief through self-mutilation was seen as a way of achieving physical well-being, as well as purifying oneself spiritually and making amends for wrongdoing.

Elaine's feelings of relief brought about by cutting herself and sometimes pulling out her hair was a Band-Aid solution that was continuously reenacted in a vicious cycle. It was only when she was able to put the secret into words that she began to own it and work it out.

In research on self-mutilators, psychiatrist Armand Favazzo found that more than half of those who mutilated themselves (like Elaine) had hellish childhood experiences involving physical and sexual abuse, and the prolonged absence of love, nurturing, and physical contact. Many who cut and burn themselves do so as a way of compulsively gaining relief that rarely lasts. As a therapist, I have found that the presence of an ongoing, empathic relationship slowly erodes these patients' defenses. When they are ready, they put the secret meaning of their symbolic self-mutilating behavior into words. If they sense that I am with them, they develop the strength and resources to expel their inner demons through words rather than actions.

Sometimes committing murder brings relief to those who are so burdened by their secret sufferings that there appears to be no other way out. In Edna O'Brien's novel *Johnny I Hardly Knew You*, the narrator is driven to find relief from the suffering she has experienced at the hands of men, beginning with her sexually abusive father. She finally murders her lover, who is also her son's best friend.

Having become involved with a man who offers her love, caring, and commitment, she casts all aside in one terrible moment in bed in which she relives the secret of her insupportable relationship with her father. Hart, her lover, appears to be having a seizure, but all she sees is her mad father frothing.

Because she never dealt with her dreaded secret head-on, her need to expel and get rid of the internalized abusive father took the form of relief through murder. She achieves revenge for her secret suffering by exorcising the paternal demon. Murder—and the feelings that accompany it—bring temporary relief. "There was unleashed in me some great find of hate and horror and I wonder now if hate had not been at the very seat of love, or fear or disgust or lovelessness," she says.

Written Confessions

Not all of us are emotionally ready or willing to risk revealing ourselves directly to others. In the eighteenth century, disclosure through letter writing reached its zenith. For many of us living in the computer age, e-mail has replaced hand-written letters as a means of quickly confiding in others as well as getting to know people on-line. Marriages have even resulted from this form of technologized intimacy.

The diary is another powerful tool for self-disclosure. Because relationships to diaries are so private and so closed, noted diarists such as Samuel Pepys and Virginia Woolf more frequently revealed hidden aspects of self to their diaries than to intimates.

It is sometimes easier to bare our souls through written confession outside the presence of a confidant. As Graham Greene pointed out in *Ways of Escape,* writing itself is therapeutic and brings relief as we unburden ourselves of our secret concerns. The diarist's need to reveal herself to herself outside the prying public eye speaks to the benefits of this form of release.

Sidney Jourard was one of the first psychologists to note that talking or writing about one's secrets could reduce and even prevent psychological and health problems. More recently, psychologist James Pennebaker demonstrated that people who write about their secret traumas, as well as the thoughts and feelings surrounding them, experience greater psychological and physiological relief, including heightened immune function. The benefits derived from written disclosure involve not just physical relief, but also self-understanding.

Telling our story to a diary or computer can bring tremendous relief, because the secret is now, somehow, out. It is widely known that keeping problems bottled up inside can cause emotional and physical stress. Writing about traumas can put some distance between us and the traumatic experience. Getting it off our chests and onto paper helps us gain mastery over our secrets in lieu of being enslaved by them.

Diary writing, like therapy, provides a confidential avenue for self-expression. The diary itself is often viewed as a specific other and may be personified by being given a name (e.g., Anne Frank addressed her diary as "Dear Kitty"). The diary here becomes a confidant and even a valued friend that cannot talk back or betray our secrets.

For many diarists, the diary becomes a constant companion. Not surprisingly, many people first begin to keep diaries in adolescence—a time of turmoil and shifting identity. One of my patients remarked, "My diary gives me a sense of stability because my family was always in chaos. In venting my feelings and exploring my thoughts, my diary was a place of comfort and relief. During moments of great despair, it grounded me. It was something to hold on to—an anchor."

Pennebaker maintains that we work through a trauma by writing about it continually over time. In the absence of a human confidant who is there to help us explore, understand, and work through the secret, the diarist is less likely to come to grips with many of the issues surrounding the trauma.

Nonetheless, written self-disclosure brings cathartic benefits. One of my patients described the relief he experienced as follows: "My diary enables me to get out my hidden feelings and let off steam. By writing important things down, they become more fixed and more a part of me. It makes me feel better to be able to go back in time and revive memories at will."

Virginia Woolf was able to gain some relief from anxiety after confiding in her journal. "Why is life so tragic, so like a little strip of pavement, over an abyss? I look down, I feel dizzy; I wonder how I am ever to walk to the end. But why do I feel this: Now that I say it I don't feel it."

Some of us come to see the diary, like the therapist, as a special confidant who is safe and affirming. Both diary writing and therapy are confidential forms of self-expression that ultimately enable us to gain relief. In each form of disclosure, we bridge time as we travel into our pasts to better understand our present selves.

The Role of the Confidant

Letting our secrets tumble out indiscriminately does not bring relief; spiritual fulfillment comes by *communicating* our secrets to our fellow beings. Relief results when we are listened to, empathized with, and accepted by confidants who are there for us.

Some of the classic work on relief involved soldiers and veterans coping with post-traumatic stress after World War II. They fell prey to their secret obsessive thoughts—of murder, bombing, leaving buddies behind in order to save themselves, and so on—which often ended in nightmares, panic attacks, and obsessive ruminations.

The relief experienced came from reexperiencing the original trauma through hypnosis or from talking about it, but *only* if the soldiers realized they were in a safe place with an understanding, non-censorious therapist. Getting out anger, fear, guilt, envy, or other disavowed feelings was only a first step toward achieving relief. Lasting relief was brought about by constructively working out these secret traumas with the help of the therapist who would stay fully engaged with the patient in the encounter with the terrors of the wartime soul.

The psychoanalyst Heinz Kohut observed that our need for affirming others is like our need for oxygen. We need others to hear us and help us work out our confessions for our psychological survival. Just as a mother who is emotionally attuned can help her child identify and accept his emotions, so the attuned therapist is indispensable in providing a climate that will help us release our secrets. Nowhere else in the world are we as free and as safe to air our dirty laundry. With confidentiality guaranteed and the hour totally devoted to our needs, we can let down the walls of reticence and pretense in the absence of danger and repercussions.

Who we confess to, along with the setting we choose—as psychologist Carol Tavris reminds us—can be more important in bringing about relief following confession than the disclosure itself. Letting out secret angers to the wrong confidants can increase tension by raising our blood pressure and make us feel angrier than we did before the confession.

Without a receptive audience, people disclosing their secrets may be worse off than if they never confessed, according to research psychologist Roxanne Silver. Her interviews with over a thousand Vietnam veterans (summarized in Beth Azar's *APA Monitor* article) revealed that, in general, those who related wartime and postwar experiences felt more relieved. However, veterans who reported that people did not want to hear about what happened to them in Vietnam expressed more stress and intrusive thoughts.

Whether we allow ourselves to fully express hidden feelings or not also depends on whether we see our confidants, past and present, as permitting or denying emotional release. During one session, my patient Faye, normally a polite, charming twenty-nine-year-old writer, burst into a rage, raised her fist at me, and paced menacingly up and down the office. A minute later, she recovered and apologized profusely to me for her emotional outburst.

Faye's mother, who was an alcoholic, insisted on two things: that no one ever discuss her drinking, and that no one in the family display any sort of emotion—she viewed emotional displays as unseemly. I conjectured that perhaps Faye thought her anger would kill me. She vigorously nodded, restating her mother's edict that nice, well-brought-up girls did not display or even have rageful feelings.

Faye needed to deny or dissociate herself from her rageful self in order to guarantee her survival in the family. As she continued to see me as separate from her mother, she was able to take more risks in therapy by letting out these secret disavowed parts of herself. When she saw that I accepted her rather than ridiculing or berating her as her mother would have done, she began to experience genuine relief.

In many segments of our society, expressing emotions is prohibited—almost as if simply having strong feelings is a terrible secret to guard. Messages that deter us from expressing emotions and thereby gaining relief abound: "Don't be a crybaby," "be a man," "temper, temper, young lady," and so on. My patient Karen's mother would banish her to her room whenever she looked sad or angry, saying, "Go to your room until you can have a smile on your face." In this atmosphere, secrets and the emotions connected with them are quickly suppressed or repressed.

Power relationships can also work against relief. If I decide to throw caution to the winds and confide my secret resentments at being treated unfairly to my boss, he may be just as likely to counterattack as to empathize, since he holds the reins of power. Angry outbursts or withdrawal, in tandem with initiation of divorce proceedings on the part of betrayed spouses, illustrates the dangers of disclosure when the impact on the confidant is not sufficiently taken into account. At other times, the expression of suppressed grievances is understood by the confidant who can forgive or make amends for thoughtless behavior. Here the self-discloser can truly experience relief as the two become closer following confession.

The confidant is not always liked; sometimes simply being there offering an ear can be enough for the discloser to go through the depths of despair in order to gain relief. The Canadian novelist Brian Moore, in *The Lonely Passion of Judith Hearne*, presents us with a memorable character, Judith Hearne, a plain Irish-Canadian woman holed up in a boarding house and increasingly giving herself over to drink after being rejected by a fellow boarder whom she saw as a potential mate.

During one of her weekly visits to a friend, she makes a desperate confession to his wife, Moira O'Neill. Covering her face, sobbing, she declares, "And I never liked you, Moira. That's the truth, I never liked you." After Moira, as confidant, accepts her despite her insults, Judith feels freer to let out her forbidden feelings of loneliness, degradation, and despair.

"Moira, I've lost my faith. . . . What am I doing with my life? . . . A single girl, with no kin, what am I doing?" Encouraged by Moira's non-censorious receptivity, Judith mentions "with confessional zeal" that Moira has not yet heard the worst: "No, no, I'm going to tell you the whole thing, Moira, the whole thing. Because I have to tell it to somebody, somebody must listen." Judith then goes on to describe herself as marked-down goods at an auction with no one bidding for her.

At this point, Moira begins to weep, as she more fully reveals her compassion toward Judith. Judith cannot stop now. She relates how any man who offers her a kind word becomes a prince, and then blurts out that the American who was courting her was only a doorman, and even he turned her down.

Moira's steadfastness as the series of confessions builds to a crescendo, as well as her heartfelt expression of compassion through weeping, allows Judith to release her secrets, experiencing relief also through crying and facial quivering. With her faith in God and the traditional confessional quickly eroding, Judith is nonetheless able to experience a measure of relief through Moira's human concern and acceptance.

My patient Maria, a forty-three-year-old administrator, demonstrated how important continually working on and working out a secret in the safety of ongoing therapy is in finding relief. Maria was shocked, forlorn, and deeply depressed when she discovered that her former boyfriend had hanged himself. After she revealed John's suicide to me, she went through months of bereavement, alternating between feelings of numbness, depression, and anger at John. One day, she came into therapy looking relaxed and refreshed. She began, "I finally feel total relief, and I can't believe what brought it on. I ran into John's cousin, who insisted on telling me every detail of how John hanged himself. It occurred to me that I should feel sick, but after every gory detail was revealed, I felt my whole body relax. And it has continued a week later.

"You see, I knew that John was an expert with ropes. He had made my bookshelves and strung them together with rope, and they held up for years. So he really planned his death so it would work. He was never successful in life, but he wanted his death to be successful.

"Now it has all finally come together. John wanted his death. It wasn't in response to any one person or thing. So I'm off the hook at last."

Maria began to feel the weight of her guilt leave her, as she was able to visualize John in the act of killing himself. She had previously wanted to leave therapy because of the pain she experienced as she dredged up her terrible problems with John in life and death. Maria often intoned, "I always thought, 'let sleeping dogs lie.'" To which I replied, "And now you see that these dogs have a habit of waking up."

"Yes," Maria responded. "I've got to continue to face his death, and that he won't be around anymore." Maria at first had been reticent to face the reality of John's death and to grieve for him. It was only when she reframed the meaning of his death—acknowledging that he finally had been successful at something—that she was able to also acknowledge the impact of his death and face the range of disavowed feelings that surfaced during therapy. As listener, questioner, interpreter, and sometimes prodder to get at secrets Maria was adept at dodging, I experienced both her rage at my relentlessness and her gratitude at my persistence in being with her throughout her ordeal.

Scottish psychoanalyst Ronald Fairbairn saw the therapist as the successor to the exorcist concerned with casting out devils. For Maria and many other patients, lasting relief comes when self-disclosure casts out bad figures whom we have internalized and who continue to exert an influence on us, even from the grave. Maria's boyfriend left her through death; yet the legacy of guilt, self-blame, and depression he exerted when alive continued unabatedly following his death. Maria was able to begin to relinquish the hold this relationship had on her only when she felt secure enough to confide in me as the loving parent she never had. She was able to rid herself of John, as well as other internal "demons," both by replacing them with me and by recasting John in the more sympathetic role of unfortunate victim who ironically took control of his life by taking his life.

A secret trauma itself is usually not enough to leave an indelible scar on our psyches. It is our inability to express our pain to ourselves and others that leaves emotional wounds. By paying attention to the discloser's plight and tuning in to her shame and pain, she regains respect as she recognizes that she is accepted and being taken seriously.

Again, relief is not simply a matter of emotional release; it comes through working out the traumatic past. As confidants, our willingness to empathize with and sometimes even be advocates for those who were neglected or abused allows our friends, relatives, or patients to gradually allow their secrets to emerge. We do not bring about relief through gimmickry; rather, we provide a safe and secure haven for secrets to be revealed or reexperienced and worked out.

The therapist or priest often becomes the gatekeeper to the wider social realm, as we try out our secrets with them in order to see whether relief is even possible elsewhere. To be heard and accepted means that we are not alone. The burden of guilt and shame is alleviated through sharing the secret. The relief that follows is indispensable to the "cure of the soul."

3

Redemption

AT LEAST ONCE in our lives, each of us has cried out to a
stranger, a beloved friend, or God: "Save me!" As sophisticated
twentieth-century people, we are sometimes surprised by the primi-
tive resonance of that plea. Yet, from what or from whom do we seek
to be redeemed—from our own sordid pasts, from the ominous dark
side of our natures, from present oppressors, or from an amorphous,
primal uneasiness lying just beyond our reach?

Many of us gloss over or assiduously avoid the role that redemption plays in our lives, yet we are all faced with themes of redemption
and transformation every day. Therapists often enter the field with
conscious or unconscious thoughts of rescuing others. Having experienced the futility of healing their own dysfunctional families, many of
them wish to rescue their patients from similar fates.

Many of our romantic relationships are based on our need to be
rescued by a "knight in shining armor" or on the need to rescue the
beloved. These motives temporarily shift the focus of the relationship
from the problems of daily living toward a loftier, more idealized plane.

When we risk confession, we embark on a journey that we hope
will end in redemption. In confession, our darker side has been ex-
posed and rendered less powerful. No longer forced into a Jekyll-Hyde
dichotomy, we see ourselves as whole persons. Like the phoenix that
rises from the ashes of its own destruction, we are freed to embark
upon a new, less constricted phase of existence.

Redemption (from the Latin *redimere*—to buy back) literally means liberation by payment of a price or ransom. The risk of confession it-self—of opening ourselves up to others with no guarantee—is the one we pay. This chapter later addresses how the relentless pursuit of the truth—no matter how painful or horrible—is another price we pay for freeing ourselves from self-deception. A third potential price: at times, we witness the death of our old, inadequate selves as we are trans-formed to a higher, more fulfilling level of being.

There is always a price to pay for redemption. But since the end product is freedom from self-deception and from a cautionary, mea-sured life not fully lived, it is truly worth the cost.

The Price of Redemption

The Bible speaks of payment of a price in order to be delivered from evil. In everyday life, facing the demonic in ourselves may be the price we pay to secure our freedom.

The risk of confession, sincerely offered to ourselves or to others, is the price we consider and weigh in the balance in our quest for re-demption. When May Karr wrote *The Liars' Club*, a memoir of her East Texas childhood, she left no holds barred in her quest for the truth. Karr reveals how her mother, married seven times and often rendered insensible by drugs and alcohol, set fire to Karr's toys and tried to kill her. To add to her misery, Karr was raped by a neighborhood boy at age seven and was later molested by a babysitter.

It was not until she was grown that she discovered some papers in the attic which revealed the secret that shaped her family. In a previ-ous marriage, her mother had two children who were kidnapped by their father and never returned. The reason for her mother's many marriages, as well as her need to escape through drugs, suddenly be-came very clear. In Karr's words, her mother "had started marrying people to get her kids back." Her mother never confided her secret to Karr for fear of alienating her further.

Karr's relentless quest for the truth and her willingness to face the family drama in all its ugliness and ignominy made redemption pos-sible. The accidental discovery of her mother's secret enabled her to retrieve a crucial piece of her past and see her mother in a new light.

Is the truth sometimes too wrenching a price to pay for redemption? Socrates', and later Freud's, core philosophies were based on the premise that only the truth can set us free. Karr was never the same again once she set out on her quest for salvation. She was able to find meaning in the chaos of her past and to discover that her life, once examined, was worth living.

Joni Mitchell's song "Circle Game" reminds us, "Something's lost, but something's gained, in living every day." When we reveal secrets that have imprisoned or deformed us by preventing us from moving forward in our lives, we gain much more than we lose. Baring our souls is part of the price we pay for redemption.

Redemption does not come without risk or effort. In the Old Testament, God redeems "with a stretched-out arm," making known God's strength. The New Testament speaks of Christ's blood as the price he paid to secure freedom for those who would believe in him; he redeemed humankind quite literally with his blood.

Effort and even agony enter into redemption. Sometimes risking disclosure may seem too high a price to pay for a redemption that may never be attained. Witness the dilemma of Hilary Burke, the hapless antihero of Iris Murdoch's novel *A Word Child*. Hilary is driving at 100 miles an hour with Anne, the wife of a university colleague with whom he is having an affair, when Anne confesses to carrying her husband's baby. Enraged, Hilary gets into an accident in which Anne and her unborn baby are killed.

Hilary ponders the possibility of redemption: "Can sheer suffering redeem? It did not redeem me, it just weakened me further." Like the branded woman Hester Prynne, doomed to wear the letter *A* for adultery in Nathaniel Hawthorne's *The Scarlet Letter*, Hilary imagines himself carrying the placard *Murderer* around his neck forever.

Dostoyevsky believed suffering was a necessary prelude to redemption. In all his novels, characters go through a spiritual cleansing process, an atonement deeply rooted in Orthodox Christianity and Russian folk tradition. This leads his cast of characters from sinful, even evil lives to redemption. His masterful last novel *The Brothers Karamazov* is permeated with the drama of human redemption. Even the family's kindly priest, Father Zossima, and the saintly Karamazov brother Alyosha have known evil and passed through it to a higher state. Unlike Murdoch's Hilary, who is paralyzed by his cowardice, Mikhail Karamazov's dramatic confession to Father Zossima redeems him.

Mikhail confesses to Father Zossima that he had murdered his mistress fourteen years ago because she wanted to marry someone else. A servant was implicated in her death but died in prison before he could be brought to trial. Mikhail, overcome with guilt, finally confesses to the authorities, whereupon he falls ill. On his deathbed, Mikhail tells Father Zossima, "There was heaven in my heart from the moment I did what I had to do."

Mikhail transcends his wretched state as he recasts himself into the mold of sufferer finding relief through a sense of relatedness with God and the human race through confession. There are no shortcuts to redemption. In Dostoyevsky's world, suffering is essential for the expiation of guilt and ensuing spiritual redemption.

Even if our lives are at risk in confessing (so often the case with Dostoyevsky's characters), the grace we receive by feeling God's love and forgiveness allows us to sense ourselves reborn as we "come clean" through telling the truth. Redemption is also a human enterprise. We seek to right ourselves with our fellow beings in order to be absolved and redeemed.

The secret many of us do not care to contemplate is that suffering often results from not even trying—from finding a thousand reasons why we should not risk revealing ourselves—even as a path to finding redemption. It is only by *doing*—by putting ourselves on the line through language, restitution, or creative transformation—that we can be redeemed.

There is no redemption when confession takes place in half-measures. Redemption comes to us when we are willing to do away with—let die—those aspects of ourselves that stand in the way of a new life, of rebirth. Freed of those malignant aspects that can threaten our very existence, we are renewed.

The mythologist Joseph Campbell identifies many examples in

world mythology and fairy tales of metaphoric death through being consumed: swallowed into the belly of a whale (e.g., the Bible's story of Jonah and similar stories from the Eskimos of the Bering Strait, the Zulus, the ancient Celts, and the Polynesians), or eaten by a wolf, as in the tale of Red Riding Hood. The lesson we learn, notes Campbell in *The Hero with a Thousand Faces,* is that the passage inward is a form of self-annihilation as a transition into a sphere of rebirth. The Bible (John 12:24) likewise refers to the cyclical nature of death and rebirth in all living things. "In very truth I tell you, unless a grain of wheat falls into the ground and dies, it remains that and nothing more; but if it dies, it bears a rich harvest." The journey inward, often undertaken in confession, can be perilous as we meet our own brand of fearsome monsters. But risking confession—even to the point of annihilation of our very psyches—allows us to emerge renewed and strengthened.

Ernest Becker, in *The Denial of Death,* underscores the paradox that we are biologically finite yet symbolically infinite creatures. We live on through our progeny, good works, and creative endeavors. Because we are symbolically capable of infinite possibilities, our secrets once revealed are not just dead artifacts that are unearthed whole; rather they undergo permutations as they are reborn in the context of our present experience and social relationships.

A vivid example of the paradoxical twists redemption can take is the "death-in-life" followed by "life-in-death" revelations faced by the protagonist in Leo Tolstoy's masterful short story *The Death of Ivan Ilyich.* Ivan Ilyich Golovin is dead when the story opens; in fact, we read his death notice. In reality, however, he has been psychically dead all his life—a cold, calculating, ambitious lawyer and judge who never really lived. He never admitted to himself how deadened his existence was, devoid of love, consideration, and intimacy.

He falls ill and endures a slow, painful fading away, with no one—not even his wife, friends, or colleagues—attempting to understand him or sympathize with him. It is only toward the end of his life that Ivan Ilyich becomes emotionally close to his young servant, Gerasim, and begins to recognize the young man's worth as a fellow being.

In his last weeks, he is transformed. Ivan Ilyich sees his wife and son in a new, more empathic way as his old, selfish self dies with his failing body. As he becomes able to open himself to others as never before, he is truly alive. He is redeemed. As the fog of self-deception is lifted, Ivan Ilyich is awakened to life as life ends. Ivan Ilyich, in a sense, finds redemption by being "born" anew, rather than from re-covering a lost, primordial part of his nature that had been hidden away.

Yet the latter is often what takes hold of us in redemption. Israel Baal Shem Tov, the great Jewish mystic said, "Forgetfulness leads to exile, while *remembrance is the seat of redemption.*" Our memories cata-pult us forward in our confessional journey; our anguish moves us in the opposite direction toward concealment.

How many victims of childhood sexual abuse or violence carry their wounds around with them and even allow them to multiply by becoming abusive adults themselves? By concealing the secret of abuse from themselves or from others, they are condemned to relive their trauma or to remain wounded in their hearts and minds.

Memory, on the other hand, is a catalyst on the confessional jour-ney toward redemption. Confession confronts us with the painful, yet heroic task of jogging ourselves out of our Lethe-like slumbers of for-getfulness into stark awareness. When we welcome rather than fear making ourselves known, we begin to deliver ourselves from the false comfort of self-deception.

The Levels of Redemption

Redemption takes place on different levels. While religious and histor-ical worldviews focus on the "great individual" or charismatic leader who saves his people (most notably, Christ, Mohammed, the Buddha, and Moses), the early psychoanalytic movement emphasized the indi-vidual who is saved from parental tyranny and self-deception by be-coming autonomous. Later approaches (notably, self psychology and object relations) have focused on our need to take initiative in concert with affirmation and support from our friends, lovers, or therapists.

I view redemption as taking place on three levels: (1) the reli-gious/charismatic model involving salvation through surrendering ourselves to a larger power or leader; (2) the self-sufficiency model in which we believe that only we can save ourselves through our own efforts; and (3) redemption through collaborating with others to pool our efforts. We experience all three levels to varying degrees at different times in our lives.

Level 1: Redemption through Merger with Another

We sometimes feel that the way to get back our true selves, or the parts of ourselves that have been too long submerged, is to give ourselves over to earthly or higher powers who will redeem us. Freud spoke of the "oceanic feeling" in which we experience blissful union with the archaic mother.

Even on this level, we are never totally passive. Organizations such as Alcoholics Anonymous and Overeaters Anonymous assume that addicts can be saved only by actively taking responsibility for their addiction while simultaneously giving themselves over to God who oversees and aids in their redemption.

Symbolic death and self-transformation begins with the common acknowledgment of "hitting rock bottom," often made in AA meetings. At times, an AA meeting is not unlike a religious revival meeting; the excitement of bearing witness is a satisfying substitute for the temporary highs of alcohol. Spirituality is a core element in Alcoholics Anonymous, Narcotics Anonymous, and Overeaters Anonymous; all of these Twelve Step programs praise God for lifting the curse of addiction "one day at a time." Six of the famous Twelve Steps of AA talk about relying on God or a "Higher Power." The experience of confessing in public and feeling accepted and applauded for our courage gives us confidence that we are on a redemptive path. For those who invoke God as a source of forgiveness, succor, and love, these Twelve Step meetings take on an aura of salvation. When redemption firmly takes hold, spiritual highs replace drug-induced highs.

Organized religions and religious cults offer redemption to those who adhere to their rituals and belief systems. Encounter therapies also bear witness to symbolic death and rebirth. The metaphoric use of words such as *reborn* and *saved* are found in evangelical Christianity in both Protestant and, increasingly, in Roman Catholic churches.

There are fascinating parallels between Egyptian mythology and

Christianity regarding redemption through merger with a higher being or hero. Both view human salvation from death as occurring through vicarious participation in the experiences of a divine hero who has experienced death and resurrection. In both, the divine hero is not a distant, omnipotent deity; rather as one who has shared the human experience of suffering and death, he is someone close to us. Merger with a flesh-and-blood hero such as Christ thereby humanizes the process of redemption.

The Janus-like face of destruction and redemption forms part of our collective religious heritage. In Christianity, with its triadic godhead, the Son gives himself up for sacrifice, dies, and rises again in order to redeem humanity from the bondage of sin and spiritual death. The link between destruction and redemption is also part of Hinduism. In the divine triad of Hinduism (Brahma, Vishnu, and Siva), Siva literally means "the blessed one." Although for Hindus, Siva represents the destructive principle in life, rebirth from the ashes is implicit. Without destruction of the old there could be no rebirth.

In Judaism, the goal of the High Holidays is not merely repentance but also renewal. Renewal is sought by continually examining our lives. As Rabbi Irving Greenberg notes in *The Jewish Way*, "The awareness of being judged for life and death is a stimulus to stop living routinely." That religious challenge finds its secular equivalent in our casting aside routine, safe living through self-disclosure in our everyday lives.

The family romance is another variant of redemption through merging with or being rescued by powerful others. As first described by Freud, the child who is disillusioned with her own parents fantasizes about having other parents who might be celebrities or royalty. The fantasy of being rescued by the "real parents" has its analog in religious conversions or membership in cults in which the believer feels redeemed through identification with idealized parents or omnipotent leaders. The price redemption brings is nothing less than dissolution of previous identity; what is recovered is a sense of specialness that comes from the feeling of being reborn.

On the secular front, women who are searching for their "knight in shining armor" or men who are looking for their Dulcinea see the idealized beloved as being able to save them from the yoke of their "toxic parents" or from toxic aspects of themselves. In these instances, the romantic partner is idealized and therefore myopically viewed as a symbol of salvation rather than as an equal partner to share in the vicissitudes of daily living. Redemption is possible only when both partners work with each other in keeping the secret bargain they have made with each other; namely, "I am willing to be saved by throwing in my lot with you and passively adhering to your view of the good life."

Our yearning for redemption often arises out of a need or deficiency. As long as the partner who is seeking to recover a primordial state of security through marriage makes these secret needs known to an accepting spouse, the needs are no longer secret, and a path to redemption becomes possible. Should the idealized partner want mutuality, or should the initially passive partner change and develop an autonomous identity, the possibility of redemption gives way to marital discord or dissolution.

Level 2: Redemption through Self-Sufficiency

A Swedish proverb states: "The best place to find a helping hand is at the end of your arm." Those who pride themselves on self-sufficiency believe they can save themselves only through their own efforts. Thus, as friends, parents, or therapists, we are faced with the paradox of how to best support those in our lives who believe we are superfluous in their quest for redemption.

In some instances, we may be viewed as hindrances or even enemies to be psychologically avoided; other self-sufficient types may deliberately choose a life of solitude, as did the philosopher Immanuel Kant, to pursue creative goals. Still others adopt the narcissistic position that only they can save others or themselves from disasters.

When we are disillusioned by our parents at an early age, we may steadfastly hold to the belief that redemption lies in our own hands. In this way, we convince ourselves that we need never be vulnerable or needy again. When a child frequently feels abandoned, neglected, abused, or betrayed, he only trusts himself to be responsive to his own needs. John Donne's "No man is an island, entire of itself" is transformed into "Every man for himself."

When they grow up, children who have been massively disillusioned with their parents often unconsciously choose relationships in which they can be emotionally invulnerable and avoid further disappointment by remaining what George Atwood terms "counter-dependent." Women may marry men whom they hope to rescue as a way of fending off their own secret neediness.

Carrie was a twenty-four-year-old graduate student bent on saving her husband, Carl, an attorney who hated his job and all authority figures. He secured a number of positions and promptly lost them. Whenever his job was endangered, he threatened suicide.

From the start of their relationship, Carrie assumed the role of Carl's rescuer. By constantly rescuing Carl through offering advice, rewriting his resume, and simply being there, Carrie controlled the relationship. She was so busy trying to save Carl from one catastrophe after another that she conveniently avoided dealing with her own problems, which went underground. These secret problems included hatred directed at her inept sister whom her parents favored and repeatedly attempted to rescue, and feelings of incompetence manifested by her reluctance to return to her dissertation and complete it.

Carrie's one-sided rescue attempts enabled her to postpone facing her own need to be saved from those parts of herself she did not wish to acknowledge. By finding a weak and incompetent mate, she was able to suppress these same qualities in herself. It was only when Carrie acknowledged these disowned parts of herself in my presence that she gradually began to relinquish her need to be self-sufficient.

Rescuers like Carrie harbor the secret of their own desperate need to be rescued. Ironically, the chosen "needy" partner often propels the first step toward redemption by holding up an extreme mirror to the rescuer/partner of her own secret neediness, ineptness, or lack of ambition. Rejuvenated in the presence of an ongoing relationship predicated on trust, the rescuer becomes brave enough to recover those parts of herself she did not dare acknowledge before.

The price of disclosure is nothing less than opening up the shutters that have too long hidden the needy, vulnerable part of the psyche. The relief that comes from no longer having to "go it alone" frees people like Carrie to seek redemption in the intimate embrace of others.

The secret part of the psyche that often comes into play in those who attempt to rescue others is that of the messianic/charismatic superperson defying all odds. My patient Sandy, a bright, articulate twenty-seven-year-old computer programmer, was one such person who spent her life trying to rescue others at great expense to her own autonomy.

She revealed, with some trepidation, that in college her favorite game was "Who would you like to be?" "I was the only person who wanted to be Christ, because I always wanted to be a superhero."

For Sandy, moreover, love had always been equated with suffering. She never felt loved as she was by her mother, and she identified with her divorced father, whom she viewed as dying alone, devoid of real love.

Sandy also confided that she was suffering from a crisis of faith. "We all are searching for God or something to believe in," she said. When I noted that our earliest gods are our parents, Sandy continued, "Yes, my mother was always a goddess—loving and beautiful—but now she and I are so different. Her New Age religion has come between us." My comment to her was, "Your world has become godless since your mother fell off the pedestal." Sandy, teary-eyed, concluded, "Yes, I know I need to believe in myself, but it's lonely."

Sandy's story contains many of the redemptive elements in confession. Her attempts to rescue men and her Christ fantasy attest to her secret grandiosity. Over time, she realized that her own redemption would only be attained when she became willing to forgo her need to rescue others.

It is difficult for us to trust others, especially when those closest to us have inflicted trauma that runs deep. Sometimes, becoming self-sufficient is a vital first step in dealing with the wounds to the soul. D. H. Lawrence grapples with these issues in his poem "Healing."

> I am not a mechanism, an assembly of various
>   sections.
> And it is not because the mechanism is working
>   wrongly, that I am ill.
> I am ill because of wounds to the soul, to the
>   deep emotional self

and the wounds to the soul take a long, long
    time, only time can help
and patience, and a certain difficult
    repentance,
long, difficult repentance, realisation of
    life's mistake, and the freeing oneself
from the endless repetition of the mistake
which mankind at large has chosen to sanctify.

Lawrence could well be extolling the healing power of confessions. Trauma wounds the soul, and secrets left untended fester as they continue to imprison rather than free us. The process of confession, beginning with the courage to reveal ourselves and mediated by relief, sometimes in the form of repentance, ideally culminates in redemption, as we free ourselves from repeating life's mistake.

Self-sufficiency is not always either a defense or a retreat from life. As true for us as it is for caterpillars, a cocoon is both something to protect us and a boundary out of which to break free. In therapy, I sometimes become a boundary extension for a patient as the two of us live with the paradox of allowing the patient to keep a secret safely ensconced within a "cocoon" for as long as is comfortable. At some point, the patient feels sufficiently comfortable and trusting to give birth to the secret with me as an unobtrusive background presence.

Self-sufficient disclosers often need the confidant to be as unobtrusive as possible with them in order to break out of their cocoon and begin healing the "wounds to the soul." Indeed, as the therapist or friend continues to pass the self-sufficient person's tests, remaining steadfast and true throughout, a subtle shift may occur as the confidant is seen more as a helpmate or collaborator, rather than an intrusive hindrance.

I am reminded of my patient Serge, a twenty-nine-year-old actor, whose self-sufficiency needs were transformed into a quest for redemption in concert with me. Serge grew up in a family whose ethos was one of self-sufficiency and control. Even when Serge's lover was dying from complications of AIDS, he felt useful and powerful in being able to come to his lover's rescue and make his last months better by ministering to all his needs. Serge was unaware until much later in our work together that he harbored a secret salvation fantasy in which only he, by virtue of his specialness, could save his lover. This secret went against the family script of being stoic and humble in all endeavors.

Following his lover's death, Serge was cast further into crisis by having to deal with his parents' divorce (after twenty-five years of marriage) and a nephew's impending death from cancer. During one session, Serge adamantly stated, "I'm not going to let myself get drawn into their problems the way I used to. They are all tugging on me for sympathy and advice, and I just don't want to get sucked in anymore. I'm just plain drained."

I then remarked, "You no longer feel as though you have to save everyone. In letting Kirk die, you saved him and saved yourself. You saved him by letting go of your need to keep him alive as long as possible." These remarks followed Serge's description of standing vigil at his lover's bedside. When Kirk became unconscious, Serge held his hand and whispered, "It's okay to die now. Don't hold on to your pain anymore. Let go." And Kirk died the next day.

Serge was able to acknowledge and let go of his secret beliefs that only he could save Kirk and that Kirk and he would always be a self-sufficient couple needing no one but each other. Kirk's death jolted him out of his solitary existence and also marked a radical change in our relationship. Serge initially used therapy to support himself through his lover's impending death and to bolster his grandiose self, which secretly held to the belief that only he could save Kirk.

Following Kirk's death, Serge was surprised at the number of feelings he experienced in rapid succession, ranging from hatred toward everyone, including Kirk, to despondency at the enormity of his loss. He was able to acknowledge his gratitude toward me, as well as his resentment at feeling dependent on me.

Six months after Kirk's death Serge looked directly at me and stated, "You saved my life," temporarily seeking redemption through idealizing me. I replied, "We worked together as a team to save your life." Serge nodded and smiled. It was important at this stage for Serge to understand that seeking help from others was fine, but that his contribution was also integral to the quest for redemption.

Serge made strides in forging a new, separate, "uncoupled" identity that needed bolstering. My acknowledgment of his contribution to the redemptive process helped him to sense the transformation made possible by working with another person instead of retreating into self-sufficiency.

Whenever therapists, lovers, or friends embark on a confessional journey with another, it is important that we resist assuming the role of savior—a role that a grateful intimate might want us to assume. We want our friends, lovers, and patients to face their conflicts and work to shape their unique solutions—*not* to avoid their individual identity struggles by identifying with an overidealized confessor/redeemer.

Moving from self-sufficiency to merger with an idealized intimate is usually *not* redemptive. We must be there for others, particularly for those who have trod the self-sufficient path, not as proselytizers, but as guides on the difficult, sometimes hazardous journey in search of redemption.

Level 3: Redemption through Our Efforts in Concert with Others

In chapter 2, confession was presented as a relational act—ideally, a form of communion between souls in which the speaker and listener are engaged in a meaningful, intimate encounter. Because we are vividly aware of the listener—whether friend, colleague, parent, or therapist—and have expectations about how our disclosure will be greeted, our secret rarely emerges in pure, undiluted form.

Sometimes we alter the secret to make ourselves appear more acceptable to others. At other times, we exaggerate the heinousness of our "crimes" in order to test whether our friends will stay with us in spite of knowing our secrets. Here the confidant is put on trial to see whether she has the courage and stamina to stick with us throughout the confessional process.

The Bible tells us, "In the beginning was the word." Words are vital to our existence; used impulsively, they can kill; chosen judiciously, they become the means of our redemption. In the aforementioned "let-it-all-hang-out" encounter groups of the 1960s, participants often wantonly revealed rage or hatred directed at strangers in the group.

Some suicides ensued that were directly attributed to these disclosures. In these instances, words literally killed!

Confessions expressed to intimates who accept and work with us to resolve our secret dilemmas salve our spirits, in part, through a frank exchange of words. This is because in an ideal confession, we—patient and therapist, parent and child, friend and friend—are partners in dialogue. As confidants, we should never simply be omnipotent interpreters or acquiescent automatons who compliantly support whatever our friend is revealing. True, there are times when our friend may primarily need quiet support; at other times, interpretations may calm the flood of uncertainty that is washing over the discloser.

The most redemptive confessional journey is the one in which my friend and I are partners in dialogue. Suppose, for example, I confide in my friend that I am planning to leave my husband after ten years of marriage. Which style of relating on the part of my friend would work best for me? My friend might comment, "You must be out of your mind. He's fantastic. You'll never find anyone even remotely as good as he is." This interpretive/punitive mode, instead of offering redemptive possibilities, shames me back into an imprisoning marriage or ends my friendship.

Alternatively, a friend might offer unqualified support, enthusiastically assuring me that whatever I do is okay with him and that I will have his support. This affirmation does make me feel comfortable in the short run, but it shortchanges me of the opportunity to look at the ramifications of my decision in greater depth. There is usually a price to pay—the disclosure itself may be that price—in redemption. But my friend's easy agreeableness allows me to avoid dealing with the harder issues radiating from the disclosure.

As a partner in dialogue, however, I am neither unduly punitive nor needlessly compliant when my friend reveals a secret. I am an active as well as an interactive questioner, explorer, interpreter, problem-solving companion, and guide who, along with my friend, uses language to gain freedom from self-deception and bad relationships.

The philosopher Ludwig Feuerbach once said that speaking is an act of freedom. Whenever we fail to reveal ourselves through speech because of anxiety, fear, or self-consciousness, we remain imprisoned within ourselves. By freeing ourselves from the tyrannical hold of the unconscious, from isolation from our fellow beings, or from constrictions to self-awareness, confession leads us toward redemption.

Prisoners in solitary confinement redeem themselves from the hell of going crazy by making up stories and reciting poems out loud. Confession—the telling of our own stories—likewise frees us from our prisons of isolation and desolation.

On this third level of redemption, therapy constitutes a special kind of cooperative team enterprise. Patients know, implicitly or explicitly, that they hold the key to their own salvation. They work with therapists to save themselves from the darkness of their own self-deception. Through the therapeutic enterprise, patients seek to transcend destructive aspects of self in order to integrate their divided selves.

Psychologist Robert Jay Lifton, in his book *The Nazi Doctors*, described the defense of "doubling," whereby Nazi doctors created an "ordinary self" in which they were healers and an "Auschwitz self" to avoid the conscious awareness that they were murderers. Moral behavior was reserved for those in the in-group among whom they were healers, while doing harm to those in the out-group was viewed as justified. Although this is an extreme example, we all occasionally split off disagreeable or repellent parts of ourselves that may hurt or even destroy others or ourselves. By increasing our awareness and acknowledging *all* parts of ourselves, we are less likely to victimize ourselves or others.

In redemption, the opposite of doubling occurs; namely, people who engage in healthy redemption have a sense of self-integration along with the ability to empathize. Unlike the Nazi doctors who engaged in doubling, we, as confidants, seek to bring the dispirited, disillusioned, or disenfranchised into our universe rather than exclude them from it. In healthy redemption, confidants act compassionately rather than dispassionately. We try to acknowledge good and bad aspects in ourselves as well as in others.

In unhealthy redemption, on the other hand, we see ourselves as coming to a less fortunate individual's rescue in order to glorify ourselves or validate our own competency. We come to view ourselves as therapeutic saviors or masters on how to lead "the good life." By respecting our friends who confess to us—that is, by literally seeing them for who they are, along with their characteristic ways of being in the world—we avoid the pitfalls involved in unhealthy redemption.

Previous discussions referred to a death-rebirth theme that occurs on both religious and therapeutic levels in redemption. This theme is illustrated in a version of the Egyptian myth of Horus and Osiris, in which the murdered Osiris descends to the underworld. He remains passive only until his son Horus, the new king, visits to tell him the old order has been reestablished. Through Horus' ministrations, Osiris is transformed into a living soul.

So disclosers, at times, are "brought back from the dead" in part through the infusion of hope by their confessors. Osiris is the prototype of every soul who hopes to conquer death. People who are depressed, disillusioned, or demoralized routinely undergo deathlike experiences. Revival requires the confidant, like Horus, to serve as a facilitator and breathe life back into the discloser who has adopted a primarily passive state of being.

Redemption is made possible by the joint efforts of the confessional pair. Spiritual or psychic death becomes the essential prelude to life as confidant and discloser together grapple with the secrets of the discloser's soul—secrets that thankfully are not permanently dormant, but rather are in a state of becoming. Freud referred to the unconscious as an active unconscious; this enables us to access and face our secrets in order to free ourselves from their dominion. Once the secret is acknowledged and discussed, it has already forfeited its passive, static state of hibernation.

As our disowned, heinous parts are owned by us and restored to consciousness through language in the presence of an intimate, the confession is *already* transformed, and so are we. Just as Horus revived his father, Osiris, so does the confidant as guide help recover and transform our secret selves in a covenant with us that promotes redemption.

Redemption as Self-Transformation

When our confessions carry us all the way to redemption, we experience ourselves in entirely new ways. We witness the birth or rebirth of a self invigorated with new possibilities for leading our lives.

When we choose to do nothing to relieve and work out the perceived heinousness of a thought or deed, guilt or shame revolving around the secret tends to escalate rather than diminish. Only by erecting and maintaining an elaborate system of defenses and subterfuge are we able to continue to keep these disowned parts of ourselves submerged. When we are locked into self-deception or trapped in a cycle of lies based on a need to live in dreams, confession becomes impossible.

Facing the tragedy of our existence is the first step on the road to redemption. In Gustave Flaubert's novel *Madame Bovary*, Emma is slowly destroyed by the intricate fabric of lies on which she has based her life, by the buildup of debt to support the vanities of that life, and, inevitably, by blackmail, so much a part of the enclosed provincial world from which she is trying to escape. With the breakdown of her illusions and the accumulation of unbearable realities, her destruction becomes inevitable. Since she could not confess and thereby redeem herself, she chose suicide instead.

Destruction (either of demonic aspects of ourselves or of psychically malignant relationships) may sometimes be indispensable for self-transformation. The psychoanalyst Wilhelm Reich, mentioned in chapter 2 as a vital contributor to our understanding of the nature of character armor and ways of finding relief, was launched on a redemptive path in response to a tragic episode in his own life. At the age of fourteen, Reich discovered that his mother was having a secret affair with one of his tutors. When Reich reported the infidelity to his father, his mother killed herself.

Reich underwent redemption through his own struggle with sexual repression, which culminated in a theory on the enlightening aspects of freedom and the nonrepression of sexuality. In *Faces in a Cloud*, psychoanalysts Robert Stolorow and George Atwood view Reich's atonement for the betrayal as taking the form of utter commitment to a theory based upon the "eradication of all those values and ways of thinking which had motivated him."

Reich's history reveals how another's destructiveness (his mother's suicide) resulted in a life devoted to redemption and transformation. In radically transforming his own mores and inner convictions, Reich's creative expression also touched and transformed others.

The theme of confession and its aftermath of destruction evolving into redemption and transformation appears in sharp focus in Reich's life. Yet following self-disclosure, many of us experience redemption without destruction as a precursor. I am reminded of Arnold Schoenburg's *Transfigured Night,* composed in 1899, based on a poem by Richard Dehmel. The music itself moves from dark to light, guilt to . innocence. In the poem, as a woman walks through the woods, she confesses to her lover that she is pregnant with another man's child, and resignedly notes that life now has its revenge, since she has met her lover too late. The lover consoles the woman, and exhorts her not to burden her soul with guilt. He describes the special warmth flowing between them that will transfigure the child and make it truly theirs.

Both the poem and the music reflect the redemptive and transformational possibilities inherent in confession. The woman risks confessing her pregnancy to her lover, who reassuringly accepts her. She then gains relief and is redeemed through this acceptance. The two are luminously transformed through the confessional bond established between them. The child will be a living testimonial to the woman's redemptive experience and to the couple's renewal.

Martin Luther, as a novice, went through the ceremony of lying before the altar with his arms spread away from him like Christ's on the cross. Erik Erikson, in his psychohistory *Young Man Luther,* notes the prior's concluding words, "Not he who began, but he who persists will be saved." Confession is the first step in a gradual process that requires faith on the part of both discloser and confessor that, through persistence and sometimes painstaking effort, we will develop a sense of redemption. It is this persistence that is so often missing in a world in which magical beliefs and quick-fix approaches intrude on virtually every aspect of life.

We come to experience ourselves in new ways through confessions that are transformed in the process of remembering and working them through. By discovering, uncovering, and owning the past, we move toward autonomy in the present. Our guilt-ridden or shameful selves shift in the direction of greater strength, tolerance, and willingness to work out our secrets. When we recover a secret, we never return to a static sameness, but rather encounter a past mastered and transformed in the light of present awareness.

Marcel Proust transports us into the realm of renewal in his masterpiece *Remembrance of Things Past*. Proust experiences inexplicable pleasure from reminiscences in which chronic depression and inertia are suddenly transformed into feelings of self-worth. In each of our lives, repressed secrets may sweep over us in such a way that the less-than-blissful past is now relived as an elated present moment in which, as strengthened and more integrated people, we triumph.

The self-transformation wrought by confession was especially striking in the case of my patient Jim, a thirty-two-year-old graduate student in physics. In our sessions, Jim usually related his life experiences in a highly intellectualized way. However, in one session, things took a dramatic turn when Jim unexpectedly made a long-suppressed, shame-inducing confession:

> When I was thirteen, I brought a little girl of six into the house to play. I told her that I would get her some artificial flowers but that in the interim, I would have to tie her up so she would not get lost. She agreed and I bound her hands. When I returned, I gave her the flowers and she left. Although I did nothing to her sexually, she told her parents and the story reached most of the neighbors. My mother never let me live down the shame. Even though I did nothing to molest her sexually, I still feel I'm evil because I later conjured up that scene when I masturbated.

While Jim voiced his conviction that this confession confirmed the evil in him, the act of sharing his secret with me and not feeling judged in the process enabled him to reexamine his attitudes and actions which were predicated on his still strongly internalized Catholicism. By freeing himself from the yoke of self-deception, Jim was able to gradually evolve new options that both redeemed him from his former idea of sinfulness and realigned his sexual priorities.

Jim began to rebuild his self-image. By altering his fantasies, he was able to alter his perception of himself. He began to will fantasies of sexual intercourse in tandem with the bondage fantasies.

Jim's self-image, bolstered by my acceptance and further exploration of his confession, enabled him to share his secret with his girlfriend. Since they then enacted both intercourse and bondage fantasies to their mutual enjoyment, Jim no longer viewed himself as a sadistic monster beyond redemption.

Like Jim, when we confess we return to the scene of the "crime" or trauma both to master the original situation and to use the episode to renew ourselves. Because the past is constantly reconstructed by the present, we are freed to transform rather than relive the past through the radicalizing (literally, returning to one's historical roots) process of confession.

The psychologist and philosopher William James introduced the concept of "second birth." In *Varieties of Religious Experience,* James differentiated the once-born from those "divided selves" who search for a second birth that will convert them in their "habitual center . . . of personal energy." A common confession that heralds the onset of a second birth concerns a sense many people get of feeling free creatively and/or emotionally only after a parent has died. I recall one patient who at age sixty began to dance and paint after her aged father died.

Erikson speaks of a second birth as the resolution of an identity crisis. If we do not find fertile ground for the establishment of our own identity, we may instead commit ourselves to ideological movements or charismatic leaders that result in a forfeiture of identity. Conversely, therapy is a kind of ideological endeavor that encourages us to find our true selves without being swallowed up in the service of a group, system, or ideology.

Confession in psychotherapy places issues of identity squarely back on our shoulders. When we reclaim our own histories, we begin to achieve redemption. In owning the past and integrating it into the present, we can see an ever-widening view of our reowned selves in relation to old and new people in our lives.

Many people experience this second birth—often saving themselves from despair and even suicide—through self-transformations brought about by commitment to their own creative work. Friedrich Nietzsche and Frida Kahlo were two creative geniuses whose art was often redemptive in nature.

In a letter to Hans Von Bülow dated December 1882, Nietzsche disclosed, "My new way of thinking and perceiving, which has been reflected in my books for the past six years, has kept me alive and almost cured me." The self-transformation brought about by Nietzsche's creative efforts resulted in redemption and renewal.

In contrast to his megalomaniacal letter in which Nietzsche experienced himself as transformed and saved through his writing, other letters disclose the despair that cast a cloud over his life. At such times, he bemoaned the fact that nothing could save him from his darker side. In a letter to Franz Overbeck dated March 1883, he lamented, "I've lost interest in everything. Deep down, an unyielding black melancholy . . . I feel so incomplete, so inexpressibly conscious of having bungled and botched my whole creative life." Nietzsche alternated between exuberance and pride in his accomplishments and suicidal thoughts and feelings of demoralization. Nonetheless, his ability to return to his creative nature enabled him to continually recreate himself out of the ashes of his despair. Nietzsche bypassed death by experiencing rebirth repeatedly through his art.

Sometimes redemption and self-transformation can arise out of the death of a marriage. Take the harrowing example from Ingmar Bergman's 1973 production *Scenes from a Marriage*. The husband, Johan, presents himself as a self-confident, extroverted, successful academician; Marianne, his wife, appears to be the quieter, more dependent, and less confident partner.

Marianne uses her diary as a confidant. In her diary, she traces her need to please to a childhood in which any attempt at self-assertion was harshly punished by her mother.

As time passes, we witness Marianne's self-transformation toward liberation, independence, and strength; and Johan's development in the opposite direction, becoming more and more insecure in his career and in his role as a man and human being.

The price Marianne pays for achieving freedom and self-transformation is the dissolution of her marriage. Redemption comes when she reclaims an aspect of herself that has survived her mother's and husband's demands to be weak and obliging. Marianne's redemption comes from acknowledging and reowning past secrets and from sweeping her more secure, liberated self into the future by ending her marriage.

The Pursuit of the Heroic

Many of us have a need to be heroic—to make a difference on a grander scale, if only fleetingly. Joseph Campbell, in *The Power of Myth*, states that the hero's objective is to save a people or a person or to support an idea. The theme of death and rebirth becomes an integral part of the hero's journey, as he might die or descend into darkness as part of his trials. He would then be born again or metamorphosed into a fruit-bearing tree sustaining his people, for example. The hero dies, but the power of his soul lives on.

Therapy itself, at times, becomes a perilous journey in which patients, as heroes, risk exposing themselves, seeing their illusions die, and facing hitherto hidden aspects of themselves as they are born in a process marked by psychic death, transformation, and redemption. The process of renewal in myth and therapy constitutes a return to our roots. In order to come to terms with our identities, we reconnect with those aspects of our parents and other intimates that are heroic and worthy of being championed.

In the process of redemption, we may also kill off those aspects of our parents and ourselves that are no longer viable, while preserving those aspects that add continuity and heroism to our life story. Rebirth on the heroic therapy journey is a process in which our self-image is reorganized along with our revitalized relationships to others.

Dreams can reveal heroic aspects of ourselves we might normally play down or not even realize exist. As avenues for spiritual awakening and redemption, dreams allow us to disclose secrets and hidden aspects of ourselves that might not otherwise see the light of day. My patient Gloria's dream in which her perils, trials, and heroism underscore many aspects of redemption is one such example.

> I was in a candy store from my youth, giving the customers information on how to heal naturally. As my son Vance and I were walking past another store, we saw a wounded dove. I had to help the bird and so I took it with me.
>
> Then we were in a rowboat, and I laid the bird down. But the bird had become a lamb whose eyes were covered over with fur. The boat was in the East River. To our left, a giant ship was being pulled by a smaller ship. I showed no fear or worry. In the wake of the large ship, many fish were jumping up. They were so close that I decided to reach over, get the fish, and put them in the boat. I also picked up a "dollar fish" that was unusual looking.
>
> I said that it was a good thing that we took the lamb, because the lamb would have been slaughtered. I thought to myself, "I've saved the lamb. Now I'll heal it and it will live."
>
> I then realized that the boat had no paddles, but I put my hands into the water and paddled back to shore. One person on shore mentioned the unusual dollar fish.

The dream began with an undisguised portrait of Gloria as a natural healer—a role that she assumed from an early age toward everyone except herself, since she secretly felt unworthy. She was constantly rescuing her younger brother, who got into scrapes with the law, as well as her older, alcoholic brother, by forcing him into rehabilitation centers on various occasions.

Gloria was the one who came to everyone's rescue, since her depressed, hypochondriacal mother was always on the couch recuperating from an operation or a host of pains that immobilized her. The secret which symbolically manifested itself in the dream was that Gloria saw herself as the would-be slaughtered lamb, since she had been physically abused by her father and her husband, as well as by her brothers. Gloria was not able to save herself from her destructive marital choice and gradually fell victim to the same passivity as her mother.

Gloria's dream, however, came at a crossroads in therapy, when she began to move from a passive to an active stance. She realized that in order to save herself, she would have to stop saving everyone else and start tending to herself. Gloria viewed the flaps on the lamb's eyes as her own blindness and self-deception when it came to doing anything to get herself out of her current predicament.

A strong redemptive theme that emerged in Gloria's dream was her own resourcefulness. She was able to paddle to shore on her own power—using her arms—and thus find a creative solution to save herself and her son from being cast adrift.

Gloria saw the smaller ship as her son. "I guess that in some ways I've used him as a whipping boy (her son was a successful banker who partly supported her) by financially bleeding him to seek revenge on all the other men who hurt me," she said, wistfully. Once her hidden rage toward the abusive men in her life emerged full-blown, Gloria started to see that her own road to redemption did not lie in staying financially bound to her son, but rather in "freeing myself to catch my own dollar fish." She was able to acknowledge that her tremendous rage toward the men who had abused her had been displaced onto her son—the only man who unstintingly gave to her with no strings attached.

Gloria was able to save both herself and her child by providing food in the form of fish. Unlike the frightened Gloria who cowered at the sight of her abusive father, in her dream she was able to save the day without fear.

Dreams—especially what Jung referred to as "big dreams" heralding major life themes and self-transformations—are one of the best ways to harvest our secrets and work them out in order to achieve redemption. When we take our dreams seriously and try to understand and integrate what is revealed into our broader lives, we can get in touch with the heroic in ourselves.

Gloria's dream represents one pivotal step in her heroic journey toward self-redemption—a journey we all risk in our dreams at critical periods in our lives. Gloria transformed herself from a woman who thrived on saving others at tremendous cost to herself to a woman who was able to tend to her own needs by revealing herself to me with all her attendant vulnerabilities.

Dreams are wonderful examples of confessions that get to the heart of secrets or secret themes in our lives which might not otherwise see the light of day. We shed our everyday defenses and inhibitions in our dreams. When we take the time—in or out of therapy—to pay attention to our dreams as confessions rich in meaning, we can continue on a confessional path toward redemption. Gloria's dream, when shared, was itself a confessional leap from self-sufficiency toward seeking redemption through a collaborative effort.

Gradually disclosing this dependent side of herself led Gloria to turn the redemptive focus toward herself instead of others. The death-rebirth theme found in many hero myths revealed itself in the imagery of the near-slaughtered lamb that was able to be brought back from death.

Whereas Campbell's mythological heroes save others on a grand external scale, the hero in therapy or, for that matter, in everyday life, sets out on an internal journey in which self-redemption becomes the heroic task. As Gloria became able to let go of self-destructive patterns and risk new ways of being that seemed, at times, frightening and awesome in scope, it became evident to me that her self-transformation was nothing short of heroic in nature. Unlike Campbell's solitary heroes, we can become the heroes of our own existence by taking the journey inward together with our intimate soul mates as fellow travelers.

· II ·

Confessions
from the Cradle to the Grave

4

The Emergence of Confessions

CONFESSION is one of the earliest forms of communication that binds us to each other in an intimate, trusting way. As social creatures, we ideally begin life attached to others who are there to meet our growing need for physical care, nurturance, and emotional closeness. Researchers have long observed the importance of emotional attunement and intimate give and take between mother (or other primary caregivers) and baby. It is that relationship between caregiver and infant that is most crucial in early life.

Pediatrician and psychoanalyst Donald Winnicott often said that "there is no such thing as a baby," meaning that we understand a baby only in relation to the mother or primary caregiver. As the channel for baby's cries, babbles, and other assorted sounds, the parent is not just a passive receiver, but also a "meaning giver." How she processes and feeds back what the baby communicates is vital for the development of trust and the child's ability to communicate at a more sophisticated level later on.

Confession is a complex outgrowth of the interaction inherent in the earliest stages of the parent-child relationship. When we share a secret, we get the most out of the experience when the confidant truly listens and tries to match our needs with a sensitive and understanding response.

If the parent is a sensitive listener (perhaps the most important ingredient for a confidant), the child, in turn, learns how to listen. When a confidant's words instruct and soothe us following a disclosure, we learn that throughout our lives we can find feedback from empathic others to help us solve problems as well as maintain a sense of well-being. Such positive early experiences provide a foundation of trust and stability.

As we grow up, we create boundaries between ourselves and others. Secrets are the cutting edge of determining and regulating those boundaries; they control the flow of information or enhance relatedness. Our right to privacy is bolstered early on by the often unspoken social rules prohibiting entering a room before knocking or disturbing family members when they are in the bathroom. This sense of privacy also carries over to secrets. Even very young children are entitled to have secrets. Children learn whom they can trust with their secrets and how friendships sometimes become alliances revolving around shared secrets.

Children who are allowed a zone of privacy by their parents have less trouble establishing boundaries for self-disclosure as adults. Privacy is a boundary control process in which we decide when to make ourselves accessible to others and when to close ourselves off.

Some of my patients and friends have related early memories of mortification in which parents, oblivious to their children's right to privacy, barged into the bathroom or bedroom. To add to these indignities, some parents who caught their children masturbating warned them about the contrived dire consequences of this behavior, including disease or even death.

In such households, parents observe no boundaries. Children are treated as extensions of their parents or nascent entities to be molded to fit parents' needs and desires. Mary McCarthy captures this sense of intrusiveness in her aunt's child-rearing practices in *Memories of a Catholic Girlhood:* "The basis, I think, of my aunt's program for us was in truth totalitarian; she was idealistically bent on destroying our privacy."

Children use secrets to subvert the oppression in these types of households. While parents may more or less succeed in destroying their children's physical privacy, secrets enable children to retain their psychological space. Secrets remain an indispensable salve to their souls even as their bodies and physical surroundings are subjected to various indignities.

When children's physical boundaries are nonexistent, they clamber to maintain at least some control over their psychological boundaries. Keeping secrets enhances autonomy and minimizes vulnerability. In families where children's privacy is respected, there is no need to guard secrets at all costs. Children learn that others close to them are trustworthy and supportive. Sharing secrets in these families is a way to become even closer without risking dire repercussions.

The privacy that secrets confer enables us to develop and maintain an identity. If I can define what is me and what is not me, what belongs to me (including my secrets) and what does not, I am better able to define and understand myself.

In adulthood, privacy continues to be a boundary issue in which we look at ourselves in relation to others and consider how much or how little contact with other people best suits our psychological and spiritual needs. When we come from families that lack privacy, we often go to extremes. Boundaries between ourselves and others are either so tightly maintained that we become withdrawn and alienated or, at the other extreme, so lax that we spill our secrets to anyone who will listen, indiscriminately revealing ourselves in a way that could endanger our social standing as well as our self-image. Early assaults on our privacy may seriously limit or even destroy our ability to trust others or make sound judgments about when self-disclosure will really enhance our lives.

Secrets are the raw ingredients for confessions. As we know, families often collude with each other to prevent secrets from emerging.

Malignant secrets, those that eat away at the soul of the victim or family, often remain locked up, off-limits to outsiders. One of my patients was repeatedly raped by her father over a period of ten years, beginning in preadolescence; her mother colluded in the incestuous relationship by remaining silent about it, by not "seeing" or recognizing it. Her father warned my patient that if she told anyone about his demands, something bad would happen to her. He also suggested that if she told, no one would believe her anyway. Her father and mother, as "partners in crime," colluded with each other to keep the secret hidden from her brother and grandmother, as well as from the outside world.

Secrets, even malignant secrets, often involve alliances. In the above mentioned instance, my patient's parents colluded against her to sustain the incest over several years. In many other instances of child abuse, the trauma is borne in silence by the child alone.

Two other common kinds of secret alliances are formed in childhood: the playful, child-centered alliance and the power-oriented parental alliance. Many of us recall keeping secret collections of rocks or other childhood treasures hidden from our parents; others had a close friend with whom a secret, imaginary world was shared. These childhood secrets and secret worlds made us feel special and temporarily outside the boundaries of our parents' world of rules and regulations.

We learn to set boundaries early on to protect ourselves against rageful, retaliatory parents, or merely to gain approval by keeping certain secrets—those that we may view as shameful or disgusting—underground. On the other hand, when we are fortunate enough to develop a sense of security through "good enough" parenting, along with a basic sense of "being okay," we are more willing to trust others with our secrets.

When children realize that their thoughts are not accessible to others, they begin to acquire the notion of privacy. Psychologist Russell Meares' research indicates that this landmark development takes place during the fifth year of life. This sense that a child has a secret that belongs to her and that she may choose to retain or reveal this secret is a major step in the development of a self-concept—a sense of who the child is and what makes her the person she is—apart from what her parents tell her.

Suppose that when a child reveals herself, she is made anxious or made fun of by parents who are incapable of tenderness. These conditions give rise to what Harry Stack Sullivan terms the "malevolent transformation" in which the child may begin to assume that she lives among enemies with whom she can risk no intimacy. To protect herself, she learns to distance herself. Keeping secrets locked inside a self made vulnerable through repeated trauma or pain becomes a means of survival in a hostile world.

Melanie Klein was one of the earliest analysts to elaborate on our internal psychic world as a powerful influence on our development. According to Klein, we do not just relate to people "out there"; we also relate to those significant intimates that we have internalized. Thus, one reason we keep secrets from ourselves is that we do not wish to offend or suffer retaliation (albeit fantasized) from our archaic childhood parents. The strength of our internalization of those earliest models can allow them to affect us even from the grave. We have only to read Franz Kafka's autobiographical "Letter to his Father" to see how childhood fears and humiliation can invade and pervade a person's psyche throughout life.

Childhood Secrets

In *The Poetics of Space*, philosopher Gaston Bachelard describes the house as a tool for the analysis of the human soul. The house has a long history as a psychoanalytic image for the body and self. Bachelard notes, "And by remembering 'houses' and 'rooms,' we learn to 'abide' within ourselves."

Many of our secrets reside within our childhood homes. The memories we retrieve often inadvertently bring forth secrets that startle us as well as the confidant with whom we are sharing them. A friend revealed that she had no recollection of feeling connected with her brother, who died of leukemia when he was eight. My friend was six at the time.

But once when she mentioned her brother, something different happened. She spontaneously started to conjure up memories of the physical nature of her brother's room and his possessions. By sensing herself in that space, she was able to dredge up her secret jealousy of the attention her sick brother was receiving, seemingly at her expense.

Bachelard also reveals how chests and caskets, their contents concealed, are witnesses of the need for secrecy. Yet they also beckon us to open them — to expose their physical contents either for our curiosity or for our betterment.

We open windows to clear the air and clear our souls. We open chests and caskets to open our pasts to ourselves. Sometimes, our secrets become evident to us only through a physical shock to our senses that opens part of a secret world to us.

Attics are repositories of childhood secrets. My patient Pat decided to turn her attic into a nursery. While rummaging through her old ballet shoes, dolls, and other toys, she experienced the kernel of a long-buried secret evoked by these objects.

When Pat was ten, her older sister would throw out her toys, along with her other possessions, and Pat would continually retrieve them from the garbage. "It was like she was throwing out my past. I discovered my ballet shoes and through them, a long-forgotten secret. When we were girls in ballet class, I had tripped my friend Isabelle before she went on stage, so that she appeared, at best, to be an awkward duckling. My audition shone by comparison and I got the part."

Bachelard surmises, "He who buries a treasure buries himself with it. A secret is a grave." Sometimes, in order to revive an important part of ourselves, we must risk digging up our secret treasures. But unearthing them is not enough. *We must share our secrets*—both to resuscitate our past and to breathe new life into ourselves by facing and truly working out those secrets in the present. The foundation for sharing secrets arises in the earliest harmonious communications between baby and caretaker. This sense of mutuality sets the tone for subsequent confessions.

Infancy and Intimacy

Babies are actively engaged with caretakers from the start, not only to express their biological needs, but also to begin to interact socially with others. Chapter 2 makes the point that confessions are primarily relational—a means of linking ourselves to others—and that in our later relationships, even when we share secrets in part to alleviate bodily tension, we are also acting to enhance intimacy.

Psychologist Daniel Stern, in *The Interpersonal World of the Infant*, asserts that as early as the seventh to ninth month, an infant has the capacity for psychic intimacy—the desire to know and be known in the sense of mutually revealing subjective experience.

Infants, of course, cannot reveal themselves through language, but

Stern asserts that their mental states can be disclosed through sharing attention with the mother. Infant research has shown that some time before the ninth month, the infant begins to turn her head to follow her mother's line of vision—mirroring her mother's inclination to move her head in the direction in which she's looking. But infants at this age not only visually follow their mothers' directions to reach a target; they also look back at their mothers' expression for feedback to confirm that they have arrived at the intended target.

Early on, infants are able to take another's perspective into account. The baby's early acknowledgment of others, along with her need for validation, becomes more subtle and refined as she grows older, bringing the confidant's meanings and perspective into her world by sharing confessions.

A second example of shared perspective can be observed in some children of eighteen months who cry and become upset when a parent cries and shows other signs of being sad. This demonstration of empathy implies that very early life experiences equip us to resonate with others in using combined perspectives to resolve confessions.

Others are sought not merely for soothing and intimacy, but also because they provide mental stimulation. The desire to unravel the mysteries of life, in concert with the desire to seek out others as partners in the process, begins early. This interweaving of curiosity and communal needs, while considerably less cognitively complex than confession, nonetheless contains the kernels of risk taking and relatedness that enters into sharing confidences.

Developmental researchers Colwyn Trevarthan and Jean Piaget have reset traditional child-development timetables, believing children can communicate a wide range of emotions and hold on to mental images much earlier in life. Because the ability to emotionally express oneself and discern others' emotions, as well as to remember critical incidents, are basic ingredients for forming and sharing secrets, the blueprint that facilitates or impedes self-disclosure is likely to be laid down in our earliest interchanges.

Hearing allows us to take in not only sounds but also impressions of our physical and interpersonal world. Our mothers' breathing and heartbeat are among the earliest indicators we have of a world beyond our own skin. No wonder hearing is so deeply associated with our emotional relationships. We know that it is *not* nursing at the breast per se, but rather hearing the steady rhythm of mother's heartbeat that soothes the baby and promotes bonding.

Psychoanalyst Didier Anzieu suggests that a sound mirror—a sound image of the self—develops at a very early age. His research implies that our earliest form of identification may derive from the baby's connection to the sound of the mother's voice—the "sound bath." The melodious bath of the mother's voice and her songs provide the baby with a sound mirror used first for his cries (calmed by his mother's voice), then for his babbling, and finally for the development of language.

What adults often seek in confidants is the kind of receptivity they first found in a sensitively attuned mother. The tone, as well as the language of the confidant, become crucial in determining whether we are attuned to, or tune out, what the confidant wants to tell us.

When we search for other early developmental markers in the evolution of confession, attachment is also a concept of singular importance. John Bowlby's and Mary Ainsworth's research demonstrates that we attach ourselves to others throughout life. The accessibility and responsiveness of the mothering figure is crucial for our attachment potential later in life, as well as for the development of trust which is required to reveal our secrets to others. Secure early relationships based on empathy and trust are a solid foundation for later attachments in which we feel secure enough to risk disclosure.

Bowlby observed that all infants, regardless of their care, become attached to a caretaker. Simply "being there" is a major component in early shared confessions. A neighborhood friend, or the parent who is seen as most accessible and empathic, may become a targeted recipient of secrets for this reason.

Attachment represents a balance between security and exploration. Psychoanalyst Margaret Mahler observed the eighteen-month-old infant's exploratory zeal in dashing away from her mother, sensing the freedom of her own actions. After a time, however, she turns around to make sure her mother is still there, as a secure base at which to "refuel." The back-and-forth movement of that early stage of infant development is much like the balance we seek in confessing later in life. We can more easily risk self-disclosure when we feel secure that our confidants are accepting and cooperative. Under these conditions, we can feel some of the exploratory exhilaration of the young child as we run through a confessional course with confidants whom we can turn to at various points along the way with certainty and love.

Stories as Confessions

From the start of life, storytelling strengthens the emotional bond between parents and children. How stimulating and comforting were those precious childhood storytelling moments. Stories were a way to be with the people we loved most in the world while risking the adventure of being transported into other worlds. As adults, we avidly listen and take in information when we become spellbound by stories; the ability we learned as children—to learn from the stories we were told, to absorb every exciting detail—can later become an essential skill brought into play in sharing and consuming confessions.

Stories enable us to experience many things: a sense of connection, emotions ranging from happiness to fear, and a stretching of our imaginations. All these storytelling elements account for our natural tendency to express confessions in story form.

Indeed, confessions almost always assume a narrative form. Confessions are our life stories—stories which shape and transform us for better or for worse.

Developmentally, storytelling is one of the earliest forms of educational, cognitive, and emotional enjoyment shared between parents and children. Children learn to construct stories about their own experiences, including their secrets, from these early stories. As was true of our childhood stories, when we relate confessions as stories, we do so to make sense of ourselves and our world by simplifying life. We hearken back to what is familiar in telling our confessional tales.

Confessions in the form of stories evoke in us childhood "once-upon-a-time" feelings of security. When a confession involves the distant past, the historical remoteness of the story makes it feel less risky. Murderous rage in a child vented against spiders is not quite as alarming as its adult counterpart.

A Roman Catholic patient disclosed how she confessed to her grandmother that she had dropped the wafer (host) on the floor while receiving communion. She was so humiliated by her clumsiness that instead of picking it up as she had been taught, she pressed her shoe onto the wafer to conceal it. Her grandmother, in a fit of self-righteousness and probably remembering the old nuns' tales of her own childhood, told her granddaughter that she was going straight to hell for desecrating the host.

Having carried around her childhood secret for more than twenty years, this young woman finally felt enough trust to tell me about it. The simple act of telling her story to a nonjudgmental listener gave her a tremendous sense of relief. Historical distance, coupled with her need to be understood rather than condemned, enabled her to risk confession. Since this patient viewed me in the transference as a benign authority figure who served as a substitute for her condemnatory grandmother, she was able to experience me as a receptive, accepting confidant.

We are continuously searching for meaning in our lives. Often, our lives take on meaning when we see ourselves as actors within our own life story, be it a family saga, a tale of heinous crime (real or imagined), a morality tale, or an exhibitionistic one-person monologue. Our secrets are stories to be told, taken seriously, repaired, and worked out as we move through the confessional journey.

Childhood Confessions

Language is our richest means of making ourselves known, through a meaningful dialogue with another person, through an exchange of ideas and feelings. From birth on, the parent interprets the infant's behavior in terms of words, creating meaning from her perspective. Gradually, as the child develops language, meanings are mutually created and shared.

Speaking becomes a shared experience between parent and child.

Disclosures made by the child to a parent become an early form of intimacy in which the child shares an inner experience. Sharing a secret becomes a way of "being with" the parent through words. The two can now share mutually created meanings about the secret by continuing their dialogue. Psychologist John Dore calls these negotiated shared meanings "we meanings."

We usually view language as a skill that helps us achieve individuality; childhood confessions connote that the opposite is equally true — that language is also used to further togetherness. Our confessions are usually shared with others to achieve intimacy and acceptance, as well as to bring the confidant's perspective into a shared pool of meaning.

Language can bring us closer, but language can also deceive us and create a world of illusions. My patient Debbie was obsessed with the possibility that her mother might die at any moment, even though her mother was healthy and only in her late forties. Exploration of this obsession revealed that when Debbie was five, her older brother left home one day and never came back. While family members attempted to hide what had happened, Debbie discovered a week later that her brother had died of a drug overdose. The little girl worried because it rained all week, and she was afraid her brother would be too cold in the ground. During the summer, Debbie worried that her brother would be too hot.

When Debbie asked her father what death was, he told her that everyone died when Jesus called them. She then asked if Jesus called on the phone, and her father said yes. As a result, she became frightened of phone calls for a long time.

Language was used by Debbie's father to conceal, distort, and falsify the actual circumstances of her brother's death, as well as the nature of death itself. These explanations increased the little girl's worries and preoccupation with death to such a degree that as an adult, separation anxiety became the pivotal theme of her relationships with people.

Many of our earliest secrets are characterized by predominantly self-related concerns. Very young children (two to seven years old) often operate on what Jean Piaget terms *egocentric principles*. These children, captive within their own viewpoint, take other people into account only insofar as they fear repercussions from authority figures. Children who pull the wings off butterflies or kill frogs get caught up in their own enjoyment without considering the pain they cause. Among the most common secrets from this period, which emerge in adulthood, are petty theft, cruelty to animals and younger or weaker children, lying, bodily control issues, sexual experimentation, and school pranks.

Salvador Dali revealed several harrowing instances of his own childhood cruelty, which at the time had served only to improve his mood and heighten his self-esteem. At the age of five, Dali helped push along a younger boy who was riding a tricycle. He then deliberately pushed the boy, tricycle and all, off a bridge; the boy landed on the rocks fifteen feet below. Dali's victim was badly injured and had to remain in bed for a week. Egocentrism predominated, as Dali admitted that the general turmoil around the incident put him into a delightful mood.

Another broad category of secrets concerns neglectful or sadistic behavior meted out to children "for their own good" by caregivers. Cruelty directed at children comes in many forms. Attempts at "soul murder" (extending Leonard Shengold's term for sexual abuse and deprivation) range from subtle manipulation to overt torture. This excerpt from Mary McCarthy's memoirs graphically depicts her then-secret sufferings: "We were put to bed at night with our mouths sealed with adhesive tape to prevent mouth-breathing; ether, which made me sick, was used to pull the tape off in the morning, but a grimy, gray, rubbery remainder was usually left on our upper lips and in the indentations of our pointed chins when we set off for school in our heavy outer clothes." McCarthy goes on to reveal how, on weekends, the children were forced to stay outside for three hours in the morning and three hours in the afternoon, regardless of the temperature. She recalls standing in the snow at temperatures ranging from fifteen to twenty-four degrees below zero, crying, and beating on the window with frozen mittens. At that point, her aunt's angry face would appear at the window and drive her away. This chilling account of maltreatment tears at our hearts and souls, especially when we realize that many victims, unlike the articulate McCarthy, are afraid to tell their stories.

Many of the childhood confessions related to me by patients involve striking instances of victimization. My patient Lucy was a twenty-four-year-old administrative secretary who reported feelings of dissociation and diffuse anxiety that made her fear she was losing her mind. At first she avoided any mention of her childhood; if the topic appeared to lead in that direction, she would deflect it back to her current symptoms and life circumstances. One day, she finally blurted out:

> I can't spend one more session avoiding the recurring event that I am afraid may have damaged me for life.
>
> My father, who was six feet, four inches tall and a corrections officer, used to get into fits. When these came over him, he would pull out my hair and bang me against the wall. Sometimes I would lose control and urinate. That would make him even more furious, and he would start to kick me and scream obscenities at me.
>
> Each time this happened, I believed I was going to die. Sometimes I would even pray for death to come and take me out of my misery. Even though he would attack me for no reason, he apologized to me only once, when my mother threatened to leave him. Yet my father would always make me apologize to him, since he said I deserved what I got.

Having adopted a self-blaming stance, Lucy would apologize for everything, including her confession that betrayed the collusive family secret. During the course of therapy, Lucy learned to see how this overwhelming childhood event pervaded her entire life. It contributed to her fear of intimacy (intimacy unconsciously being equated with violence); anxiety, especially in closed spaces like the subway (involving feelings of being unable to escape a situation of impending doom); and depersonalization (hearkening back to her wish for death to escape her father's brutality).

Expressing and exploring the childhood secret helped Lucy acknowledge a still more deeply hidden secret: her hatred of and murderous feelings toward her father. As she began to see herself in a new light, as a person who did not have the power to control her father's murderous tantrums, she was slowly able to understand that she was not to blame. Further, Lucy's bonding with me enabled her gradually to expel the toxic, internalized father. Lucy's secret virtually paralyzed

her during most of her life. While her symptoms (anxiety and depersonalization) immediately began to diminish following confession, re-
building her self-esteem and relationships with others has been a
slower process.

Childhood secrets may constitute either discrete, discontinuous
episodes (e.g., stealing a candy bar one time) or recurring life themes
(e.g., Lucy's story). In this latter instance, disclosing the secret in
adulthood led to the first break in a repetitive pattern of unsatisfying
"no-win" relationships.

Family secrets, such as abuse, frequently involve family members
colluding with each other to hide the secret from the outside world.
These secrets are frequently "crazy-making," since parents often choose
to act as though nothing is wrong, refuting the evidence that children
have. For example, children with alcoholic fathers are told their father
is "a social drinker." Or when their mother is placed in a mental institution, this gets translated into, "Mother is away on business."

Other family secrets revolve around issues of reproduction. It is sad
but true that in the late twentieth century, some parents still tell their
children the stork brought them. Miscarriages are sometimes dismissed as God's wanting to be with the baby.

As much as these lies debase the child's intelligence and destroy
trust, telling secrets indiscriminately can be destructive when they are
not presented in a sensitive enough way to enable the child to handle
them. Suppose that one day a child is told by the woman she has always known as her mother that she is really not her biological daughter but her stepdaughter. Fearing an emotional scene, the terrified
stepmother runs out of the room, closing all further discussion. No
one is immediately available to handle the child's inevitable questions
and upset feelings.

In *Children's Secrets*, sociologist Thomas Cottle contends that keeping
secrets perpetuates family myths that lend a semblance of normalcy
and harmony to the family. My patient Tara was, for many years,
locked into the myth of her family's stability. Only in her twenties did
she inadvertently become privy to the secret of her grandfather's infidelity and abandonment. Tara found out that her grandfather left her
grandmother during World War II, married two other women in differ-

ent countries, and never returned home. Her grandmother constructed an elaborate narrative about the necessity of his departure on a patriotic mission and tied his subsequent disappearance to the highest patriotic motives. Tara remarked, "She loves him to this day and resents any intrusion of reality." In Tara's family, only her grandmother preserved the myth. Intergenerational discontinuity was especially strong, with Tara and her sister refusing to collude with their grandmother in preserving the myth.

Secrecy is bound up with our childhood play. The charm of play is enhanced by making a secret act of it — "us" and not "the others." Think of the game of "doctor," in which children sometimes explore each others' private, "forbidden" sexual parts. Only certain children are allowed to play, and no adults must ever find out about these secret goings-on. Children also find private areas — tree houses, places in the woods, nooks and crannies in the house — where they enact secret rituals and games that are off-limits to others, especially parents. By keeping secrets and inhabiting secret places, children develop a sense of their own individuality and specialness, while preventing parents from controlling them in these areas.

Despite the need to sometimes keep secrets from parents, children also may come to their parents with secrets, especially when the parents are seen as highly nurturant. Researchers Duane Buhrmester and Wyndol Furman found that parents, especially mothers, were important confidants for children in grades two and five, but became less important among eighth-grade adolescents. Parents may be more sought out by second-graders because when children are at this stage, their parents are better listeners and providers of advice than peers.

Other studies have revealed that children from low-nurturant homes disclosed more to friends than parents. Children may find it hard to disclose certain secrets to parents, especially when the secret involves family members, because they — like their adult counterparts — see disclosure as a risky venture. Suppose you are an eight-year-old who is so jealous of your new baby brother that you are thinking of ways to kill him. Although your parents appear to be nurturant, you nonetheless fear recriminations if your plans to murder your brother are revealed. These types of quandaries beset the growing child throughout development.

Friends grow in importance as confidants, particularly between the ages of six and ten, which is considered by many developmental psychologists to be the most crucial period for the formation of friendships. Even at kindergarten age, children begin to share secrets with special friends, rather than with their peer group at large, as a way of enhancing intimacy. By the time children reach fourth grade, personal topics are sometimes related solely to friends, as the boundaries between intimate friends and everyone else become more firmly drawn. Friendship connections solidify the sense of "us-ness" against the adult and out-group worlds.

Preadolescent and Adolescent Confessions

During preadolescence, self-disclosure to friends becomes even more important as parents are seen, to a much greater extent, as sources of power and retribution. Because, as preadolescents, we are more concerned about others who are close to us, keeping secrets from parents is seen as a way to protect ourselves as well as our friends.

Psychiatrist Harry Stack Sullivan refers to the same-sex "chumships" of preadolescence. In these friendship groupings, the communal nature of endeavors frequently results in secrets involving several people. Sharing confidences with a chum becomes a basic friendship activity, promoting intimacy and lessening loneliness. The sense of equality, mutuality, and reciprocity experienced in peer relationships diminishes dependence on older authority figures as confidants.

Herman Hesse's novel *Demian* captures the redemptive value of friends as confidants. When the protagonist Emil Sinclair is ten, he and two neighborhood boys run into the much bigger and intimidating boy "from the wrong side of the tracks," Franz Kromer. Each boy boasts about his schoolboy pranks. Sinclair relates a false confession in which he steals a sackful of apples from the mill. Kromer demands to know whether this story is true. Sinclair swears to its veracity "by God and the grace of my soul." Kromer then turns around and blackmails

Sinclair, stating that the mill owner is offering two marks to anyone who finds the thief.

Sinclair at first succumbs to the threats, bringing Kromer what he can. But then Sinclair's luck turns around. He is befriended by the mysterious Max Demian who seems to be able to read his mind, sensing that Sinclair is being blackmailed, as well as knowing who the perpetrator is. Demian assures Sinclair that he will find a way to stop the blackmail.

The soul-to-soul communion and the release from isolation arising from Demian's divining the nature of the secret is apparent. Sinclair relates: "I found my way home and it seemed to me that I had been away for a year. Everything looked different. Something like a future, like hope, now separated me from Kromer. I was no longer alone. Only now did I realized how terribly alone I had been with my secret for weeks on end."

Emboldened by his friendship with Demian, Sinclair confesses to his mother and then to his father; he gains relief through their acceptance. Parents are still important sources of comfort and support to the preadolescent who, nonetheless, may first confide in a friend as a test run for the parental disclosure, which is often seen as riskier.

Common confessions from the chumship years related by adults often concern group issues, such as "peeing contests" in which boys vie to see who can urinate the farthest; communal stealing; spying on older siblings "making out"; and assorted pranks at the expense of parents to enhance one's standing in the group.

Secret-sharers frequently maintain self-esteem and a sense of collective identity through these secrets. In Mark Twain's *The Adventures of Huckleberry Finn*, Huck's harboring of the slave Jim concerns a collective secret in which Jim's very life is at stake. The secret life adopted by the pair also provides Huck and Jim with an identity as freedom-loving fugitives outside the social order.

My patient Andrew, a thirty-two-year-old insurance salesman, haltingly confessed that he had been raped by a group of neighborhood boys when he was nine. "The reason I never told anybody up until now," said Andrew "was that I feared my father's reaction and was afraid that once the word got out about what had happened, these boys would continue to take their revenge on me. They did rape me more than once, but the fear of even more dire consequences happening to me if I should tell made me keep my mouth shut until now."

The need for peer acceptance and inclusion in groups often makes confession a risky venture. Should the bond of secrecy be broken, Andrew was convinced that he risked either ostracism by the group or a spiraling pattern of revenge on their part. The group's persecution was already exacting a fearful toll on his feelings of self-worth. As such, confessions from this period frequently are revealed many years later when the person is no longer involved with the group, yet feels compelled to confess in order to be free from the burden of these internalized albatrosses.

Many secrets from preadolescence revolve around sexual or physical abuse that remains underground, leaving scars and broken lives that sometimes never are mended. Because of the preadolescent's feelings of guilt or shame, as well as his fear of breaking up the family or hurting other family members, the victim of abuse is not likely to disclose the secret. The incest survivor mentioned earlier was silenced by her fear that she would not be believed or that the even more dire consequences threatened by her father might occur.

To further ensure that the paternal abuse remained secret, children were not allowed to come to her house, and she was discouraged from making friends. Although this patient was trained to be isolated, she fortunately felt nurtured and loved by her grandmother who lived with the family. Yet she never could summon up the courage to reveal her horrendous suffering to her grandmother, since she feared that the shock of disclosure might kill the elderly woman.

Although abused children often keep the secret of their abuse hidden, clues to abuse frequently appear, including bruises, burns, backaches, urinary problems, ringing in the ears, and more. In all states, doctors, teachers, psychiatrists, psychologists, and social workers are legally required to reveal even suspicions of foul play to the requisite authorities. Those of us in such professions become witnesses to the child's nonverbal disclosures of abuse and so become child advocates breaking through the abuser's enforced wall of silence. Children who have been abused can be helped when they find adult confidants who have the courage to come to their aid and defend them. Such support helps children see that they have been wronged and thus brings to an end the vicious cycle of self-blame.

During preadolescence, secret keeping can be just as important in maintaining a sense of well-being as confessing. In Jung's autobiography, *Memories, Dreams, Reflections,* he recounts how at the age of ten he carved a manikin on two inches of his ruler, wrapped it in wool, placed a stone by it, and put everything in a case that he hid in the "forbidden attic" of his house. He wrote letters to the manikin in a secret language, and left them in the attic for the manikin. Jung concludes: "I contented myself with the feeling of newly-won security and was satisfied to possess something that no one knew and no one would get at. It was an inviolable secret which must never be betrayed, for the safety of my life depended on it. . . . This possession of a secret had a very powerful formative influence on my character: I considered it the essential factor of my boyhood."

The lonely boy created a manikin, which he could control and communicate with in secret. As children, we often create fantasy playmates or have toys or pets that become the repositories of our innermost secrets. They can never hurt us or tell our secrets to our fathers or mothers. Loyalty is absolute. Friendship is guaranteed. Our prized secret is safe.

Adolescents are often worlds apart from preadolescents in their confessional outlook. Many adolescents see parents as foes or competitors. As such, adolescents may in fact relish revealing secrets to their parents, either verbally or by their actions, as a way of asserting their autonomy or rebelliousness.

Nonetheless, many secrets are still hidden, only to be revealed later in psychotherapy or among adult friends or lovers. My patients have reported a variety of adolescent secrets: drinking all the liquor in their parents' liquor cabinet; taking drugs under their parents' roof; standing in picket lines protesting against a parent's cause or occupation; and becoming a groupie or a follower of a religious or social cult that is strictly antithetical to parental values.

Since the secrets of adolescence are frequently flaunted before parents, we can well wonder why these issues recur as confessions in therapy years later. While adolescents act upon their thoughts and feelings in order to get a reaction from parents, the "real secret" involves the underlying dynamic between adolescents and their parents.

Thus, an adolescent who spitefully confesses to his parents that he drank all their liquor is only revealing the surface secret. Imbedded in this communication may be the adolescent's desperate need for attention and to feel different and special. Should such incidents not result in the expected parental reaction or change the adolescent's life in the desired direction, disillusionment and esteem deflation may ensue.

It is these internalized thoughts and feelings that constitute the more profound secrets which are obscured by the acting-out behavior. The more deep-seated secrets impel adult patients to dredge up these adolescent incidents in order to address the incompleted parental battles.

Another side to the adolescent coin is idealism. Many adolescents strive to avoid selling out through being phony or counterfeit; instead, they strive to be true to themselves. While they despise parental lies and hypocrisy, they also recognize that much in life is a sham. So idealism exists side by side with disillusionment. Thus, when adolescents engage in collective family secret-keeping, they mention feeling inauthentic and phony. They feel trapped into adopting a stance of secrecy that runs counter to their ideals.

Although the adolescent often wants her own room in which she can madly scribble in her diary, she may gleefully tell the same secrets to her best girlfriend or even to her girlfriend's mother. In this regard, I remember my friend Shelley when we were both seventeen. While she viewed her mother as a "square," she would eagerly come to my house and tell her latest sexual exploits to my mother, whom she viewed as a liberal, supportive confidant.

I thought she went too far, however, when one day she blurted out that her boyfriend had plunked her down on the table where he avidly had his way with her, all of which was depicted in graphic detail to my mother.

My mother listened seemingly impassively. After Shelley left, my mother exclaimed, "What a slut!" As a seventeen-year-old, the lesson I learned was, "Never confide in a parent about sex." Yet it did not deter me from disclosing many other things to my mother, whom I loved dearly and whose advice I often sought. To this day, Shelley believes that sharing her sexual secrets with my mother helped her through her stormy adolescence. My mother's silence was interpreted as affirmation; she provided a needed adult ear as a counterbalance to my friend's stern, critical mother.

Adult Confessions

As our world expands, the number of people involved in secrets, as well as the number of potential confessors, dramatically increases. While childhood confessions generally involve family or egocentric issues, adult confessions (e.g., homosexuality, addictions, abortions) move from a primarily individual focus to wider social concerns.

A case in point is the person who confesses his homosexuality in psychotherapy but shies away from revealing his sexual orientation to family, friends, employees, and the larger community. I recall one gay patient who wished to become a minister in a conservative parish, and so had to contend with a fundamental secret that concerned not only his immediate family but also the community of parishioners.

Sexual confessions are often risky ventures. These secrets can be so emotionally charged that some couples have an explicit rule that they are not to reveal sexual secrets about their pasts. Revelations concerning being picked up by a stranger or participating in orgies are often thought to tarnish the beloved and thus blight the wholesomeness of the relationship.

As adults who can now assume multiple perspectives, we are able to participate in collective family secrets in a far more complex way than our childhood counterparts. Adult secrets may recapitulate parallel childhood secrets that emerge in situations in which we feel enough safety to disclose them. The secret sharer is able to risk disclosure, bolstered by the realization that others will not retaliate. This was the case with my patient Lana, a twenty-nine-year-old homemaker who originally sought therapy after she became a victim of assault. After being attacked by two teenage boys, she was unable to travel by herself and would quiver uncontrollably several times a day.

Lana readily revealed her current secret in order to gain relief from her symptoms, which had become overwhelming. What was more difficult for Lana to acknowledge was the familial violence that pervaded her childhood, the memory of which reemerged following her victimization.

Whenever I would ask Lana about her family, she would either divert the conversation to the present crime or describe her parents in vague, amorphous terms. What finally prompted her to break the familial code of silence was the rage she experienced when her mother, five days after the attack, minimized the incident by saying, "You should be over it by now."

Lana angrily exclaimed: "My mother's motto has always been, 'The family is sacred. Never let anyone know the family secrets.' I remember when my mother broke a plate over my head and threw a knife at me. My grandmother saw what happened, but was told to keep her mouth shut, since she should be grateful that she was allowed to live with us. Since no one ever acknowledged my mother's violent nature, I grew up feeling isolated and alienated." In Lana's family, not only was the violence concealed from the outside world, but the members also colluded with each other to disavow or ignore the mother's outbursts, which were attributed to "that time of the month" or "a temper."

The strength of the symptoms brought about by the crime prompted Lana to confess the current victimization, which unwittingly brought to the surface the hidden maternal crimes that no one had dared acknowledge. The adult secret evoked the even more painful childhood secret in which Lana was the ongoing victim of a sadistic mother.

Adult confessions between bosses and employees can be powder kegs ready to explode. It is always dangerous for employees to be seduced by their boss's disclosures. Power does not always corrupt, but power always has the edge.

How well I remember my patient Georgette's blow-by-blow description of the close, confiding relationship she had with her boss over the year she worked on a women's project. Georgette recounted, "The first time we went to lunch, my boss leaned across the table, looked me straight in the eye, and revealed the horrifying story of how her daughter had been abducted by a religious cult and how her husband managed to get her back and deprogram her.

"I was so impressed by my boss's candor that I immediately opened up, telling her funny and harrowing stories about the vicissitudes of single life in New York City. She seemed genuinely interested and supportive."

These mutual confessions went on for the year that the program was funded. Then one day Georgette's boss called her into the office and told her she could not possibly recommend her for another year. After a few seconds of stunned silence, Georgette asked her boss why. "Frankly, I don't approve of your lifestyle," her boss blurted out, self-righteously. "You shouldn't get yourself into these situations with me."

"When I disclosed how hurt and angry I was, especially since we were working on a women's project that encouraged women to accept themselves in multiple lifestyles, she only shrugged and said she had work to do," Georgette told me. "A week later, she ascribed some of her harshest statements to being out of sorts due to her period. Can you imagine the disillusionment and hurt I experienced, especially having looked up to my boss as a feminist role model?"

This exchange of secrets that went on over a period of a year between a boss and her employee illustrates the dangers of reciprocity in confession when the two participants do not share equal status. Georgette's boss shammed empathy only to use Georgette's disclosures against her. The boss's revelations were of a graver nature, yet Georgette lost out. Because she chose to turn her boss into a mother/confidant, Georgette deceived herself into believing that power relationships, especially between women, were really friendships. The *folie à deux* that ensued cost Georgette her job.

Confessions by employees to employers are indeed risky business.

This is so, primarily because the employer's relationship with the employee is one of power. Bosses have what sociologists call "idiosyncrasy credit" enabling them to confess to employees with impunity. Credits represent status, allowing for deviation and the assertion of independence. Regarding confessions in the workplace, this translates into bosses having more latitude than employees to "break the rules" of conformity by disclosing secrets about themselves. Employees who are not in positions of power have much more to lose by confessing or getting embroiled in the employer's confession.

We have all seen cartoon characters with the overhead balloons revealing what they really think of the boss. Even when employees know the boss is engaging in self-destructive behavior, confrontation is generally ill-advised, since the employee's job may very well be in jeopardy. On the other hand, if the boss gets wind of an employee's drinking problem, for example, he is likely to confront the employee with "the secret," often more out of concern for his work performance than for his personal welfare.

Chapter 1 outlined the risks of confessing to co-workers, including the possibility of becoming part of the office gossip. Nevertheless, there are also benefits derived from disclosure. Co-workers often confide in each other, especially when they are allied by grievances directed at their boss or their immediate superiors. Mutual concerns and shared work space make co-workers naturally gravitate toward each other as confidants for support and understanding.

Adult confessions often are a self-reflective product of age and experience. Such confessions may take the form of self-abnegation or reproach—a cognitive state that is commonplace in adult confessions, while relatively absent from children's revelations. Note the self-loathing in this excerpt from Antonin Artaud's letter to Doctor Allendy written in 1927: "There is something rotten in me. In my mental process there is a sort of basic evil which hinders me from enjoying what destiny offers me."

We can sense equally vitriolic self-recrimination in Søren Kierkegaard's 1839 *Journals*: "The whole of existence is poisoned in my sight, particularly myself . . . no man can console me, only God in Heaven and He will not have mercy upon me." Extreme loneliness, futility, and self-abnegation run through Kierkegaard's self-reflections. When confessions are reflections on our lives rather than concerned with discrete events, they are often accompanied by more intense emotions.

The complex nature of adult confessions makes us search between the lines to find the secrets involving the very core of our being. Gerald's case illustrates how a confession involving drugs may be seen as a state of being that becomes the person's major, and sometimes only, ongoing confession. Gerald, a thirty-two-year-old designer, became heavily involved in a single weekend drug-filled marathon in which he progressed from marijuana and cocaine to a dangerous mixture of drugs, including LSD, amyl nitrate, and a number of amphetamines. While he initially discussed the motivation of his drug patterns in terms of a need to escape, have fun, be paid attention to, and be admired, he showed little emotion when he told me about his preoccupation with drugs, nor did he make any efforts to desist from or diminish drug use.

During one session, Gerald suddenly adopted a very serious demeanor and pondered out loud, "I wonder what these drugs can do to me?" I quietly said, "I wonder." Gerald became silent and then burst into tears. "These drugs can kill me. Sometimes I think I want to die. Why am I really taking these drugs? To escape from myself. I loathe myself. And the drugs aren't working to change that."

When his hidden "loathsome" self emerged, Gerald realized that he was faced with the difficult decision of delving further into this hidden aspect of himself or continuing to exist on the precarious, frenzied edge of life.

Gerald began using drugs to fill a void; he was waiting for the drugs to work their magic and change his life. Through the therapeutic dialogue, Gerald came to the startling realization—not too late—that drugs as a way of life enslaved rather than liberated him. The drug-induced illusions of omnipotence, charisma, and fearlessness provided only a fleeting state of well-being that unsuccessfully masked Gerald's sense that his true self was loathsome.

Other adult confessions are entered into courageously or even defiantly in a spirit of liberation and *joie de vivre*. No nineteenth-century writer surpassed Lord Byron in the revelation of his sins and foibles without apologies or hypocritical repentance. In a letter to his friend Richard Belgrade Hoppner, dated October 29, 1819, Byron proclaims, "I am all for morality now—and shall confine myself henceforward to the strictest adultery—which you will please to recollect is all that that virtuous wife of mine has left me."

The Role of Language in Confession

Language is our single most important confessional liberator as we wend our way from childhood to adulthood. As we develop greater comprehension and facility with words and their nuances, our confessional possibilities vastly expand. The change from concrete to abstract thought not only broadens the potential range of secrets, but also provides us with more sophisticated defenses to disavow secrets.

The move toward abstract thought and greater awareness is evidenced, for example, in confessions pertaining to our reassessment as adults of parents' influence on us. In a remarkable letter to his father, Kafka confesses: "You have been too strong for me. . . . Sometimes I imagine the map of the world spread out and you stretched diagonally across it. And I feel as if I could consider living in only those regions that are not covered by you."

In a sense, our secrets and our confessions form a map depicting critical incidents in our lives, along with the significant people who guided us and propped us up, or disappointed and betrayed us, along the way. Our stories, especially our confessions, are landmarks in our development, pinpointing who we are as well as the kind of people we are likely to become.

5

Why We Need to Confess

E ACH OF US is equipped with an inner eye that measures us
against our peers. Chapter 4 pointed out that, as we develop, we
are able to chart our growth and change by listening to our own confessions and monitoring the reactions of our confidants. In so doing,
we are able to find our place in the world.

If our childhood confessions are met with parental censure, we
may grow up with the sense that we do not have the right to express
our innermost selves to others. We may be convinced that those selves
will strike others as repugnant, bizarre, or less than human. Given a
childhood legacy of dread or ambivalence surrounding confession, we
might wonder why we are motivated to confess at all. The need to reveal ourselves to another person fundamentally different from our
punitive childhood confidants can, in time, override the need to protect our vulnerable selves.

While unique childhood histories impel or repel confession, societal currents seem to favor self-disclosure. As anthropologist Ruth
Benedict remarked, perhaps too simplistically, ours is a "guilt culture,"
and guilt invites both disclosure and atonement. Confessions by public figures who make restitution for their addictions, sexual peccadil-
los, and other indiscretions tend to be greeted with public sympathy.
From the bedroom to the boardroom, from the pulpit to the political
podium, confession is a time-honored tradition that is cherished in
our society. The Judeo-Christian tradition emphasizes that confession
is good for the soul. "Coming clean" is a way to heal both the division
within our soul and our broken relationships with others.

Confessions come in many stripes and sizes, and we confess our secrets for a variety of reasons. This chapter explores our major motives for revealing our secrets, including the need to alleviate our guilt or shame, the need to transform ourselves, the need to relate, and the need to be special.

Guilt

Guilt presents us with a special problem. We do not want to be plagued and overrun by guilt, making it the essential fuel that drives us, nor do we want to be part of a culture that tries to excise guilt from our psyches, thereby undermining moral stability.

Nietzsche, in *The Genealogy of Morals,* represented one extreme by viewing guilt as a weakness to be eliminated. Freud also viewed a relentless conscience as a personal liability. According to this perspective, people who internalized overly critical, rigid parental values developed crippling guilt as a result, which in turn needed to be assuaged. While psychoanalysis acknowledged the existence of real guilt, the emphasis in analysis was placed on "neurotic guilt," in which the punishment did *not* fit the crime.

O. Hobart Mowrer was one of the first psychologists to proclaim precisely the opposite; namely, that we suffer from real guilt and should therefore confess, atone, and make real restitution. It is not enough to merely confess and say we're sorry. Being good involves doing good through the act of reparation.

Mowrer maintained that guilt is good when it awakens our moral sensibilities and signals our dormant conscience that we did wrong and must therefore set our house in order. As a signal of a deep unrest in our souls, guilt can help clarify a secret. When we experience guilt, we often force ourselves to thoroughly explore the dark side of our natures—to crystallize the secret and come to terms with it as a means of resolution and absolution. Acknowledging the secret and taking responsibility for it satisfies our longing for spiritual harmony as well as relief from guilt. Guilt is the clarion call to restore moral balance in our lives through reparation.

Mowrer viewed the collaboration of psychology and psychiatry with religion as the most fruitful means to heal both broken relation-ships and the divisions within ourselves. Real guilt was implicated as the core problem in psychological distress. As such, when patients dis-close guilt-saturated secrets in therapy, therapists should not try to as-suage their guilt or to help them feel better. The aim of treatment should be to have the patient confront the guilt and come to terms with it by finding constructive ways to remedy wrongdoing.

The guilt stemming from a bad conscience is a gift of grace that helps us understand ourselves and explore our psyches, according to Jung. Jung viewed the divine as a powerful force in helping us con-front our guilt. Included in the idea of grace is that a divine power ex-ists to help us live a moral life. Grace is God's love—God's gift enabling us to grow spiritually by acknowledging and working through our ad-versities and traumas.

The sting of a bad conscience is seen by Jung as a catalyst for con-fession. Children can develop stronger consciences in response to guilt; unfaithful spouses can rediscover their love and responsibility toward their spouse because of guilt. Confession and restitution to al-leviate guilt sets us on the path to becoming better human beings.

On the other hand, guilt is bad when it is either nonexistent or ra-tionalized by a mentality such as cult leader Charles Manson or the murderer Raskolnikov in Dostoevsky's *Crime and Punishment.* Guilt is also corrosive when we are so harsh on ourselves that we become crippled with rigid morality that far exceeds the extent of our mis-deed. We become consumed by a guilt that eats away at us in a self-defeating, destructive manner.

We need to consider the nature of our guilt in deciding whether to confess and make restitution. In many instances, the guilt-ridden dis-closer is actually the wronged person (e.g., child abuse survivor) who has gone through life punishing herself. Bryan, one of my patients, would often tiptoe into his sleeping sister's room to gawk at her ex-posed breasts when he was an adolescent. The nature of Bryan's "ac-tual" wrongdoing—incestuous voyeurism—was disproportionate to the punishment he meted out to himself—placing himself in unsatis-fying relationships with rejecting, yet seductive women.

Once Bryan embarked on the therapy journey, he discovered the long-buried secret that had previously catapulted him into self-destructive relationships predicated on unremitting guilt. Through therapy, Bryan acknowledged his secret along with his guilt. Over time, his recognition that he did not irreparably harm his sister, yet was continuing to hurt himself, resulted in a gradual turnabout of his dating patterns.

In this case, confession produced not only relief from guilt, but also self-forgiveness and redemption from a life of futile, unsatisfying relationships. The self-punitive cycle that plagued Bryan for most of his life was broken at last.

Freud rendered the Oedipus complex the central secret of the child's existence. As the story is told in Sophocles' *Oedipus* trilogy, Oedipus' parents are informed by the Delphic oracle that their son will kill his father and marry his mother. In order to avert this tragedy, the infant Oedipus is sent away to be killed; however, the helpless baby arouses the pity of his would-be assassin, who saves him. As a man, Oedipus unwittingly runs into his father and kills him. He later becomes king and unknowingly marries his widowed mother. When he finally discovers the horror of his deeds, he blinds himself and goes into exile. Although the patricide and incest are not strictly his fault, Oedipus takes responsibility for his role in his family's tragedy, experiences guilt, and cruelly punishes himself.

Freud's first mention of the Oedipus complex (the child's desire to sleep with the parent of the opposite sex and do away with the parent of the same sex) appears in the Fliess correspondence on October 15, 1897. Once Freud was able to acknowledge his own Oedipus complex, he was able to contend with the centrality of oedipal secrets in his patients' lives. "Everything I experience with patients I find here," Freud confessed.

While oedipal secrets have tended to be weighted in the direction of children's feelings toward parents, some of the most guilt-ridden secrets concern parents' counteridentifications with their children. Parents' erotic or rivalrous feelings toward offspring are considered especially dangerous secrets to reveal, since legal and moral sanctions against incest and child abuse carry far-reaching repercussions. We are less reticent to confess analogous, veiled secrets involving feelings such as a father's hatred for his daughter's boyfriends or a mother's flirtation with her new son-in-law.

Oedipus' unwitting incest is one of the two major secrets (patricide is the other) that doom his existence. The covert crossing of generational boundaries puts the incest victim in a double bind in which a message of sexual equality is transmitted to the unequal child/partner. The child who is threatened or bribed to hide the secret often internalizes a "blame the victim" attitude. If the child is at all aroused by the forbidden venture, feelings of guilt and shame increase. Only recently, with the emergence of victim advocacy, assistance, and support groups, have incest survivors and victimizers risked confessing these deeds in order to come to terms with their guilt.

Because they are subject to the adult's brainwashing aegis, child victims often accept the adult's lies and denial. Like Oedipus, they are blind—blind to what is actually going on and to any explanation other than the parent's official version.

Oedipus' blindness catalyzed by unbearable guilt for patricide and incest actually enables him to see—to acknowledge and come to terms with—his tragic fate. Those who take on the "sins of the parents" or spouse as their own guilt remain blinded by their "soul murder," to use Shengold's term, as long as they see no way out.

Patricide is the second great secret that was kept from Oedipus, either due to the gods' machinations or his own denial, preserving his self-interest by hiding the damaging secret from himself. Psychoanalyst John Steiner points out that Sophocles' text contains evidence to suggest that certainly Tiresias (the blind soothsayer), and even Jocasta (Oedipus' mother/wife), suspected that it was Oedipus who had killed his father and married his own mother. Steiner asserts, "One can argue further that each of the participants in the drama, for their own reasons, turns a blind eye to this knowledge." Like Oedipus, many of us disavow or deny the meanings that might be garnered from our secrets.

While the wish to murder our mothers and fathers is pervasive, the actual deed is a rarity. Our guilt at the *thought* of murder is sometimes as great as if we had committed the crime. We have only to think of sibling rivalry in which older siblings sometimes pray for the death of the new usurper of parental attention. On those occasions when the baby or child actually does die, the guilt stemming from the thought "I killed the baby" leaves the surviving child saddled with guilt derived from the alleged omnipotence of her powerful thoughts.

The ancient Greek philosophers and dramatists recognized the powerful role of guilt in confession. In Aeschylus' trilogy, *The Oresteia*, Orestes, encouraged by Apollo, kills his mother Clytaemestra and her lover Aegisthus. Orestes metes out this revenge following Clytaemestra's murder of her husband, Agamemnon, and his mistress, Cassandra.

Orestes' action was sanctioned by a god and rationalized by the reality that Clytaemestra was indeed a double murderess, yet when Orestes displays the bodies of his mother and her lover and defends his murder of them, the Furies—spirits of retribution—appear to him and drive him out of Argos. In the play *Orestes*—Euripides' version of Orestes' murder of his mother—Orestes' confession to Menelaus after he is driven mad by the Furies, is vividly described.

> Menelaus: Ye gods! What am I looking at? Some ghost from hell?
> Orestes: What you describe is outward; my torments are real.
> Menelaus: Words could not picture such ghastly disfigurement.
> Orestes: This is myself—my unhappy mother's murderer.
> Menelaus: What is the disease that ravages you?
> Orestes: Conscience. I recognize the horror of what I did.
> Menelaus: I advise you to be clear, not clever. What do you mean?
> Orestes: This: what destroys me more than anything is grief.

When Orestes is ultimately acquitted by the jury, Apollo—the symbol of intellectual detachment—demands the Furies' expurgation. Athena points out, with her traditional wisdom, that the Furies—spirits of anger and revenge—are also part of life. The greatness of the *Oresteia*, according to Rollo May, resides in Aeschylus' insight that we need both Apollonian intellect and the daimonic in order to develop insight and compassion. Athena persuades the Furies to remain in Athens, and their name is changed to the Eumenides—the gracious ones. As May comments, "The hated daimonic can be a guardian and a channel of grace."

Expiation of guilt following confession concerns coming to terms with and acknowledging *all* aspects of ourselves—even the Furies in us. Athens is enriched by accepting the Furies; we are transformed and renewed by acknowledging the rageful, even murderous, sides of ourselves, then accepting responsibility for our actions and dealing with our guilt head-on instead of trying to escape from it.

Guilt invites confession. Yet the mere act of confession in the absence of reparation may actually exacerbate guilt and hasten one's downfall. Lady Macbeth, swept away with ambition for her husband's aggrandizement to gain the crown of Scotland, pushes him over the brink to murder. She suffers guilt and remorse over her deeds, which drive her to self-revelation in the sleepwalking scene. "Out, damned spot! Out, I say!" She later continues, "Here's the smell of the blood still. All the perfumes of Arabia will not sweeten this little hand."

Lady Macbeth's compulsive hand-washing ritual cannot remove her guilt; indeed, the more she attempts to assuage her guilt, the more she is reminded of the guilt, even in her somnambulistic state. Since she can neither undo her act nor confess to anyone by the light of day, her compulsion to confess finds partial expression through actions revealed only in an altered state of consciousness. A hinted suicide becomes her ultimate repentance for guilt that cannot otherwise by relieved.

Psychoanalyst Theodore Reik wrote about the compulsion to confess in order to alleviate unconscious guilt. This need, evidenced in criminals, is also present in all of us. Lady Macbeth's guilt is betrayed through her hand-washing ritual. Criminals may leave behind evidence that incriminates them.

Reik viewed the need to confess "sinful" or bad deeds as a desire for punishment to expiate unconscious guilt emanating from oedipal wishes. Early on, the child realizes a link between atonement for wrongdoing and the restoration of parental love after being punished.

In a related vein, Alice Miller poetically draws on instances of guilt evoked in the child who attempts to be a separate person rather than an extension of a narcissistic parent. The person who dares to risk becoming a separate being may harbor secret guilt-inducing fantasies, such as "my parents will die" in the mistaken belief that she is needed for parental sustenance. One of my patients, who had made great strides in becoming her own person, poignantly related how her mother sent her a birthday cake on which was written, "In fond memory of the daughter you used to be." The patient exclaimed: "She can never just let me be. As long as she's alive, she'll never let me forget my place as my mother's daughter." As therapy progressed, she began to understand that the guilt she had assumed for herself was not based on her own deeds but was unconsciously induced in her by her mother as punishment for attempting to be herself.

Thus far, I have spoken a great deal about guilt and less about repentance. While guilt is a feeling and state of mind associated with acknowledgment of wrongdoing, repentance involves remorse for wrongdoing along with actions designed to change one's ways. On the confessional journey, it is repentance followed by restitution to others that releases us from our prisons of guilt; relief from guilt can then give rise to redemption.

Anne Tyler's novel *Saint Maybe* chronicles the guilt and eventual redemption of Ian Bedloe, a seventeen-year-old college freshman who blames himself for the sudden "accidental" death of his older brother, Danny, who has smashed his car into a wall. Ian's guilt stems from his comments to Danny that his wife, Lucy, was having an affair. Following Danny's death, Lucy commits suicide, leaving behind the children.

Depressed and demoralized, Ian is burdened with unbearable guilt: "Sometimes he tried to believe that everyone on earth walked around with at least one unbearably guilty secret hidden away inside. . . . Maybe if he . . . confessed to his mother, she would say, 'Why, sweetheart! Is that all that's bothering you? Listen, every last one of us has caused *somebody's* suicide.'" Mulling this over in his mind, he convinces himself that confessing to his parents would make things worse and would possibly even kill them.

One evening, he notices a neon sign for the Church of the Second Chance. Ian then confesses to Reverend Emmett, convinced that God forgives everything. But the minister tells Ian that he is mistaken — being sorry is not enough. Ian must offer concrete reparation by dropping out of college and helping his parents raise the children.

Ian discovers that forgiveness for wrongdoing must be earned through love and sacrifice. Plagued by overwhelming guilt, Ian goes through an entire confessional journey discovering ways to make reparation to redeem himself from guilt. His external repentance and sacrifice results in internal healing. By doing better, Ian becomes a better person—and through this lesson the reader learns about the nature of confession and redemption.

Guilt results from the realization that we have broken important social or ethical rules we have come to accept. Activities such as stealing, killing animals, or lying frequently induce guilt. Shame results from failure to realize our aspirations. Defects we perceive in ourselves may be physical (e.g., being deformed or anorexic); psychological (e.g., feeling lazy or inept); or behavioral (e.g., being caught "playing doctor" as a child or hiding liquor as an adult). When we know we have done wrong, we feel guilty; when we fall short of our ideals, we feel ashamed.

Shame

Until recently, ours was a culture that encouraged disclosure of guilt, while treating shame as something to be hidden and kept secret. The word *shame* is derived from an Indo-European root *(skam* or *skem)* meaning "to hide." Thus, shame is very much connected with secrecy. Times and attitudes have changed, however, to the extent that some are now advocating public exposure and reparation to chasten wrongdoers and to deter them from repeating their crimes. Shame has entered our national consciousness in part to restore a sense of values which makes it easier for people to feel part of a community. Public exposure in tandem with reparation sensitizes both the criminal and the community to the importance of facing one's crime, fully experiencing shame, and making restitution as a means of returning to the community.

Like guilt, the coin of shame has both its positive and negative sides. History presents many instances of cruel, unwarranted exposure of innocent victims. In Europe, for example, it was common to insert a bar sinister—a diagonal band going from the bearer's left to the bearer's right—on the shield of the family coat of arms to indicate illegitimacy in the family. The stigma that results from such exposure has no redemptive value and, in fact, encourages us to keep our secrets closeted.

When techniques to provoke shame are rooted in compassion, however, the result can be redemptive; restoring a sense of shame makes our moral boundaries clear. Justice Walter Williams, who presides over the municipal court in Chattanooga, Tennessee, often requires public acts of contrition and restitution from offenders. A prankster who set off fire alarms at a busy hotel, for example, was ordered to polish the fire department's trucks. Williams has found that public exposure and retribution has resulted in "good conformity," the kind that makes it easier for people to form communities. Shame has proven effective in other states as well. A minister in Wisconsin persuaded a man who burglarized his church to stand up before the entire congregation to apologize, and then to help repair the church. A federal judge ordered a defendant convicted of tax evasion to purchase computers and teach parolees how to use them. These successful approaches depend not on imposing shame but on imposing punishment. The person then has a choice of feeling shame as a way back to the community's fold.

Part of the problem in looking at "good" and "bad" shame is that we constantly receive double messages. On the one hand, we have been encouraged to hide feelings of inferiority or incompetence, which is one reason why married folk rarely divulge secrets about the relationship to friends. In shame, our ideal image or ideal marriage is revealed to be not quite up to the mark. Marriages without sex or generally devoid of passion are secrets partners often collude with each other in keeping from the outside world. Each partner's desire not to hurt the other renders disclosure an unthinkable betrayal.

On the other hand, we have become a "shameless" society, canonizing the intruding investigative reporter who digs up the most lurid scoops. When we glorify exposure, we devalue shame. Cole Porter's song "Anything Goes" begins with the refrain, "In olden days a glimpse of stocking/Was looked on as something shocking/Now heaven knows/Anything goes." Written in 1934, it is just as true today. In this kind of topsy-turvy shameless world, we have the sense that there is no moral compass guiding us.

Yet, Ken-Ichiro Okano, a psychiatrist who is conversant with both American and Japanese cultures points out that shame is one of the most hidden states of all for Americans. Because our core sense of who we are and how we feel about ourselves is so bound up with shame, we are more likely to hide secrets involving feelings of inadequacy or inferiority.

When an unwitting confession renders me stupid, incompetent, or an object of ridicule in others' eyes, I may experience temporary psychic death—or worse. Have we not all thought at the height of an embarrassing moment, "I wish the earth would swallow me up," or, "I wish a trapdoor would open beneath me."

The Japanese believe that power and competence should not be flaunted; thus, for them what is hidden is powerful. In our more openly narcissistic society, "in your face" displays of assertiveness and abilities are encouraged as a way of attaining the good life. Shame is often viewed as something unhealthy to be diminished or eliminated. We are encouraged to hide our feelings of shame behind a grandiose facade; thus the underside of our grandiosity is our secret sense of being inadequate, inferior, or shameful.

Charles Dickens, despite his fame and accolades, was haunted throughout his life by the shame he experienced working for six months at a blacking bottle factory after his father's financial ruin. Dickens remonstrates, "No words can express . . . the secret agony of my soul as I sink into this companionship. . . . My whole nature was so penetrated with the grief and humiliation of such considerations, that even now famous and caressed and happy, I often forget in my dreams that I have a dear wife and children . . . and wander desolately back to that time of my life."

Secrets revolving around shame, humiliation, and embarrassment cut to our very souls. While guilt is usually bound to specific actions that we can atone for, shame is more difficult for us to deal with since it is related to our self-image—to our very sense of being.

Because ours is a society emphasizing displays of strength, competence, and control, it is no wonder that some of our most formidable secrets involve moments in which we see ourselves as weak, vulnerable, or disgusting. In *Moments of Being*, Virginia Woolf disclosed to the Memoir Club, a group of close friends, how her two half brothers played humiliating sexual games with her until she was eleven. She felt that she would be blamed if she confided in anyone. The year of her death, she wrote how she still shivered with shame at the memory of one of her half brothers standing her on a ledge when she was six so he could more conveniently explore her private parts. Woolf's agony of shame was only partially alleviated through her writings; her lifelong aversion to many things sexual can be traced at least in part to this early sexual humiliation.

The risk of being blamed for confessing makes many sexually abused children, in particular, reluctant to confess. An equally deadly risk concerns exposing oneself in vain to others who then turn a deaf ear. Meeting with the confidant's indifference can be enough to make the vulnerable soul hide from the world, with invisibility being preferable to mortification.

Because so many today suffer from narcissistic problems in which feelings about oneself alternate between invulnerable grandiosity and a sense of emptiness and worthlessness—we see both the danger of suppressing shame and the pitfall of indiscriminately glorifying grandiosity. Until we realize that we have the need and the right to come forward with *all* parts of ourselves, we cannot begin to accept love and heal the divisions within ourselves; nor can we break down the facade of invulnerability preventing us from being authentic with each other.

Friedrich Nietzsche and Charles Darwin noted that humans are "blushing animals." We often lower our eyes or avert our gaze when embarrassed. Where shame is involved, the body sometimes discloses secrets better than speech. Freud and Breuer's *Studies on Hysteria* discusses how Fräulein Elisabeth von R. showed arousal when Freud pressed her thighs during a physical examination. Her face flushed; she threw back her head and closed her eyes, allowing herself to experience the sexual pleasure she denied herself in conscious life. Breuer spoke of sexual conflicts that were regarded as so shameful that they were hidden from the patients themselves as *secrets d'alcôve*. Although Elisabeth's symptoms eventually disappeared through Freud's "talking cure," it was her body language, initially registering shame and pleasure, that paved the way for further clues to her secret life and desires.

We all need and want affirmation from others—"mirroring," in Heinz Kohut's words. As early as fourteen months of age, infants show a range of emotions, which include embarrassment and "showing off," as a result of being the focus of attention. Both shame and exhibitionism become major forms of self-expression, often even before the infant can talk. One reason for the onset of shame is that the delightful experience of self-awareness converges with the awareness of ourselves as objects of criticism. As children, our pride in our bodies as joyful sources of exhibitionism can rapidly shift to shame when met with critical rejoinders by cold parents. A patient wistfully recalled, "I secretly felt like superman, strong and proud, until my father told me to put on some clothes and stop acting so silly."

While many of us shy away from shameful confessions that penetrate to the core of our being, the relentless nature of shame can eventually promote confession as we move from self-consciousness (the heart of shame) to consciousness of ourselves as worthwhile people.

Our parents' body language—their ease with their own bodies and pleasure or displeasure with their children's bodily displays—sets the stage for the emergence of good or bad feelings about ourselves. Should our parents respond to us with disgust or excessive modesty, we are likely to view any hint of our own grandiosity or exhibitionism with disdain. As adults, we may avoid or deride displays of exhibitionism, while secretly yearning to divulge our own grandiosity and be accepted.

One person who fit this profile was Mary, a twenty-seven-year-old administrative assistant who could never fully relax and enjoy sex because in her words, "Part of me is always scrutinizing myself, hoping my partner won't notice my bulges, and checking myself to see if I am doing everything right." Mary's self-conscious examination masked a secret desire to shine and be admired, bulges and all.

"When I was five, my friend and I used to 'play nun,'" Mary confessed. "Since we figured nuns were supposed to suffer, I suggested we put twigs in our underwear. Much to my surprise, it felt good. But when my friend's mother noticed the twigs when my friend went to the bathroom, my friend told on me. Her mother called me a bad and dirty little girl. I was so humiliated, I just wanted to crawl into a hole and disappear."

So severe was Mary's shame that she never again did anything sexual until the age of eighteen, when she met her husband. After she had finished her story, I remarked how difficult it must have been to listen to her friend's mother's tirades against her and how lonely it must have felt to live with the unexpressed secret for all these years. This empathic interpretation brought forth a flood of material pertaining to how Mary, as an only child, felt isolated from her parents and was ashamed to ask them anything personal for fear of disapproval or retaliation.

When the eleven-year-old Mary innocently asked her father what the word *fuck* meant, he slapped her across the face and told her never to say that word again. Mary was incessantly made to feel that adults were the authorities and that children had no rights, not even the right to know. Such treatment often makes children feel invisible and expendable.

After Mary revealed the twig incident to me, along with the memories of shame and loneliness, I commented that the nun game seemed to be a creative use of play. The delighted patient said she never expected me to say that and in fact feared my reproval. My words helped Mary feel appreciated. She no longer felt the need to retreat into hiding.

The Need to Transform Ourselves

By facing the unacceptable in ourselves, we can become more integrated, creative beings. Drug addicts, in acknowledging their addiction, reach a turning point heralding a transition from one phase in their lives to another. Religious conversion experiences—indeed all rites of passage in which we are willing to stand out and be counted—

are profound statements of identity. "Coming out" as a member of the gay community or confessing one's religious affiliation to a hostile regime represent ardent declarations of commitment. No longer content to live in the shadows, those who declare themselves are willing to risk public censure, or even death, in order to stay true to their values and identity.

Some confessions that may appear to be trivial or banal to the outside observer are experienced by disclosers as guiding lights that signal turning points in their lives. Saint Augustine, in his *Confessions*, castigates himself over a childhood theft of pears. This seemingly minor childhood prank becomes a powerful motivating force in strengthening his will to follow a lifestyle and ideology that call for sacrifice and endurance.

The confession as rite of passage may serve as a signpost marking a person's transition from one phase in life to another. Leo Tolstoy, in his *Confession*, speaks of the existential boredom and discontent he was experiencing at a time in his life when (ironically) he was successful, rich, and enjoying the love of his wife and children. It was through his acknowledgment of this unnamed void that Tolstoy was able to begin the search for enlightenment, a quest that dominated the rest of his life.

Like Tolstoy, many of us confess in an effort to find new meaning in our lives. We may reveal our deepest doubts and darkest secrets in order to risk "the courage to be," in Paul Tillich's words. The courage to be sometimes encompasses the courage to be different; that is, to move out of an ossified existence and risk new modes of being which challenge the traditional internalized parental voices.

Confessions that constitute rites of passage are often perceived to be the most dangerous and difficult to reveal, because our sense of identity itself may seem to be on the line. Patients who enter therapy with the hope of resolving their "secret life" sometimes spend months and even years examining issues that are deemed safer to reveal in this arena than to confidants in the "outside world." This is often the case because, even though the secrets pertain to one aspect of ourselves (e.g., sexual orientation, alcoholism, espousing a controversial political cause), we see the integrity of the whole self as bound up in the would-be confession.

When I acknowledge to another that, "I am an alcoholic," "I am a homosexual," or "I belong to a cult," I am changed forever. Because in allowing a major aspect of my identity to be public, I become more committed to my principles and stronger in my resolve.

When we declare ourselves to be part of a community of like-minded adherents, confession is, of course, less difficult. Declaring that I am an alcoholic, overeater, cocaine addict, or sex addict within the context of a sympathetic, understanding community sets me on the paradoxical path of changing that designation even as I declare myself to the group. Acknowledgment of the addiction commits the discloser to lasting change without ever taking the addictive nature for granted. This entails working every day to monitor oneself and remaining vigilant about never again succumbing to one's addiction.

In other instances, declaring oneself to an uncertain or possibly hostile audience can strengthen one's identification with the in-group, which may in turn become the accepting surrogate family. When acceptance follows disclosure to family and friends, a mutual outpouring of love occurs. Appreciation for being authentic carries its own special rewards. Affirmation from empathic confidants enhances identity.

Erik Erikson viewed "person identity" as being contingent upon others' and our own perception of our self-sameness and continuity over time. We have a sense of who we are, as well as the goals, values, and beliefs to which we are committed. Confessing signals that we are willing to commit ourselves to the discovery and rediscovery of who we are. A newfound liberation transforms us into the people we already are, untrammeled by phoniness and fear of being ourselves.

Psychoanalyst Heinz Lichtenstein views identity as "invariance within a process of transformation." We have all had the experience of sensing changes in ourselves resulting from all the people and events that have had an impact on us over the years. At the same time, we think of ourselves as fundamentally the same in personality despite external changes.

This aspect of sameness or invariance integral to identity is also talked about by Carl Rogers and Rollo May, who view therapy as a process of becoming who we are—that is, retrieving and getting back to our essential natures. In the practice of Zen, the feelings of continuity most often occur during the *satori* (enlightenment) experience, capped by the overwhelming realization that we are what we have always been. Individuals can see themselves as they really are. When people confess that they are gay, for example, a continuity is added to their lives. The enlightenment that comes with acknowledgment and acceptance of the secret (by the discloser as well as confidants) lends continuity and credence to identity.

In a famous passage quoted by Daisetsu Teitaro Suzuki, a Zen master remarked, "When I began to study Zen, mountains were mountains; when I thought I understood Zen, mountains were not mountains; but when I came to full knowledge of Zen, mountains were again mountains." In explaining this passage, Suzuki maintains that the mountains are really mountains when they become assimilated into our being. The secret often seems alien until it becomes part of our ongoing selves through confession. The secret is a metaphorical mountain until it is acknowledged and thereby transformed into a real entity through confession.

The act of confiding in others begins to transform us immediately. Secrets (sometimes even from ourselves through denial or rationalization) can now be openly and authentically acknowledged. The resolution of secrets of this kind—secrets closely bound up with our identity—resides in accepting who we are and integrating what was before a secret into our very nature. The mountains really are mountains; gay people can acknowledge who they are without the need to live a counterfeit existence.

The Need for Community

By sharing our secrets we break through to the community. The more isolated we are, the more destructive is the power of the secret over us. In the blackness of the unexpressed, the secret can poison our whole being.

We become grounded in anxiety when we lose our sense of relatedness with others. In shunning intimacy, we choose isolation. And isolation can ultimately become the death of our spirit, a spirit which instinctively seeks communion with others in order to become centered.

Psychologist Sidney Jourard observed, "No man can come to know himself except as an outcome of disclosing himself to another person." If disclosure to oneself were enough, no one would ever cry on a bartender's shoulder, regale the hairdresser with confidences, or seek therapy. Telling our tale to a confidant helps us understand ourselves better. We cannot really know ourselves unless we risk disclosure to others. Freud wrote to his friend Wilhelm Fliess in May 1894: "You are the only Other, the alter." Freud revealed his innermost secrets to Fliess on paper and in person.

A large part of the motive to confess is the desire to be heard and accepted; another major component is the need to tell the truth and be believed. When we tell the truth, we need others, as well as ourselves, to acknowledge our experience and give it meaning. Survivors of date and marital rape, as well as survivors of child abuse, are often reluctant to reveal their secrets, since they fear that others will not believe them or that they will be devastated by not being heard. Truth telling is also difficult when the abused, tormented, or neglected have trouble labeling their experiences and giving them meaning. For many oppressed spouses, the term "marital rape" is seen as an oxymoron. Abused or neglected children sometimes equate suffering with love, especially when they are isolated from loving families. They, too, may have trouble acknowledging the truth of their abuse.

The Bible also emphasizes the truth-telling function of confession. It is a special form of communion with God, maintains theologian Dietrich Bonhoeffer. God is viewed as loving the sinner, but hating the sin. God wants each of us as we are. "My son, give me your heart" (Prov. 23:26). While we can wear a mask before each other, nothing can be hidden from God. We can dare to be sinners; our liberation arrives through being truthful in our confessions and our contrition before God. We sense God's presence in the confessions that break through the seclusion of our hearts.

Dostoyevsky's novel *Crime and Punishment* brings the confessional motif to a new level in literature. The student Raskolnikov kills Alyona, the old pawnbroker, and Lizaveta, her stepsister, as a way to test his theory that the superman can stand outside common conventions. As soon as the murder is completed, his first thought is to confess; the last confession is to Porfiry, the chief investigator of the crime.

From the moment Raskolnikov commits the crime, he thinks of confessing prompted by his fear of being discovered. While his theory of crime was based on the idea that crime isolates one from society and that the superman should be able to withstand solitude, his experience following the crime belies these notions.

Raskolnikov does not, however, confess to his friend Sonia out of feelings of guilt. On the contrary, he presents a series of rationalizations to "explain" the murder to her. Thus his confession is an attempt to win her sympathy and understanding. He confesses to Sonia in order to return to the stream of life and to the community. No longer alienated following this confession, he is freed to tell Porfiry.

Raskolnikov's isolation and estrangement catalyze his confession. His idea that the superman would be able to stand alone proves to be wrong. After the murders, Raskolnikov is punished rather than exalted by his state of solitude. His final confession to the police stems from his realization that he cannot live alone. Raskolnikov's crime has isolated him from everyone; by confessing, he can at least rejoin humanity. He belongs again, however vilified, to the community.

Confessions propel us into the larger community. When ritual and ceremony are added to the mix, our sense that we are not alone is further magnified. As noted, Judaic and Christian religious traditions offer ritual, community, and meaning that help those who confess find peace of mind.

Many Native American and African peoples use elaborate ceremonies led by medicine men or shamans to cure troubled souls who confess in the presence of a supportive community. The Navajo, for example, use a diviner to discover the origin of a person's affliction. Although confession in the Navajo world may fix or assign blame, the person confessing is not made to feel a great deal of guilt; ceremonies are designed to reduce anxiety and restore the person to a state of spiritual balance.

The discloser's belief in the efficacy of treatment, along with repetitive chanting, reenactment of the curing of the ancestor/hero, and herbal medications, all contribute to the positive changes following confession. It is the discloser's idealized relationship to the medicine man, as well as the community's support, that makes confession such a meaningful experience. Ceremonies make the discloser feel connected to ancestors while grounding him to his present community in a meaningful way. This group focus has also found expression in Catholicism recently, where there is a new emphasis on penitential serving within the worshipping community.

In our modern Western traditions, the priest and therapist—unlike the shaman and medicine man—usually deal with confessions on an individualized basis, often behind closed doors. Rather than being embraced and sanctioned by the entire community, many patients, until recently, entered therapy secretly, fearing the negative reactions of parents, friends, or employers.

In the absence of community support, the individual therapist often becomes the most important confidant, since confidentiality and continuity are virtually guaranteed in this relationship. Freud and Breuer's *Studies on Hysteria* established the relational context for confessions. The analyst is described "as a father confessor, who gives absolution . . . by a continuance of his sympathy and respect after the confession has been made."

Confession creates a bridge that connects patient to therapist. The bond is strengthened as the confession becomes a means for the patient to dispense with the pretense of "bad faith," to use Sartre's term, in becoming authentic. The act of sharing an intimate secret itself helps the patient combat feelings of alienation and depersonalization.

Jung described the relational nature of confession when he wrote, "There appears to be a conscience in mankind which severely punishes the man who does not somehow and at some time, at whatever cost to his pride, cease to defend and assert himself, and instead confess himself fallible and human. Until he can do this, an impenetrable wall shuts him out from the living experience of feeling himself a man among men." Confession erodes the walls that cut us off, not only from the therapist, not only from the wider community, but often also from our true natures.

Sullivan noted that the pain of loneliness is more damning than that of anxiety. The need to relate is even stronger than the need for absolution in Albert Camus's novel *The Fall*. The novel's protagonist, Jean-Baptiste Clamance, having stolen a valuable art object and eluded the police of three countries, is obsessed with the idea that he cannot die without confessing. "Otherwise, were there but one lie hidden in a life, death made it definitive. No one, ever again, would know the truth on this point, since the only one to know it was precisely the dead man sleeping on his secret. That absolute murder of a truth used to make me dizzy."

Clamance, the lawyer/thief, needs to draw himself into the confidence of others in order to justify his life. He seeks to confess not primarily to alleviate guilt, but rather to break through the wall of solitude.

Sometimes high-risk confessions are preferred by patients who elect to drive a wedge through their loneliness in lieu of continuing to exist uneasily in their psychic cocoons. Paula was a forty-four-year-old patient with schizophrenia who, in the receptive stillness of therapy, slowly began to display her troubled inner world to me. At first she risked providing small bits of information pertaining to her dissatisfaction with living with her tyrannical mother and brother. Whenever I said anything, she would take issue with it or would regard my words as interference and withdraw. I soon realized that only total silence would fulfill her aching need to be understood and accepted.

The next level of risk assumed by Paula concerned her confession about my powers over her as manifested by my body language—facial expressions and bodily movements indicating approval or disapproval to her. When she continued to test my loyalty through these challenges, and when I passed her tests, she revealed what she considered to be her most threatening confession: the existence of Alex, her inner voice and companion, who gave her orders and criticized and taunted her. What frightened Paula the most, and the reason she had kept me from hearing her secret, was that she thought I would think she was crazy and have her hospitalized.

Paula continued: "I first recall Alex appearing in the window when I was seven. He has been with me off and on for almost my entire life. Even though Alex tells me to do bad things [Paula had sometimes pulled out her hair and was given to anorexia] and tells me how stupid and boring I am, I feel empty without him."

The need to escape unbearable loneliness in part fostered the appearance of Alex in the first place. Yet the imaginary companion/tormentor was not enough. Patients like Paula need the therapist both as an ally to protect them from powerful inner voices and as a nurturant figure to understand their loneliness.

The desperation of being trapped in a world of strangers impels such patients to take perceived catastrophic risks in letting the therapist in on their forbidden, secret world. The telling itself fosters intimacy and lessens the unbearable loneliness.

Ingmar Bergman's 1961 film *Through a Glass Darkly* weaves a number of confessions together that help the characters break down their walls of solitude and meaningfully connect with each other. Set on a remote island in Sweden within a twenty-four-hour period, we witness a young woman, Karin, descending into madness. Her helpless husband, Martin, who is the "saintly" doctor; her cold, self-involved father, David; and her teenage brother, Minus, initially relate to her and to each other in ways that sustain their spiritual isolation. The physical isolation of the island is a stark reminder of the personal anguish of human isolation experienced by each character.

Karin reads her father's diary, inadvertently discovering that her illness is irreversible, along with his misgivings about his desire to chart the course of her schizophrenia in order to use these observations in his own writing. These discoveries force Karin to see her father's true nature—a voyeur fascinated by the course of her illness.

After Karin shares these secrets with her husband, Martin, he confronts her father about his cold, exploitative nature. Karin's father then confesses that he had attempted suicide, and when it failed, he realized that he did love his children and that love is the most important thing in life. Unfortunately, this love is a secret that cannot break through the walls of reserve and distance he has erected.

The relationship between Karin and her brother, Minus, undergoes profound changes as the distance between them is diminished in shocking, unforeseen ways. Karin takes her brother to the attic, where she believes the walls are inhabited by "The Others"—creatures who want her to join them in waiting for the arrival of God. Terrified of her stark revelation of madness, Minus leaves her writhing on the floor.

Karin disappears, and Minus finds her in the rotting hull of an abandoned boat. As he goes to comfort her, she draws him into incest. When Minus tells his father, his father finally talks to him. Minus is comforted, not so much by what his father says as from the fact that his father cares enough to speak to him.

This film richly confirms the value of confession as a special form of communication, giving meaning to life and breaking down the walls of solitude. At various points throughout the film, we want to shake the characters out of their lethargy and shout at them E. M. Forster's prescription for England: "Only connect!" Confession, both unintentional and intentional, is the conduit enabling the characters to connect.

Bergman once remarked, "What matters most of all in life is being able to make contact with other human beings." A theme running through the film is the necessity of establishing human contact. We see how each character is trapped behind different walls: Karin by her madness, Minus by his confusion and repressed sexuality, David by his self-absorption and inability to communicate loving feelings, and Martin by his "saintliness" that drives Karin to the point at which she cannot stand him.

The loneliness and hunger of the human soul is revealed to us throughout the film. Confessions allow each character, with the exception of Martin, to break through the walls.

The Need to Shine and Be Special

Narcissistic confessions—esteem-enhancing confessions that make us feel unique or special—sometimes represent exaggerated attempts to mask or compensate for shame. At other times, the nature of these confessions, as well as their manner of presentation, sets narcissistic confessions apart from all other confessions.

Narcissistic confessions provide the arena for our grandiose selves to emerge with pride and impunity. Tall-tale outpourings enable us to exaggerate our importance by parading adventurous, forbidden, or daring aspects of ourselves to enthralled or flabbergasted audiences. Such confessions heighten our self-esteem.

Talk show confessions, for example, are often self-serving narcissistic confessions, especially when they are presented to create an impact rather than to alleviate a burden. While the secrets of victimization or abuse the "guests" on these shows relate are often (but not always) true, in retelling them for mass media consumption, the disclosers' intent is often to impress others with their misery—and even capitalize on it—rather than to authentically convey a secret to gain relief or to be understood. After all, it is hard to be intimate with millions of people. Guests' cravings for their "fifteen minutes of fame" and the "five minute wrap-up" offered by psychological experts speaks to the late twentieth century's hunger for fast relief and instant gratification. This "fast-food approach" often belies the willingness of guests to truly confront their problems and commit themselves to working them out.

The one-to-one intimacy of the confessional or therapy session gives way to a grandiose public display of bravado in which a vast audience instantly becomes privy to the most horrendous secrets. TV hosts sometimes take on the aura of preachers, asking questions, sermonizing, and whipping the studio audience into a frenzy. Through a combination of charisma and the authority vested in them by the Age of Information, they function as latter-day evangelists.

Some TV disclosers genuinely seek to be understood and forgiven or condemned by the larger audience, as well as by God. Let us not forget, however, that the confessional media, more often than not, reflect guests' exhibitionistic natures matched by the audience's need to voyeuristically experience forbidden thrills.

While the media glorify outlandish confessions, many of us shy away from such broad-based exposure, especially when confessions concern our own bodies. Feelings about our bodies give rise to confessions that often become a barometer of our self-esteem. This is clear in Shakespeare's play *Richard III*. Richard's bodily deformity justifies anything to him, including murder, as a means to enhance his self-esteem. In the opening soliloquy to *Richard III*, Gloucester, who subsequently becomes the king, reveals that he is "Cheated of feature by dissembling nature,/Deformed, unfinished, sent before my time/Into this breathing world." He goes on to justify his villainy: "And therefore, since I cannot prove a lover,/ . . . I am determined to prove a villain."

Through this soliloquy, he reveals that nature has done him a grievous wrong in denying him the beauty of form that wins human love. Richard believes that life owes him reparation for this, and he will make sure to get it. He is convinced that he has the right to be an exception, to disregard the scruples by which others let themselves be held back. His bodily deformity—an extreme wound to his narcissism—fuels him to rationalize wrongdoing to others, using the justification that wrong has been done to him.

Disappointed by the body nature gave him, his grandiosity turns toward his sense of specialness—of not being subject to the laws of ordinary mortals—as a justification for the pursuit of his ambitions, even when murder is involved. Richard's flaws represent a magnification of some of the things we can see in ourselves. We use our secret narcissistic injuries, real or imagined, to heighten our grandiosity or to justify thoughts or acts of villainy. The questions we endlessly turn over in our minds address these "Richard the Third-like" concerns. "Why was I born into a middle class home instead of to royalty?" "Why did nature give me a puny body instead of the physique of Hercules?"

"There but for the grace of God go I," becomes our plaint. Behind these often unexpressed narcissistic injuries may lurk grandiosity of unparalleled dimensions. In John Updike's memoirs, his essay entitled "At War with My Sin" talks about his lifelong bouts with psoriasis, which he contracted at age six, prompting him to alternate between embarrassment and grandiosity. Updike notes, "Strategies of concealment ramify, and self-examination is endless. You are forced to the mirror again and again; psoriasis compels narcissism, if we can suppose a Narcissus who did not like what he saw." Updike goes on to confess how his self-consciousness was transformed into feelings of specialness. "Only psoriasis could have taken a very average little boy and made him into a prolific, adaptive, ruthless-enough writer."

When children are rebuked or humiliated by parents instead of being appreciated by them, their grandiosity goes underground, turning on itself, even as the yearning to be special and affirmed remains. On the other hand, grandiosity develops and flourishes in the presence of mirroring and affirmation from empathic confidants.

The very young Sartre, in his autobiography, *The Words,* learns that being special can garner adult adulation. Sartre muses: "Am I therefore a Narcissus? Not even that. Too eager to charm, I forget myself. . . . Happily, there is no lack of applause. Whether the adults listen to me babbling or to the 'Art of the Fugue,' they have the same arch smile of enjoyment and complicity. That shows me what I am essentially: a cultural asset." The need to fascinate, seduce, or entertain confidants may result in grandiose confessions that are embroidered, shaped, and otherwise transmogrified to make us more interesting to others and, by extension, to ourselves.

For many people, narcissistic confessions temporarily go underground. Shame—the flip side of narcissism—often impels us to retreat from certain confessions until they are ready to burst forth in all their narcissistic splendor. Sexual topics often initially induce conflicts regarding whether to confess.

Many individuals shy away from discussing sex altogether. Religious upbringing and sexual trauma in childhood leave a legacy of shame along with hidden grandiosity. Ruby was a twenty-nine-year-old graduate student with a severe conscience that made her feel that she was too "kinky." At the same time, she had a secret grandiosity that contributed to her feeling of being special *because* she was kinky. Ruby told me that although she knew she would be discussing sex, she was shying away from it. When I asked her if this might have something to do with her feelings toward me, Ruby replied, "That question made me think of my mother. Strangely, my mother was not moralistically evaluative, but she was intrusive. She had to know everything, including the details of my sex life. She once asked me what percentage of times I had orgasms with my boyfriend, and I told her it was none of her business."

Ruby remembered me inquiring about her sex life in an earlier session. I gently reminded her that I had asked her whether there was anything she would not tell me about, and Ruby unhesitatingly mentioned sex. She laughed in retrospect and said, "You're right. The funny thing is, I have brought up sex before in dreams and even told you how, as adolescents, my friend and I fondled each others' breasts. I guess this time the difference is that I remembered that you initiated the discussion and that felt intrusive.

"You see, my sex life is my only secret from my mother. Yet, since I broached the subject last week, I noticed that I had great sex with my boyfriend this weekend. It's like my boyfriend is loosening me up physically and you are mentally."

Ruby felt that sex was the only sphere of activity in which she could totally separate from her intrusive mother. At the same time, she sincerely wished to reveal her sexual side to me in spite of her misgivings about the appropriateness of her sexuality.

Confessions initiated with confidants who are empathically receptive can be transformed from shameful secrets to narcissistic snowballs that grow larger as the discloser's excitement and enjoyment increase. Our grandiosity, set free, elatedly expands as it gains momentum.

To this end, Ruby, in a breathless, anticipatory manner, proclaimed, "Okay. Here goes. My boyfriend bought me a vibrator on Saint Valentine's Day. Even though I love it, I wonder if my girlfriends use this prop, but I don't dare expose myself to them." In this narcissistic snowball effect, the confession not only demonstrates Ruby's increasing elation, but also embodies the thrill of disclosing a new forbidden, special deed or thought to an appreciative confidant.

Few of us display the effervescent grandiosity of a Dali, who confessed that at age seven he wanted to be a Napoleon and that his ambition had been growing steadily ever since. Freud demonstrated the adaptive value of parental affirmation in the development of greatness when he revealed, "A man who has been the indisputable favorite of his mother keeps for life the feeling of a conqueror, that confidence of success that often induces real success."

Confession is ultimately about relating—to intimates, to God, to ourselves. When we open up to others to unburden ourselves of guilt or shame, we atone or make restitution in order to heal the breach with others as well as the wounds to our souls. Acknowledging who we are grounds our identity. We reveal ourselves to others in order to tear down the walls of estrangement and be accepted *in toto*, including our dreaded and flawed aspects. Finally, we tell secrets to be outrageous and zany, to allow our outlandish sense of uniqueness and specialness to have their day. Our confidants' love and appreciation flow back to us, enhancing our sense of well-being.

6

Ethical Dilemmas

SECRETS are the sacred charge of priests, therapists, lawyers, and doctors. Each of us as tellers and listeners also has responsibilities, however. When secrets present us with ethical dilemmas, we must search our hearts and our minds to determine the underlying moral and possibly legal ramifications of either disclosing or retaining controversial secrets.

The ethical dilemma we face goes beyond "to tell or not to tell." We have to sort out and come to terms with our own philosophy, since confession is an acknowledgment of who we are and how we view ourselves.

How do we resolve the ethical dilemmas in confession? Ethical questions—questions of right and wrong, good and evil—are not the special province of philosophers or priests. Ethics do not emerge from philosophical abstraction, but from concrete existence in the world. We are born into a world of meanings and values full of "goods and bads," "do's and don'ts."

Early on in our lives we become ethical animals, with the ability to reflect on our moral judgments and actions. The values we acquire in our families become our earliest ethical guideposts. Only later do we look to rules and social norms to help us decide how to resolve our secrets. Later we acquire still greater mental acumen and subscribe to abstract principles such as justice, love, freedom, loyalty, and truth.

John F. Kennedy observed that the tough decisions are not between right and wrong, but between different rights or different wrongs. Behaving ethically is no simple matter. It involves transcending one's own personal viewpoint and examining the prospective decision from a wider perspective—a perspective that includes not only confidants but also rules and principles that are widely shared.

Ethics and Customs

Confessions are often linked to the domain of ethics—how ethical "oughts" either impel us to confess or to continue to conceal our secrets. The word *ethics* comes from Greek and Latin roots that mean "custom." This implies that we behave in an ethically correct manner when we do what custom dictates. We can well question whether there is now a prevailing set of customs by which we all live. A major problem is that in today's world of multiple perspectives we are not united as a society on custom or convention, and thus on what constitutes "correct living."

Changing times often dictate additions or alterations to moral principles. The eighth-century prophets added ethical precepts to address the changing social conditions that occured after the time of Moses. Concerns with social justice then prevailed, including Ezekiel's notion that in God's sight every person is morally responsible for what she does and should not attribute blame to her heredity or environment (Ezek.18:20 ff). How strongly this principle speaks to us today! The existential tradition as well as many approaches to psychotherapy espouse the view that whether or not we choose to reveal our secrets to others, we are ultimately responsible for our decisions about how to deal with them and with the inevitable consequences of those decisions.

Despite the multiple perspectives now available to us, there are three major traditions addressing ethical concerns. The philosophies we subscribe to in large measure help us decide what we "ought" to do—the ethical stance we adopt in choosing to reveal or conceal our secrets.

Religion

The religious tradition is the first great ethical system binding believers to the community and to God through confession. Religious confessions empower us to express our secrets as we "try on" words to fit the sinful experiences of our lives. Faith provides the glue that binds us and our confessions, freely offered, to the Almighty, who then favors us with love, grace, and forgiveness. In the Roman Catholic and Greek Orthodox churches, religious confession is one of the few areas in believers' lives in which they can truly reveal themselves with impunity, secure in the knowledge that the ancient seal of confession guarantees confidentiality in every situation. Believers are ethically drawn toward confession both by the rituals and traditions of the church, and by the knowledge that confession can be an instrument that propels them toward actively working at transforming themselves and finding redemption through genuine remorse and the resolve to do better.

Following Luther's split from the Catholic Church, in part resulting from his disillusionment with the system of indulgences exchanged by rich penitents and confessors, the new Protestant churches were very cautious about individual confession. While the nineteenth century witnessed the Oxford Movement growing out of High Anglicanism attempting to reconstitute individual confession, in more recent times, the Oxford Group (unrelated to the Oxford Movement) arose emphasizing sharing confession as a mutual encounter either in a group or with a single person. This practice in which congregants get to know each other intimately has also been adopted by Christian Scientists, Baptists, and Quakers.

Confession in Judaism is linked in most people's minds with Yom Kippur, the Day of Atonement; this holy day involves communal confession. The two great elements in Jewish confession are language and relationship. In confession, the words used convey the need for God's healing. It is language that sets redemption in motion. The ethical imperative to confess is strong in Judaism. Sins are disclosed to God in the belief that God will help mend wrongdoing in the process of believers becoming better, more spiritual beings.

In the Judeo-Christian tradition, confession marked a great revolution in human consciousness, because it forced people to become more self-aware in order to become better selves and more conscious of others. We become more ethical beings through confession. Virtually every religion stresses our need to make reparation for wrongdoing to our neighbors as a way of showing true remorse and finding redemption. In the religious tradition, the ethical life and confession are inextricably linked to each other.

Philosophy

Secular philosophy is the second great tradition that has a profound impact on our ethical consciousness. Socrates believed that there were basic principles of right and wrong and that inquiry into our actions would help us discover what is good. In *The Phaedrus,* Plato argued that reason governing our will and desires was the key to the good life. Even Epicurus, who taught that all life is oriented toward pleasure (a doctrine presented in his disciple Lucretius' poem "De Rerum Natura"), stressed the long-term pleasures of the mind as more gratifying than short-term physical pleasures.

Enlightenment philosophers such as Immanuel Kant continued in the rational tradition, emphasizing that morality is not given to us by God or society but is dictated by humans as rational beings. Kant's basic premise was, "Do your duty." In *The Critique of Practical Reason,* he assumed people knew the rules and agreed upon what duty entailed. Stressing the primacy of reason, Kant believed that if each of us acts as if his own acts would become the principles of everyone else's behavior, each person would always know the difference between right and wrong.

From the Greek philosophers through Enlightenment philosophers such as Kant, this strand of philosophy maintained that our reasoning faculty should govern our decisions regarding ethical dilemmas in confession. In this liberal, individualistic tradition, a great burden was placed on each of us, by virtue of our cognitive competence, to know the right thing to do.

Kant suggested that we possess inherent mental abilities which enable us to be ethical beings. In today's technical parlance, we might say we are innately programmed "to do the right thing" when it comes to disclosure. Yet, how can we know that each of our personal "takes" on moral standards does indeed reflect societal needs?

The emotional life is conspicuously missing from rational approaches—an omission that has been the primary focus of psychologist Carol Gilligan's work. Gilligan has observed in her research that men and women generally emphasize different moral concerns. While men tend to employ more impersonal, universal principles of justice, for example, women tend to have a more personal, relational focus. A woman's decision whether or not to disclose that she had an abortion, from Gilligan's perspective, is likely to focus primarily on how others might feel about her.

Our sense of concern—of compassion for our fellow beings—renders them "thous" rather than "its" in our eyes, to use Martin Buber's terminology. As long as we view others as human—like ourselves—rather than objects to be manipulated, we are less likely to demean them. We are more likely to treat them as we would like and expect to be treated. Thus, a decision *not* to be unfaithful to one's spouse springs both from religious beliefs and from a humane philosophical viewpoint such as Buber's and a psychological tradition like Gilligan's, that places empathy on a par with rational considerations.

In *The Will to Believe*, William James emphasized consulting our hearts, rather than science, to resolve questions of good and bad. "If your heart does not *want* a world of moral reality," avers James, "your head will assuredly never make you believe in one." Our current emphasis on "emotional intelligence," as Daniel Goleman calls it, addresses the importance of our emotional skills in dealing with critical life issues. The pendulum has swung from cognitive, impersonal approaches toward compassion and relational considerations, in Gilligan's view, in resolving confessional dilemmas.

The emotional aspects of morality are grounded in relationships. Because our social natures are integral to our sense of being ethical creatures, those of us who operate primarily in the relational mode are more likely to seek out confidants to help us come to terms with our moral decisions. A profound shift occurs when children move from obeying rules for external reasons, such as fear of punishment, to obeying rules for internal reasons, because they will feel guilty or ashamed of behaving badly. Now moral decisions take other people into account and thus depend more on empathy. When we feel guilty for causing another person's unhappiness, "what's in it for me?" morality ("I won't tell Mom I stole the quarter because she'll punish me") gives way to empathy-based morality ("I'll feel bad for hurting Mom, who is good to me").

The Psychological Revolution

In addition to the religious and philosophical traditions, the third great current in ethics already alluded to is the psychological revolution. Freud believed that our moral sense—the superego—was based upon our identification with parents who, in turn, serve as filters of society's values. Good and evil become a matter of internalized parental rules.

While it is true that our first exposure to morality is through family values, what if the parents themselves do not conform to traditional values? What if the parents are cruel—psychopaths, abusers, alcoholics, or simply neglectful and self-involved? We are all too familiar with the likelihood of abused children becoming abusers. Family history is a strong determinant of alcoholism and psychopathy; yet not all children of alcoholics and psychopaths inevitably follow in their parents' footsteps. Indeed, some children of alcoholics become overly conscientious teetotaling achievers, while children of psychopaths might break the family mold by becoming hell-and-brimstone preachers.

Although our moral values begin with the family, later influences (peers, school, religion, social movements) can take hold of us and transform us into ethical beings in the process. Fortunately, many who were born into dysfunctional families are able to transcend inhumane family practices. Finding empathic, supportive confidants in and out of therapy enables these individuals to confess family secrets in a secure environment. Confidants also expose people from dysfunctional families to different values and ways of being.

The major fear voiced by many adult patients who were sexually abused or neglected as children is that they might treat their children as badly as they were treated. By entering therapy and choosing to disclose what many regarded as an ethical dilemma ("betraying" the abusive parent), they broke the parental spell along with the cycle of potential intergenerational abuse. Because these patients are so aware of familial patterns of violence, abuse, and torment, they have already taken steps to show concern for their children's welfare rather than mindlessly following their own parents' abusive patterns.

Facing our past makes us more aware of the direction our future ethical decisions are likely to take. We choose to respond with care over abuse, concern in lieu of manipulation. On the other hand, shrouding our pasts in secrecy is likely to doom us to be clones of our parents.

A final major contribution to the psychological approach to ethics emerged with Jean Piaget, who as early as 1932 maintained that our sense of right and wrong does not arise from biblical or parental teachings, but rather from the reasoning abilities that develop from our social experiences with the world. Piaget observed that as we get older, our morality moves increasingly inward and we police ourselves instead of looking to authority figures to police us. As adults, our secrets pertaining to wrongdoing should motivate us to draw on our spiritual or philosophical reservoirs to satisfy an internalized conscience rather than an externally based "will I get caught?" morality.

When we grapple with a secret involving our emotional and spiritual well-being, most of us combine reasoning with emotional and relational considerations in deciding whether to confess. We may know, for example, that infidelity is wrong, yet we allow our emotional vulnerability and feelings of neediness to sway us into having an affair. Social psychologists have observed that there is a *psychological lag* between what people say they believe and what they actually do in their lives. The term "psychological lag" refers to the time between conscious acceptance of a new behavior (such as a woman's right to succeed professionally), and the dissipation of unconscious resistance to it. For example, psychologist Matina Horner showed that while female college students reported that women had every right to succeed professionally, many of these same women completed stories in which a woman at the head of her medical school class was destined to fail socially and possibly professionally as well. While these women believed in a woman's right to professional success in the abstract, the *unconscious secret* they could not confess to themselves was that in ac-

tual situations in everyday life, they were afraid that bright women were destined to fail.

When it comes to ethical decisions regarding disclosure, our actual behavior in the resolution of secret dilemmas such as whether to be unfaithful or whether to deliberately fail professionally often differs dramatically from our idealized moral judgments about "correct behavior" we list on questionnaires. As creatures with strong emotional as well as cognitive components to our personalities, we rarely rely solely on rational principles in resolving confessional dilemmas.

Further, why should we assume that "justice-based" reasoning in which one subscribes to abstract principles is inevitably better or higher than "care-based" reasoning in which our primary concerns are compassion and care for others? Kohlberg might well cite Saint Augustine as one who reached the highest moral stage because of his commitment to universal principles of faith and devotion to God. Yet Saint Augustine, who abandoned his wife and son in his quest for "universal love of God," failed to meet Gilligan's care-based person-centered moral criteria. For those who value friendship and intimacy more than rugged individualism and self-sufficiency, empathy and social concern for others is both common and desirable.

In short, when we search our hearts and souls in deliberating on what to do to resolve a secret dilemma, we are placed in a particular situation and a particular social context. A friend who operates primarily on care-based principles of empathy might choose not to divulge the spouse's known infidelity to her friend out of concern for hurting her. Another friend might choose to confess the same secret to the unsuspecting friend. The second friend's decision to confess is based more on abstract principles of justice better being served by revealing the infidelity. In justice-based morality, gaining insight into the true condition of the marriage is deemed more important than living a false, illusory existence.

Of course, we simply do not use the same moral reasoning in all ethical dilemmas. Saint Augustine's decision to pursue universal principles of devotion to God hurt others in their wake, perhaps inevitably. In choosing to love God, Saint Augustine acted callously toward his family.

Select Clerics' Dilemmas

Many literary critics consider Nathaniel Hawthorne's *The Scarlet Letter* to be the best-known account of a philandering minister in American fiction. Unfortunately, life seems frequently to imitate art these days. Victims' shame, as well as the embarrassment of congregations and of the institutional church itself, often conspire to make sexual abuse by clergy second only to incest as a taboo to be kept secret.

For centuries, these secrets remained behind closed doors; ethical dilemmas were unsatisfactorily resolved as both participants chose to keep quiet. Recently, however, churches across the ecumenical spectrum are recognizing that clerical sexual offenders represent a serious problem. Of greatest concern are local clergy who seduce congregants relying upon them for spiritual guidance. Some churches have adopted policies to deal with such sexual harassment issues—fueled in part by moral concern and in part by the skyrocketing rates of institutional insurance companies which must deal with the resulting settlements.

Psychiatrist Glenn Gabbard, cited in Woodward and King's *Newsweek* article, notes that clerical seducers are often middle-aged men who are disillusioned with their calling. When a young woman comes for pastoral counseling, her perception that the minister is like God makes her a vulnerable sexual victim. In churches with a strong Pentecostal or revivalist tradition, the power ascribed to the minister during revival meetings or emotionally charged "altar calls" can be linked to or confused with sexual passion. Because ministers predominantly still make house calls and have colleagues who are often female church volunteers, the potential for seduction is large. Seductions or ongoing sexual relationships often result in an uneasy pact of secrecy between the partners. Exposure through confession can have catastrophic consequences. When congregants and clerics are married, disclosures of infidelity affect not only their families, but also their standing in the larger community.

Much has also emerged about homosexual seduction by clergy, as well as sexual dalliances with children or young people by heterosexual and homosexual clergy. These sexual secrets pose ethical dilemmas for both clergy and parishioners. Yet many clerics are so absorbed in their own narcissistic gratification and sexual pleasure that they opt for secrecy.

The congregant/victim, on the other hand, is often more caught up in the moral dilemma wrought by the sexual secret itself. Disclosure would betray the idealized cleric, but continued secrecy would escalate feelings of guilt and shame.

Sometimes these dilemmas are resolved by a third party who discovers the secret or by the congregant's selective disclosure to a friend who then "blows the whistle" on the affair, either out of anger or in the interest of greater justice. In some instances, both cleric and congregant may search their souls to arrive at a resolution that will minimally hurt the other and, at the same time, salvage each participant's self-worth. For example, both may turn themselves in for counseling; in this way, they can be redeemed rather than continue the cycle of torment and punishment.

Of course, not all clerical dilemmas are sexual in nature. There are priests and ministers who irreparably harm young congregants by suggesting that hell awaits them when they confess to masturbating, for example. Because young children's morality is often based on the "rightness" of authorities, they are caught in the bind of either submitting to the terrible fate allegedly awaiting them in secret or the shame of telling their parents. As alternative authority figures who hopefully will disagree with the cleric's judgments, parents can ease their children's pain and fear by setting the record straight. Should the parents fail to vigorously disagree with this brand of sadistic cleric, the child's disclosure will only heighten that child's anxiety, and weaken the child's belief in the goodness and trustworthiness of authority figures, and of confession itself.

The 1995 film *Priest* captures many of the personal and interpersonal dilemmas that can potentially confront priests. The film follows social conservative Father Greg Pilkington as he arrives in Liverpool and goes on secret homosexual adventures, changing out of his ecclesiastical garb and putting on his stereotypical leather jacket. We see him picking up a man in a gay bar and then having sex. In juxtaposition to the young, conservative, guilt-ridden Father Greg is the middle-aged, liberal Father Matthew who has a sexual relationship with his housekeeper.

As if these sexual secrets brimming with ethical issues are not enough, a fourteen-year-old girl comes for confession and tells Father Greg that she is being raped regularly and secretly by her father. Father Greg is caught in the priestly dilemma of how to see justice done while preserving the sanctity and confidentiality of the confessional.

Father Greg advises the girl to tell her father she has confessed and that the abuse cannot continue. Her father then comes to the confessional and warns the priest to stay out of his life, even as he elaborates on his obsession. "Incest is human. It's the most natural thing in the world. It's the one thing we all like to do."

Throughout the ordeal wrought by the rape victim's confession, Father Greg is caught in an ethical dilemma. He wants to help the girl as a fellow human, but is bound by the seal of the confessional. Yet this dilemma, faced by many priests, is not as dire or unresolvable as the film would have us believe. Many priests whom I interviewed mentioned that while they could not directly reveal confessions of sexual abuse or murder to the authorities, they could counsel disclosers on a right course of action or ask discrete questions that might set them on a new ethical path. The sensitive cleric adopts similar tools—questions, support, advice, and interpretations—to those used by therapists in helping confessants arrive at ethical decisions without violating the rule of confidentiality.

In the film, both priests grapple with their own sexual secrets differently. The older priest seems to have no personal conflict about the ethical aspects of his behavior. He deals with his seemingly morally unacceptable behavior by separating the institutional church, comprised of rules and regulations, from his interpretation of the teachings of Christ based, in his view, on more humane loving.

Father Greg is forced to deal with his homosexuality when he is caught committing sodomy in a car and sent off to a Jesuit retreat for punishment and moral cleansing. His ethical dilemma is never resolved, yet we sense that, through his relationship with Father Matthew and his dealings with the teenage girl, he is humanized. Like Father Matthew, he becomes governed by love and less subject to self-abnegating guilt and feelings of worthlessness.

Some might take exception with how both priests dealt with their sexual dilemmas, particularly Father Matthew rationalizing his. We might wonder why he does not play by the rules and why he became a priest in the first place. In this regard, Saint Paul in 1 Cor. 3:18 remarks, "If any one among you think that he is wise in this age, let him become a fool that he may become wise." This text points to the complexity and many facets of truth.

Difficult moral dilemmas are never facilely resolved. We realize that conflicting moralities offer no easy answers nor clear-cut resolutions.

Select Physicians' Dilemmas

Physicians, like priests, have long been the keepers of secrets. Because they believe confidentiality is an inviolable right, patients feel secure revealing their most dreaded secrets to the doctor/confidant they trust and respect. When doctors graduate from medical school, they take the oath of Hippocrates, declaring: "Whatsoever I shall see or hear in the course of my profession . . . if it be what should not be published abroad, I will never divulge, holding such things to be holy secrets."

Doctors are sometimes the sole confidants for patients who reveal intimate details they may be unwilling to share with anyone else. The patient's trust is often an integral element in the healing process. In most situations, confidentiality is guaranteed as a sacred duty—keeping the "holy secrets" of the Hippocratic oath. Yet increasingly, doctors are faced with the ethical dilemma of breaking confidentiality when disclosure is in the interest of the public good. Here community interests are pitted against the individual's right to privacy.

Many ethical dilemmas have emerged around HIV and AIDS. There have been cases in which a wife demands to know whether her husband carries the virus that leads to AIDS, especially since she is pregnant and does not want to give birth to a baby who is HIV positive. If she finds her husband has HIV, she intends to have an abortion. Suppose the doctor has also treated the husband who tests positive for HIV. The doctor urges the husband to tell his wife, but he refuses, stating he always uses condoms and that if she found out about his situation, she would leave him.

What should the doctor do? Should he confront the wife, knowing that she and the fetus are in jeopardy? Or must he protect his patient's confidentiality? In one such case, the doctor, believing he had a duty to protect his patient's confidentiality, did not tell the wife that her husband carried HIV. He did remind her, however, that she and her child were at risk of becoming infected because of her husband's drug abuse. The doctor also advised her to get tested.

A new policy of the American Medical Association holds that when people test positive for HIV or AIDS, doctors have a responsibility to ensure that these patients' spouses and sexual partners are informed. Psychiatrists Michael Wilkes and Miriam Shuchman argue that there is no public policy reason for a general exception to confidentiality in all HIV/AIDS cases, since AIDS is already a reportable disease.

There is a delicate balance in HIV/AIDS cases between the patient's right to privacy and the rights and needs of others. One of the strongest reasons for keeping AIDS information confidential is to enable patients to speak openly with doctors, without fear of having the information used against them. Fear of reprisal through indiscriminate disclosure may not only prevent AIDS patients from coming forward for treatment, but also may stop their participation in research that will ultimately benefit everyone. Further, the stigma of wanton disclosure can carry over to social relations and employers. Ostracism and job loss often follow such revelations.

The ethical dilemmas mentioned thus far involve the physician's conflict over which situations dictate that confidentiality be breached in the interest of the greater community's good. Doctors face yet another kind of ethical dilemma regarding their own impulses and behavior behind closed doors. As many physicians' activities go unmonitored, there is often no way to disclose questionable practices hidden from public scrutiny.

Physicians have long been considered the trusted guardians of medical wisdom as well as the expert purveyors on how to lead a good, healthful life. When physicians in specific instances fail to live up to the ideals embodied in the Hippocratic oath, we feel betrayed. (See chapter 7 for a detailed account of betrayal.) For example, doctors warn elderly people with failing eyesight that they should not be driving. This issue becomes more complex, however, in a situation in which a radiologist with poor eyesight is entrusted to make diagnoses by examining x-rays. This real-life situation was related to me by a hospital worker who befriended such a radiologist.

As she became increasingly aware of the radiologist's eye problems, this worker confronted her friend, suggesting that perhaps he consider leaving his specialty and turning to general medicine. He angrily explained to her that radiology was a family tradition—his grandfather and father had been radiologists. In addition, he had worked hard to attain his present status, and he had no intention of demoting himself. When the hospital worker responded with the issue of the well-being of his patients, the radiologist replied that he was already getting eye training and expected his problem to improve.

Should my colleague have reported the radiologist for the greater good? Or should she have continued to appeal to his ethical sense "to do the right thing"? In fact, she did neither. Having agonized over whether to disclose this doctor's condition, she chose to remain silent, sustain the friendship, and avoid being the cause of disciplinary actions. While some might condemn this decision, each of us can only speculate on what we would do in a similar concrete situation in which friendship considerations ("care-based morality") are pitted against universal principles of life ("justice-based morality").

These kinds of ethical dilemmas are agonizing both for us and for the physician. We often have higher ethical expectations for those in the helping professions. When a priest or physician lets us down, we wonder whether anyone is trustworthy or anything is sacred anymore. Yet when we condemn the many for the infractions of the few, we unfairly degrade those who have honorably ministered to our bodies and souls.

Therapists' Dilemmas

There was a time, not so long ago, when diligent therapists learned theories of development and principles of technique, and practiced psychotherapy without worrying about ethical or legal considerations. For many years Freud set anxious analysts' minds at rest by espousing the doctrine of scientific objectivity as the sole permissible analytic value.

In recent years, however, therapists have come to realize that, as human beings engaged in a human enterprise, values and ethics inevitably enter into therapy. Some problems encountered in therapy are inevitably moral ones involving religious, political, economic, or sociocultural issues whose outcome may have a direct impact on the patient as well as on society.

Ethical "oughts" and legal "musts" have intruded into the privacy of treatment. Confessions that involve issues of drug trafficking, child abuse, or sexual perversion present an overtly ethical and sometimes legal dimension. Therapists are best able to handle such confessions by being aware of the laws pertaining to confidentiality and privilege, and by paying close attention to their own reactions, including fear, repulsion, revulsion, disapproval, or even envy (if such confessions evoke the therapist's own forbidden secret desires).

The celebrated Tarasoff case cogently demonstrated to therapists that the therapeutic domain of confidentiality could no longer be separated from larger societal concerns. Since 1976 (the year of *Tarasoff* v. *Regents of University of California*) a number of states have mandated that a psychotherapist must make public, under certain circumstances, what a patient has confided to the therapist.

This precedent-setting case can be described as follows: On August 20, 1969, a student outpatient at the University of California named Prosenjit Poddar told his therapist in a session that he intended to murder his girlfriend, Tatiana Tarasoff, when she returned to the University of California at Berkeley after her vacation. The psychotherapist contacted the campus police with this information, who took Poddar into custody but later released him due to lack of evidence. Poddar subsequently terminated his therapy.

On October 27, Poddar did, in fact, kill Tarasoff. Neither Tarasoff nor her parents had been warned. Her parents filed suit against the university, certain employees at Cowell Memorial Hospital (where Poddar also was an outpatient), the chief of the campus police and four officers, and the psychologist. The case was dismissed by the lower court, but on appeal the California Supreme Court ruled that the psychotherapist and his supervisor failed to provide an adequate warning of Poddar's intended homicide to either the victim or her parents. Specifically rejecting a defense based on patient-therapist confidentiality, the court wrote, "The protective privilege ends when the public peril begins." When the therapist has cause to believe that the patient's mental condition makes him dangerous to himself or others, disclosure is necessary to prevent the threatened danger.

The decision rocked the therapy community. Patients could no longer indiscriminately follow Freud's injunction to say whatever comes to mind. The therapist, in turn, would now have to function as a "double agent," selectively splitting the role as the patient's private confessor with that of a public citizen charged with assessing the "larger benefit" the community could gain by disclosure. Uncertainty about how to balance the two often incompatible roles can affect the therapist's treatment capacity, especially if anxiety and fear of censure interfere with her professional attitude.

The *Tarasoff* decision raised questions regarding which circumstances require therapists to exercise their "duty to warn." Many patients routinely express their desire to harm a significant person in their lives. Because many types of therapy focus on the expression of forbidden, often socially unacceptable material, therapists may be faced on a daily basis with confessions that go beyond therapeutic scrutiny into the legal domain. Moreover, therapists' predictions of violence have been found to be notoriously inaccurate, with false positives approaching 80 or 90 percent.

What is often minimized in the *Tarasoff* decision is the continued importance of protecting the patient's privacy. The California Supreme Court cautioned that "the therapist's obligations to his patient require that he not disclose a confidence unless such disclosure is necessary to avert danger to others, and even then, that he do so discretely, and in a fashion that would preserve the privacy of his patient to the fullest extent compatible with the prevention of the threatened danger." In other words, therapists should not pit the patient's privacy against society's rights; rather their ethical decisions should consider how to protect third parties from serious harm while minimizing the intrusion on the patient's privacy.

As consumers, patients must be aware of the therapist's duty to warn in select instances of confession and must also be cognizant of their right to expose the therapist if their integrity is being violated.

Nevertheless, since many patients enter therapy unaware of its goals, procedures, and policies, it is the therapist in the role of professional who is ethically responsible for setting limits and providing the structure for treatment. The therapist must educate the patient/consumer not only about exceptions to privilege predicated on the therapist's duty to warn, but also about the possibilities of therapists' misdeeds that may call for disclosure.

While the flow of confessions from patient to therapist to supervisor is an expected occurrence, therapists cross ethical boundaries when they disclose patients' confessions to the media or socially to colleagues. There have been cases in which therapists have named famous people as patients and identified their personality characteristics in newspaper interviews. In one case concerning a nationally publicized murder trial, a psychologist evaluated the accused, then provided a personality profile of this person to a local newspaper. The psychologist was censured by the American Psychological Association's ethics committee for his unprofessional breach of confidentiality.

Therapists disclosing their patients' confidences for financial gain, or to promote themselves, blinds them from acknowledging that such behavior is ethically questionable and detrimental to their patients. Such violations are not solely confined to therapists. Almost everyone uses gossip at some point to enhance one's self-importance by betraying a confidence. Suzi spilling Nancy's secret to Bobby on the playground demonstrates how children early on begin to leak each other's secrets to each other.

When therapists use patients' confessions as gossip, they are violating the canons of confidentiality. Though gossiping therapists may try to navigate between guarding patients' confidentiality and inadvertently disclosing their identity, they usually provide sufficient clues to enable the audience to piece together the identities of famous patients.

These so-called disguised disclosures, while affording a social avenue for collegial repartee, are ethically questionable, especially in instances where the patient's identity becomes obvious. The therapist gains the attention and perhaps the false admiration of other professionals and friends at the patient's peril.

The patient and therapist cannot ignore the ethical dimension in human interaction. Faced with value-laden issues such as whether a patient might be violent or might deliberately infect others with a sexually transmitted disease, the therapist as a first step ought to consult supervisors, more experienced colleagues, or ethics committees. Further, therapists would do well to pay close attention to their own values when reactions are evoked by the confession. Therapists who experience the red light of ethical disquietude can best serve the patient and protect themselves by squarely confronting their own and the patient's values in the treatment situation.

Values become especially obvious in confessions of patients' intentions or deeds that involve large-scale social issues. Take the hypothetical case of a patient who confesses to having painted a swastika on a subway wall as a child and now states that he has the urge to do so again. He also confesses to fantasies of defacing or bombing synagogues.

A number of treatment and ethical issues are immediately raised. Can this confession be treated on a strictly personal level within the context of the patient's history, avoiding the moral and social implications altogether? Alternatively, while the patient may be expressing hostility toward, for instance, a specific Jewish therapist, might his intentions not also endanger others?

With the "rule" of confidentiality no longer sacrosanct, therapists are increasingly faced with the ethical and legal dilemmas of deciding which situations call for disclosing patients' confessions. The balance between the patient's right to privacy and the public's right to be protected does not carry a long list of legal precedents to guide patient and therapist in this decision. Since precedents are being set on a case-by-case basis, confessions are helping to shape history.

Because every form of therapy contains an implicit value system and every therapist has an acquired set of personal values, therapists must learn how to treat patients whose values clash with their own. For example, therapists, whether feminist or not, have acknowledged to me their annoyance with, hatred of, or contempt for male patients who confess to abusing women. These therapists must be particularly aware that their values impinge on the ethical domain.

Therapists can never be value-free "blank screens" that "correctly" question, support, and interpret the patient's discourse in computer-like fashion. In John Dewey's words, "Human beings are not machines," nor do we aspire to be like machines.

Yet how much free rein should we give to our personal values? For example, should I become an advocate for my patient or offer advice that would indirectly put me in this role? Or should I sidestep the issue and throw it back into my patient's lap as much as possible?

These concerns quickly surfaced when a colleague gave me a detailed account of her patient Rowena, a thirty-four-year-old financial consultant, who revealed the circumstances that brought her to therapy:

> I was seeing a male therapist who came highly recommended by my mother, who was also seeing him. We had a couple of sessions together, and then I started to see him in individual treatment. All seemed to be going well until I started to voice my impression that my mother was a prude unable to relate to my sexual conflicts.
>
> To my surprise, my therapist then launched into a lengthy narrative involving my mother's affairs as I was growing up, including her ongoing relationship with my pediatric dentist whom she insisted I see well into my teens. After he finished, I was dumbfounded. Not only did I see my mother in an entirely new negative light, but I felt trapped between two forces. Clearly, my therapist — the expert — must have had his reasons for telling me, so how could I confront my mother and violate his trust? Yet, didn't he violate my trust?
>
> I finally confided in a friend who gave me your name. I feel as though I was raped by my former therapist. His words penetrated into my psyche, ripping me apart. My relationship with my mother is strained, but I am most angry at him. He should have known better. What could he have been thinking when he acted "like a loose cannon"? Please help me sort this out. I don't know what to do.

As Rowena's dilemma unfolded, my colleague's own strong feelings emerged — outrage at the therapist's unprofessional conduct, empathy with the patient's plight, and a strong desire to come to the rescue. I have already discussed the dangers of the therapist's need to rescue in chapter 3. Suffice it to say that my colleague's feelings gave her a powerful message that what was called for was helpfulness tempered by restraint rather than overzealous advocacy.

She therefore adopted an educational stance as a first step, informing Rowena that psychologists have ethical guidelines that are in place to help work with patients in as ethical a manner as possible. She told Rowena that her former therapist certainly violated these boundaries, but she might first wish to read through the guidelines in order to arrive at a more informed decision regarding whether to report him or not.

She did so, also consulting an attorney friend on her own. Armed with information obtained from the ethical guidelines along with her friend's legal advice, Rowena was able to tell my colleague what she was going to do. "I have decided to call and confront him with his despicable behavior. That's enough punishment. I don't need the additional pound of flesh that a professional hearing would grant."

Rowena's solution was to temper justice with mercy. Because my colleague provided her with educational materials rather than rapid advocacy or advice, Rowena was able to arrive at her own decision.

Therapy, by its very nature, is a confessional endeavor sometimes brimming over with ethical dilemmas. When a therapist is seeing both a mother and a daughter in separate therapies, the tendency for the therapist to cross over boundaries by inadvertently disclosing confidential material "across therapies" is ever-present. For this reason, many therapists refuse to see members of the same family or even close friends in separate therapies. Rowena's experience with her former therapist was particularly disillusioning in that he deliberately disclosed upsetting material about the patient's mother. She felt betrayed both by her mother (for her unseemly actions) and by the therapist (for violating confidentiality).

The patient in the grips of an ethical conflict should not succumb through directives or suggestibility to the charismatic therapist's value system. Should absolution for confession be contingent upon adoption of the therapist's brand of morality, the therapist becomes a secular priest preaching a new gospel.

Ethical Dilemmas in Everyday Life

Ethical dilemmas are not the special province of priests, therapists, lawyers, and doctors. We have all faced moral questions of varying magnitude. Unlike those confidants in the helping professions who can often resort to laws or ethical guidelines to help them sort out moral decisions, the average person arrives at ethical decisions in very different ways.

What happens when a friend mentions she is having an affair and you are also a good friend of her husband? Suppose your cousin brags to you about how every weekend he transmits the herpes virus to another woman to "get back at that bitch who infected me"? When you discover that your father-in-law, who is a pilot, is also an alcoholic, what course of action (if any) should you take?

Such thorny dilemmas do not allow for clear-cut solutions. Does our responsibility lie with our friend, relative, or lover, or with the greater community's welfare? And when does candor become a violation of privacy? We do not have national organizations dictating ethically correct guidelines for decision making in everyday life. At the same time, we do not have to resort to the demoralizing position that everything is relative, or worse still, that "anything goes."

How, then, do we make moral decisions regarding our own secrets or the confessions disclosed to us? We do not operate solely through objective universal principles, such as justice, truth, and fairness, nor solely through rules for right living, such as the Ten Commandments. This is not to say that principles and rules do not enter into our decisions regarding secrets, but rather that we begin the process of deciding whether to confess through our everyday practical activities. Our personal histories and culture provide us with our first understanding of ourselves, each other, and the world we live in. Values are first transmitted to us by our parents acting as filters of societal notions of good and bad.

As our social world widens and we are exposed to friends, friends' families, schools, clubs, and religious institutions, we sense our place in a larger social arena that expands our horizon of values as well as our value choices. Our morality lies not solely within ourselves (in our minds or in human nature), nor is it primarily a product of how our parents raised us.

Moral principles are filtered through families, workplaces, schools, religious institutions, and social movements. Thus, how we choose to resolve confessional dilemmas is part-and-parcel of our traditions and our social environment.

As previously mentioned, each confessional dilemma we face is set within the context of our everyday lives and social practices. Rules and norms enter into our moral reasoning with some regularity. Ethical rules for right living, however, are often filtered through the consciousness of social groups or social movements—pro-choice versus right-to-life; right versus left; feminist versus "traditionalist."

The values of the social movements we subscribe to sometimes clash with those of our families. While a gay adolescent might hide his sexual orientation from his family, as an adult, membership in gay pride movements provides enhanced self-esteem and acceptance. The sense of belonging often fuels confession to redress past grievances, stemming in part from hiding such an important part of one's identity.

Our travels through the morass of ethical terrain are sometimes filled with roadblocks. When we seek rules and norms to help us resolve our secrets, we realize that we live in an age of moral pluralism in which there are few agreed-upon ethical directives. If there is no clear imperative instructing us what to do, we are likely to experience moral perplexity instead of moral clarity. Moreover, even if we want to share our dilemma with others, we realize that we belong to multiple subgroups, each of which may subscribe to different values.

Take the conflict over abortion as it affects an unmarried career woman who finds herself pregnant. Friends who understand her unmarried status and career aspirations advise abortion; her parents and church community recoil in horror at abortion and advise that she see her pregnancy through and give up the child for adoption. The multiple voices assimilated into one's conscience, with their own ideas regarding how to achieve the good life, cast doubt on how effective several confidants with widely diverging philosophies can be in helping us reach a decision. For this reason alone, many choose to keep such secrets underground. Yet, our internal voices naggingly refuse to be silenced.

The confessional dilemma concerning abortion is twofold: whether to confide in others or keep one's secret to oneself, and a basic personal decision as an expression—a confession—of one's moral identity on this issue. While the right-to-life forces appeal to the principle of the sanctity of the fetus' life to ground their opposition to abortion, pro-choice advocates appeal to the personal principle of freedom in terms of the woman's right to control her own body. Acting according to one principle necessarily means violating the other.

The actions and stands we take on important social issues are nonverbal confessions of who we are and what we believe. The resolutions to our confessional dilemmas are often directly connected to the social movements to which we belong. Through our actions, we frequently disclose who we are now as well as who we are likely to become as members in a supportive community that fosters pride in disclosure.

We are never truly isolated when we make moral decisions. Even when we are deliberating alone, we are conversing with the various voices of our conscience: parents, church, and friends topping the list of "internalized consultants." Through these dialogues with our external as well as internal confidants, it becomes clear that our ethical decisions regarding confession are relational or "multi-relational" rather than isolated reflections.

How does this work in dealing with ethical dilemmas in everyday life? One of the goals of therapy is to internalize the therapeutic process—to carry it around with us wherever we are. We might say out loud or think to ourselves, "What would I say to my therapist? How would she respond? How would we collaborate to resolve this difficult issue?"

Sometimes we ask God for guidance in prayer. We may go to our parents' graves and pour out our hearts to them, using their spiritual presence to evoke memories of how they might help us get through difficult moral problems. These dialogues with confidants as well as with the internal voices of our conscience suggest that we never have to be estranged and alone with our moral dilemmas.

Our characters, what the Greek philosophers called "ideals of virtue," also help us deal with ethical dilemmas. The issue of character enters into all domains of social and moral life, ranging from the qualities we look for in a political leader to what we look for in a teacher, babysitter, or prospective employee. Being good and just and loving makes it easier to do right for oneself as well as for others. In psychiatrist Robert Coles' descriptions of children caught in moral crises, he observed that it was the combination of character and of the social situation in which the children found themselves that evoked moral behavior.

I am here reminded of a confessional dilemma that brings to the fore many of the previously mentioned factors that enter into ethical judgments made in everyday life. A friend began, "I have a lesbian friend who boasted to me and to many other people of the affair she was having with a heterosexual woman who also happened to be a friend of mine. The issue for me was whether to warn my heterosexual friend about her homosexual liaison being bandied about in a cavalier manner by my lesbian friend.

"After agonizing over what to do for a considerable period of time, I chose not to tell my heterosexual friend about her lesbian lover's disclosures regarding their relationship." When I asked my friend what entered into her decision, she continued, "For me, betrayal is the worst thing. I lived through the McCarthy era and knew real and imagined Communists who were blacklisted. Even though I would never tell, this still puts me in conflict with my belief that it is wrong for my lesbian friend to boast and gossip about her relationships with other people. Now that my heterosexual friend has started to date a man seriously, I am afraid that this gossip could really hurt her."

How did my friend arrive at her decision not to tell? Although she is very person-oriented and empathic—qualities that would seem to lend themselves to disclosure to stop her heterosexual friend from being harmed—her broader principles, combined with her personal history, held sway. Her strong beliefs in political freedom, justice, and loyalty, born out of her concrete experience of living through the McCarthy era, resulted in her conviction that it was wrong to betray a confidence. She showed strength of character, then and now, in holding to her vision of an ethical world—albeit still a world of conflict in which no decision could ever meet the Platonic ideals.

I end this chapter with a recollection of the day I was faced with one of the most difficult ethical dilemmas of my own life. My childhood friend Carla and I had spent an enjoyable evening together. As we stood side by side washing and drying the dishes, Carla, who was in remission from cancer, straightforwardly turned to me and asked, "When the time comes and I am in terrible pain, would you do something to help me die peacefully?" Shocked and perturbed, I muttered something noncommittal such as, "Let's see what happens."

When she left, I felt torn inside. What should I do? Should I confess and consult anyone? My good friend had entrusted me with a secret wish that it was clear no one else knew. I intuitively understood that I had to face this dilemma alone, and I deliberated about the right thing to do.

Several scenarios went through my mind. Perhaps her cancer was permanently gone. Maybe others after all might have been confided in as well. Neither of these sat well with me; I knew I was rationalizing to avoid facing one of the most difficult decisions of my life.

As the months went by, I knew in my heart and soul that I could not—would not—do anything to hasten her death. Although relationships, especially friendships, have always been a top priority in my life, the thought of assisting in another human being's death violated every moral fiber of my being. In the end, a potpourri of influences—upbringing, the Ten Commandments, legal repercussions, self-reflection, personal identity—went into my decisions not to confide in anyone else (out of respect for my friend) and not to assist in her death.

Both concerns for the relationship and abstract principles entered into my decision. I was also struck with how my early upbringing emphasizing the Ten Commandments as guiding lights in everyday living came into play along with the biblical injunction to consider one's neighbor's welfare.

This dilemma emphasizes the complexity of confessions involving ethical concerns. It became clear to me that this dilemma was not resolved by pitting empathy and concern for others against abstract principles, or religious values against secular ones. They all came into play. My life is richer for having had to confront the dilemma I was so unexpectedly presented with that day.

Ethical dilemmas revolving around disclosure concern issues much broader than simply our individual psyches or family histories. The social, philosophical, and spiritual horizons of our existence enter into disclosures that often impact not only ourselves but also our communities. The reverse is also true; namely, the ideologies and socializing forces of our adult lives—sometimes running counter to the values and beliefs we grew up with—often are crucial in helping us resolve ethical dilemmas concerning whether we "ought" to disclose an important secret or secret part of ourselves to the world. Social movements that promote pride in identity, such as feminism or gay rights, propel members in the direction of disclosure as ethically and often legally justified. Sexual harassment on the job, for example, while against the law, had previously often remained a secret, largely because of the employee's fear of being fired. Adherence to feminist principles, along with greater awareness of their legal rights, now makes it easier for many employees to disclose sexual harassment.

We entrust confidants with our most intimate secrets, expecting them to honor confidentiality and guide us through our spiritual, physical, or emotional crises. Our special confidants—best friends, lovers, priests, or therapists—are usually there for us as helpful way stations on our confessional journeys; when they violate our trust, we feel betrayed. Betrayal, of course, is endemic to all intimate relationships. Chapter 7 takes us into the broader reaches of betrayal as it relates to confession.

· III ·

Healing the Self;
Healing Relationships
with Others

7

Betrayal

W HO AMONG US has not experienced the sting of betrayal? Betrayal not only provides the subject matter for tragedy and melodrama, but also touches each of our lives. The word *betray* derives from the Latin *tradere*—to deliver or hand over in the sense that Judas betrayed Jesus. Judas delivered Jesus up to his enemies secretly, by craft, in exchange for money. The secret Judas betrayed was the meeting place of Jesus and his disciples in Gethsemane. The sign of betrayal with which Judas agreed to identify Jesus, to separate him out from the disciples, ironically was a kiss.

In the biblical tale of Samson and Delilah, Samson's infatuation with Delilah proved to be his undoing. Here we find a double betrayal: Samson betrays himself in revealing that the secret of his strength lies in his hair; Delilah betrays Samson by collaborating with the Philistines to extract from Samson the secret of his strength.

The Bible presents betrayal in order to convey lessons in morality. Judas is ultimately remorseful and commits suicide. The archetypal villain repents. The victim (Jesus) ultimately becomes, as the risen Christ, the conqueror; the betrayer becomes the guilt-ridden victim of his own actions. In the story of Samson and Delilah, Samson is presented as a sinner with overbearing hubris and sexual desire. As such, he falls victim to his own lust and resultant vulnerabilities, even though his faith in God enables him to be the ultimate victor.

In our day, we cannot be delivered from betrayal by placing ourselves in the hands of idealized lovers, friends, or therapists who come to our rescue. The challenging task we face, together with our network of empathic confidants, is to unravel the web of betrayal into which we have fallen prey over a lifetime.

Betrayal involves disclosure of information or plans that should be kept secret. There is a breach of faith in which the confidant is false or disloyal to the discloser. The material that is *confessed* in a betrayal can be either true or false. Delilah's disclosure of the secret of Samson's strength was a true confession involving a breach of trust.

False confessions involve the dissemination of misleading or erroneous information. The biblical tale of the twin sons, Esau and Jacob, born to Isaac and Rebecca, vividly portrays this type of betrayal. Jacob was his mother's favorite, but because Esau was born first, he was entitled to the major portion of his father's inheritance. Isaac was almost blind when it was time to give Esau his blessing. Rebecca colluded with Jacob in betraying Isaac by dressing the smooth-skinned Jacob in his brother's coat and covering his smooth hands with goat hair. When Isaac touched Jacob, Jacob made a false confession to his father by declaring, "I am Esau." Another form of betrayal involves the *failure to confess* information vital to the discloser's well-being. Carriers of the herpes virus who deliberately withhold this information are betraying their partner's trust.

In adultery, deceived spouses often extract confessions from each other when the adulterous partner is backed up against the wall or when the cumulative evidence is incontrovertible. Confessions of infidelity, in such instances, are reluctantly evoked. When injudicious disclosures of adultery are made "to clear the air," often little is gained and everything lost. A serious rift in the relationship, if not divorce proceedings, underscore how high the stakes can be in such risky confessions.

The notion of betrayal as deception is common in politics, epitomized by the infamous traitor Benedict Arnold, as well as in literature. In Shakespeare's *Othello*, Iago's blackness of spirit and deceptive nature ("I am not what I am"), sharply contrast with Othello's naïveté. Iago is the epitome of deception as he attempts to turn Othello against his wife, Desdemona, by inducing the false belief that Desdemona is unfaithful.

While we try to be open and convey the truth as we see it in confession, in betrayal we try to fool others. We are authentic and spontaneous in confession; we are untruthful and guarded in betrayal. Confession draws us toward others; betrayal distances us from our fellow beings.

Yet ironically, without trust and intimacy, there can be no betrayal. The moment our destinies become linked with others, the potential for betrayal is established.

Betrayal gains the upper hand when our confessions fail—when they are used by confidants to blackmail us, cajole us, threaten us with loss of love, or otherwise manipulate us. Yet, betrayal does not inevitably have catastrophic results. When the betrayed and the betrayer work toward forgiveness, mutual respect, and reconciliation, rocky relationships can be strengthened as destructiveness gives way to redemption.

The link between confession and betrayal is satirically taken up in Steven Soderbergh's 1989 film, *Sex, Lies, and Videotape*. Deception and betrayal are the *modus operandi* of the successful lawyer John Millanay, who is cheating on his beautiful, frigid wife, Ann, by having an affair with his wife's sister, Cynthia. On the scene comes the husband's old college buddy Graham. With only a car to his name ("I only like to have one key"), Graham draws the wife into the confessional mode by asking how married life is. Ann, caught off guard, replies, "Oh, I like it. I like it very much." When Graham proceeds to ask what she likes about it, Ann mentions the security of owning a house and having a husband who made junior partner in his law firm.

This reply is curiously guarded. There is no mention of love or any aspect of intimacy. Ann's guarded statement is in sharp contrast to her videotaped confession to Graham later on in which she discloses her emotional and sexual dissatisfaction with her husband.

Confession begets confession as Graham discloses he is impotent. He draws both sisters into revealing sexual secrets on videotape, which he then uses to attain sexual satisfaction. Graham, like the husband, is betraying both women since they are both pawns in his game of sexual pleasure. His deception is a subtle mind game as opposed to the husband's overt betrayal of his wife through infidelity.

Graham elicits confessions for the purpose of mental seduction and control—twin aspects of betrayal. When he verbally seduces both sisters into revealing their most intimate sexual secrets, he now exerts a kind of power over their lives. They become more emotionally dependent on Graham as they feel closer to him through their confessions. Control is exercised through knowledge of the two women's intimate lives. An atmosphere is created where the threat of betrayal through disclosure to the husband is an ever-present possibility. The husband, by contrast, dreads the possibility of confrontation through forced confession.

Like a modern fairy tale that requires a moral, both sisters' candid confessions give way to rapid insights and change—the younger sister ends her affair and the married sister leaves her husband and takes up with the videotaper. The film has powerful things to say about how easy it is to get involved in daily self-deception regarding our marriages and our lives in general. While celluloid and videotape often are metaphors for emotional distance and lack of involvement (think of Marshall McLuhan's designation of television as a "cool medium"), videotape paradoxically becomes a tool of devastating intimacy and sexual candor that allows both sisters to shed their false personas and pretenses in favor of authenticity.

Freud observed, "No mortal can keep a secret. If his lips are silent, he chatters with his fingertips: betrayal oozes out of him at every pore." Betrayals can range from deadly to ludicrous. Simone de Beauvoir infuriated Nelson Algren when she published his love letters to her, thereby rendering their private intimacies public currency. Tolstoy betrayed sexual partners by failing to confide in them that he had contracted a venereal disease and might still have it.

Betrayal was viewed as the ultimate infamy by the ancients. Punishment meted out to the traitor was regarded as harsh, but just. When Tantalus, the mythological king, revealed the secrets of the gods to his fellow mortals, punishment was swift and severe. As he stood under a fruit tree, up to his chin in water, the fruit and water retreated whenever he tried to satisfy his hunger and thirst. The gods of antiquity were equally merciless on Prometheus, who divulged to mortals the gods' secret of how to make fire. Bound to a rock, his liver was unremittingly pecked at by birds of prey each day. To add to the cruelty of the punishment, the gods saw to it that his liver regenerated each night to become a fresh target for the assault of the birds with the coming of each new day.

Punishment for these infractions never ends. These myths convey a lesson that inappropriate confession of a secret results in everlasting pain.

In our daily lives, betrayal at the hands of parents is more subtle and less easily discerned. Parental betrayal is often denied or repressed. Indeed, parental stratagems may be too sophisticated to be processed and evaluated by the young child.

Conversely, children may confess their parents' secrets to outsiders. Early on, children learn they are not autonomous beings, but rather creatures bound like all of us by loyalties and alliances. These bonds multiply as friends, lovers, spouses, children, and business associates come into our lives and make their claims on us.

As with the traitors of mythology, history, and literature, the stigma against betrayal in everyday life is strong—so strong that we have developed laws to rescue our traditional confessors from the dilemma of knowing too much. Husbands and wives are exempt from testifying against each other in court, while codes of confidentiality, for the most part, protect the special status of doctors, lawyers, therapists, and the clergy.

Many of us have encountered betrayal in the form of blackmail, duplicity, or other ruses at the hands of such high-risk confidants as parents, friends, or lovers. Early betrayals impede the development of trust as a necessary foundation for the confessional experience. When a betrayal involves disclosure that has resulted in disappointment, deception, and disillusionment, we become reticent to confess to anyone. Only when we gain awareness of the roots of betrayal can we again feel empowered to develop trusting intimate relationships and pursue aspirations in which our authentic selves can thrive and prosper. And only then can we grow in the direction of redemption that begins with confessions sincerely offered and sincerely accepted by trustworthy confidants.

Childhood Roots of Betrayal

Since many of us remain unaware of the existence of treachery on the part of parents who manipulated or deceived children "for their own good," in Alice Miller's words, it is important to begin to understand the origins of betrayal. Parents feel betrayed by children who simply want to be who they are instead of play along with their parents' agenda of how children "ought to be." Those children who often become compliant extensions of needy parents dare not realize how they are being robbed of an authentic existence, and thereby are betrayed by their parents.

The parents that Miller so ably depicts in *Prisoners of Childhood* and *For Your Own Good* view their children's efforts to separate from them physically or psychologically as a betrayal to be countered by withdrawal of love or by other forms of psychological warfare.

Betrayal may be experienced at different stages of the life cycle by both members of the parent-child pair. The parent all too often feels betrayed by the "willful child" who persists in being herself despite threats of reprisal. Maggie Tulliver, George Eliot's child heroine in *The Mill on the Floss,* continues to be a nonconformist in the eyes of her rural Victorian family, cutting her hair in a "nonladylike" manner and briefly running away to join the gypsies. Maggie finds her contemporary equivalent in Molly Bolt, the heroine of Rita Mae Brown's *Rubyfruit Jungle.* Molly is a gutsy southern girl who acknowledges her lesbianism and becomes a film student despite the restraints of provincialism that pervaded her childhood.

Both heroines decide to be their "true selves" in Donald Winnicott's term despite everything. They betray their parents through disloyalty to the parental credos for proper comportment, even as they remain true to themselves. Such heroines capture our imagination and win our approbation precisely because they refuse to betray themselves (that is, to be disloyal to whom they are) in order to maintain a tenuous relationship with parents they cannot respect. Because both of them had fairly supportive fathers, they were able to offset their maternal deprivation.

The eleven-year-old Molly's strong sense of herself becomes apparent in her interchange with her not-so-bright cousin, Leroy. Leroy begins, "You say you're gonna be a doctor or something great. Then you say you ain't gettin' married. You have to do some of the things everybody does or people don't like you." Molly retorts, "I don't care whether they like me or not. Everybody's stupid, that's what I think. I care if I like me, that's what I truly care about."

Molly, in part, is able to be self-confident because her father, Carl, supports her. Carl adheres to the one pedagogical principle that Alice Miller advocates: the need to respect the child. Many of us experience the resentment, rage, and sadness inherent in never being allowed to express the full range of thoughts and emotions deep within ourselves. By contrast, heroines such as Molly and Maggie were able to avoid being betrayed by reaping the benefits of a second chance at being appreciated by loving, empathic fathers.

Many adults are unable or unwilling to recognize the parental betrayal in their own childhood. Children's dependence on their parents' love often makes it impossible in later years to identify the early traumas that may remain hidden behind the child's early idealization of parents.

In *For Your Own Good,* Miller cites the methods employed in "poisonous pedagogy" to suppress vital spontaneity in the child: "laying traps, lying, duplicity, subterfuge, manipulation, 'scare' tactics, withdrawal of love, isolation, distrust, humiliating and disgracing the child, scorn, ridicule, and coercion even to the point of torture." Many who were thus manipulated and whipped into compliance remain unaware of being betrayed and hold fast to the image of the saintly parent. A sixty-year-old patient who had enshrined the memory of his deceased mother one day revealed the method his mother used to "cure" him of his fear of the dark. She locked him in a dark room, and the terrified nine-year-old boy forced his hand through a window in order to escape.

Many such adults who have repeatedly experienced childhood betrayal deny even glaring parental defects in order to preserve the image of the idealized parents. Some may even retrospectively legitimize the form of betrayal to which they fell victim. To this end, I recall my patient Brigitte, whose father was a philanderer who rarely came home, but did manage to get her mother pregnant during one of his visits. When Brigitte was ten, her mother dressed her in maternity clothes and sent her on errands. Passersby would make comments, such as "that poor child."

While Brigitte was empathetic to her mother's needs and was able to rationalize this bizarre maternal manipulation, she at first was unable to empathize with the little girl who was subjected to public humiliation. For a long time, Brigitte could not experience the rage, pain, and sadness which went along with the realization that her mother had betrayed her on three counts: first, her mother had misrepresented and manipulated the mother-child relationship; second, her mother had knowingly and willfully deceived everyone by shifting the shame of her own unwanted pregnancy onto her daughter; third, her mother manipulated her daughter into making a "false confession" by dressing her as though she were pregnant.

Many betrayals assume the complexity of three or more people emotionally attached to each other. A common familial example of betrayal concerns siblings who report each other's wrongdoings to their parents in order to curry parental favor. Unfortunately, children discover that such stratagems are short-lived as each, in turn, falls victim to disclosure of his misdeeds, thereby giving the other siblings temporary leverage. Only in retrospect are siblings able to discern that their parents were the ultimate victors in being able to wield control through the constant round of betrayals perpetrated by siblings upon each other.

Every family contains alliances and misalliances (alliances that backfire). Parents ally themselves against children, children against parents, and siblings against each other. Parents can also ally themselves with children against each other.

Family members outside the "alliance loop" are frequently betrayed. For example, sadistic parents band together in keeping secret the abuse of their children. Betrayal here involves failure of anyone in the family to confess abuse to the authorities. Children who disclose parental gambling or debts betray their parents' shortcomings to the outside world. Siblings reveal each others' misdeeds to parents to try to gain parental perks. Finally, divorced parents frequently attempt to curry favor with their children and power over the former spouse by betraying each other's flaws to which children would not normally be privy.

Betrayal in families involves confession arising out of the need for manipulation and control. All these alliances predicated on betrayal of family members outside the loop destroy trust, giving members temporary power over each other at the expense of goodwill and loyalty.

Fundamental Themes in Betrayal
Control

The key element of betrayal is the power to disclose or reveal. In Harold Pinter's play *Betrayal*, Emma, who is having an affair with her husband's best friend, Jerry, is clearly the character with the most power since she is the one with the most knowledge. For example, Emma reveals her infidelity to Robert, her husband, four years before she tells Jerry about the confession. Thus, Jerry lives under the assumption during those years that they are deceiving Robert and that his friendship with Robert is unaffected. Over the course of seven years, the original betrayal—the woman's betrayal of her husband, the man's betrayal of his best friend—begets others, so that deceit and betrayal enter into other relationships, including that of the lovers themselves.

Adrienne Rich writes, "Lying is done with words, and also with silence." In *Betrayal*, each character knows how to manipulate the others by timing the disclosure of secrets or deceiving the other with the silence of withheld information.

Like the characters in *Betrayal*, narcissistic parents use deception and other manipulations to keep secrets from their children. Parents' attempts to keep siblings away from each other is another way to exert power. Each child can thereby give her undivided attention to the parent. In such families, the narcissistic mother often functions as the hub of the wheel, with all sibling spokes directly connected to her. She dares not allow emotional attachments between siblings, since she views such cross-currents as disloyal, a threat to her expectation that others be there unconditionally for her. For narcissistic mothers, their children's involvement in relationships with others constitutes, by definition, disloyalty, a dangerous infringement on their own need to be the center of each child's universe.

Ruth is a twenty-six-year-old copywriter whose mother operates on the principle of "divide and conquer." Ruth and her two siblings grew up believing they disliked each other, only to discover as adults living apart from their mother that they really did like each other. The mother's need to exert absolute control by having all information filtered through her made each sibling realize, with sadness and regret, that their mother had sabotaged virtually all of their childhood relationships.

Ruth was now debating whether to reveal to her mother that her aunt (her mother's fraternal twin) was coming to visit her, since the two sisters had been estranged for years. Ruth felt the need to protect her mother from the knowledge that she wanted to have a relationship with her aunt, because she believed that her mother was "not strong enough" to accept this fact.

Ruth came to realize that she had the right to have relationships with both her mother and her aunt, and she was not going to feel guilty for allegedly betraying her mother. She told her mother and was amazed to discover that while her mother did seem hurt and did attempt to trick her into reconsidering, Ruth was able, for the first time, to resist this maternal maneuver.

Family relationships began to shift in the direction of choice, openness, and mutuality in lieu of control. As the siblings no longer cooperated with their mother's need to have exclusive relationships with each one, the mother, through her own therapy, was able to recognize her desperate need to control the world around her.

Ruth's decision to risk revealing her aunt's visit to her mother put her in control of her life. She chose not to perpetuate her mother's divide and conquer strategy. As an adult freed from the oppressive maternal hold, she was able to develop intimate relationships with her siblings and her aunt based on love and trust.

Each relationship yielded disclosures about family secrets that made family members feel closer to each other and even aroused some sympathy for Ruth's mother. Ruth's aunt disclosed that her mother (Ruth's grandmother) had been an unbearable termagant who ruled over her children through threats and intimidation. This disclosure helped Ruth understand her mother's desperate need for control in the wake of her own nightmarish childhood.

Victimization: Self-Destructive and Other Destructive Confessions

Ill-conceived confessions can result in the ultimate self-destructive act—suicide. Judas Iscariot's remorse following his betrayal of Christ results in death at his own hands. Iago's false confession of Desdemona's infidelity renders both Desdemona and Othello victims of Iago's perfidious nature. Othello kills his wife and subsequently kills himself.

When we confess in good faith, we hope that the expression of our authentic natures will be the first step on a journey toward redemption. Destructive confessions, in contrast, are made in bad faith to hurt and destroy others for the discloser's self-aggrandizement or quest for power. Iago presents a false front to achieve his aims. Authenticity and spontaneity give way to manipulation and the posed performance.

Betrayal does not always arise from the deliberate machinations of evildoers. The moral ambiguities giving rise to betrayal in everyday life frequently are less clear-cut than the biblical portrayals of Judas Iscariot and Delilah would have us believe. In Louis Malle's 1987 film, *Au Revoir Les Enfants,* a betrayal takes place that changed Malle's real life forever. The film is set in Occupied France in 1944, when the twelve-year-old Malle, represented by the character Julien, attended a Jesuit boarding school. To Julien's surprise, three new boys appear in the town toward the end of the Christmas holiday. One of them, Jean Bonnet, becomes Julien's chief competitor for scholastic honors and, briefly, his best friend.

The three new students are, we discover, Jews disguised with new names and identities in an attempt to hide them from the Nazis. Julien goes through his friend's locker where he discovers the secret of Jean's identity. His real name is Jean Kippelstein.

While Joseph, the kitchen hand, is the actual informer, it is Julien's quick, inadvertent glance at Jean, "tipping off" the Nazi in the classroom, that may have cost four people (the three boys and the headmaster) their lives. When they are arrested, Julien realizes that his glance, proffered in one tragic second, will haunt him for the rest of his days. Julien's glance was a nonverbal confession. Through his body language, Julien betrayed his friend by revealing his identity as a Jew to the Nazi.

What could have possessed Julien? The senselessness of the betrayal, along with the ambiguity of his motives, forces us as the audience to wrestle with our own unresolved issues involving betrayal, guilt, and regret.

In George Bernard Shaw's play *Mrs. Warren's Profession*, Mrs. Warren first confesses to her daughter, Vivie, that her rise out of poverty was achieved through prostitution. But it is Mrs. Warren's two subsequent confessions that embitter Vivie. Vivie finds out that she and Frank (the rector's son) are brother and sister, thereby abruptly ending a budding romance. The final coup cementing the destruction of the mother-daughter relationship is Mrs. Warren's disclosure that she is still a madam with "hotels" in various spots in Europe.

Vivie is unable to reconcile and integrate past transgressions with present happiness. Not only does she feel a victim of deception, but she also finds her hopes and dreams dashed in the wake of learning the truth about her mother's "secret life." Vivie's illusions about maternalism, respectability, and conventionality are smashed.

The sociologist Georg Simmel, advising against indiscriminate disclosure, comments, "An ideal sphere lies around every human being . . . this sphere cannot be penetrated, unless the personal value of the individual is thereby destroyed." Every person is entitled to a zone of privacy. People who unswervingly trust others, baring all to everyone, are especially prone to betrayal. Often prey to their own self-deception, they are more likely to be victims in others' schemes of deception.

Confessions primarily enable us to connect intimately with others; privacy is one of the best ways for us to maintain or regain a sense of relatedness to ourselves. We sometimes have to remind ourselves that we benefit from our private spaces where we can mull over secret concerns away from outside intrusions and the risks of betrayal.

Confession can lead to redemption; yet indiscriminate confession not only is not redemptive, but also can be harmful. People who indiscriminately confess to everyone have no boundaries—no idea of when confession might result in betrayal in lieu of redemption.

Shakespeare's tragedies *Othello* and *Hamlet* reveal to us how the protagonists' self-deception ultimately results in self-destruction and destruction of others in the aftermath of rage evoked by betrayal. Othello's childlike naïveté enables Iago to enjoy Othello's blind trust; Iago's false show of loyalty enables him to betray Othello. He succeeds in the destruction of the innocent Desdemona, followed by Othello's suicide.

Hamlet expresses his rage in being "played upon" by Guildenstern: "Why, look you now, how unworthy a thing you make me! You would play upon me; you would seem to know my stops; you would pluck out the heart of my mystery. . . . Do you think I am easier to be played on than a pipe? Call me what instrument you will, though you can fret me, you cannot play upon me." Hamlet is enraged at the manipulations of those who seek to destroy him. His awareness of impending betrayal momentarily helps put him in charge of his life.

Abandonment

Those who have been psychologically or physically abandoned in childhood often come to rely on objects, rather than people, to counteract massive feelings of betrayal. Psychoanalyst Harold Searles has written extensively about patients' relationships with the nonhuman environment of objects and nature as an antidote to loneliness and vulnerability to hurt and abandonment at the hands of humans. Meaningful connectedness with the nonhuman world of nature and the nonsentient world of objects can console us and give us strength, knowing that we are unique and, at the same time, part of the universe.

For Michael, a twenty-seven-year-old engineer whose father died when he was seven, "things" helped him pass the time as he experienced the urban loneliness that was his lot as an only child in mid-Manhattan. His toys were his constant, faithful companions which, unlike people, could not betray him. One of Michael's earliest memories concerned the playful activity of mixing colored water in test tubes that his father had given him. Test tubes later came to represent his deceased father and to provide an actual link to one of the few instances in which his father's smile of approbation touched the young child.

This same patient became enraged when he perceived that "things" abandoned him. When his two-month-old shirt started to unravel, Michael angrily exclaimed, "I felt betrayed and let down. I put my faith in things, since people are so fickle. Now it seems that things can be fickle too. I take good care of them and expect them to do the same by me."

Over time, it became clear that things represented an extension of Michael's self, with which he could identify and control. Michael periodically stated, "I see things as a radiation of self—who I am and what I am. That's why I feel so betrayed when things break down or fall apart."

For Michael, things not only served as an extension of himself, but also hearkened back to a deceased father who came alive for him when he used his chemistry set for experiments or played with his model trains and camera equipment. Commerce with things strengthened Michael's sense of self and kept alive his identification with his deceased father.

For many people who lost a parent in childhood, "thing constancy" comes to lessen the betrayal they experienced through this premature loss. Especially for the very young child whose expectations encompass parental omnipotence and even immortality, death is the ultimate betrayal. Yet these feelings often remain outside of awareness, partly because the child is not given the opportunity to process the death with empathic adults or is not mature enough to conceptualize the meaning of death. In addition, the child may feel responsible for the death and thus believe that he has no right to such sinister feelings. Since the child's perceived disloyalty (in thought or action) makes him feel, in part, culpable for the parental abandonment, he dares not become aware of the betrayal that has been experienced.

Betrayal in Therapy

Both patient and therapist can experience actual or fantasized betrayal in the course of treatment. In the latter instance, betrayal at the hands of significant others from the past insinuates itself into the therapy relationship. The therapist or patient is then perceived as the traitor.

Therapists may, in fact, engage in sex with their patients, break the rule of confidentiality, financially exploit patients by billing services not rendered or waiving fees to indulge a rescue fantasy, and so on. Sometimes the therapist adopts a dual relationship with a patient, compromising "neutrality." Getting a house or acquiring a painting through a client is an insidious form of relationship betrayal.

When a therapist withholds vital information such as having a terminal illness or planning to move, the patient's implicit trust that therapy will continue uninterrupted is violated. When the therapist acts "out of character" by making sexual advances or asking the patient for favors, the patient again feels used and abused by the therapist, who allegedly is different from the betrayers in the patient's past.

In therapy, patients trust that surrendering—letting out their secrets—will bring relief and healing. Patients need to believe that the therapist can tolerate disturbing secrets. When therapists withdraw from confrontation and steer their patients away from secrets the therapist finds hard to deal with, the patient's trust is again betrayed.

Instances of sexual betrayal at the hands of renowned analysts give us insight into therapists' tragic weaknesses as well as insight into the kernels of creativity that sometimes spring from the detritus of betrayal. Sigmund Freud, Carl Jung, and Sandor Ferenczi—titans of psychoanalysis—became entangled in messy relationships in which female patients became pawns in a powerful net of betrayal. In the first volume of the Freud-Ferenczi correspondence (1908–1915), the largest number of letters give a detailed account of Ferenczi's love affairs with "Frau G." (a married Hungarian woman with a strong interest in psychoanalysis) and her daughter, Elma, who was then in her twenties. In October 1909, Ferenczi confided in Freud that Frau G. was not only his patient, but also his mistress. In July 1911, he notes that he had also begun to see her daughter who was suffering from depression. By December, he admitted that he had fallen in love with Elma. "I was not able to maintain the cool detachment of the analyst. . . . Perhaps in the end my sight was clouded by passion."

Ferenczi pleaded with Freud to take over Elma's treatment, but after three months, this therapy reached an impasse when Elma discovered that Freud was writing to Ferenczi about her. She had now been ensnared, abandoned, and betrayed by two "great" analysts! She begged Ferenczi to resume her analysis, only to again feel rejected and abandoned when he eventually married her mother.

Both Freud and Ferenczi colluded with each other in knowingly betraying Elma, even though they were tormented over the venture. Muddling real-life and transference relationships to a shameful degree, neither man was able to maintain the professional boundaries necessary for the good of treatment. Ferenczi subsequently traced his betrayal of both mother and daughter to infantile revenge against his own mother.

Patients' confessions offered within the confines of the therapy relationship are appropriate and desirable. They constitute one of the basic ingredients in the development of intimacy and trust. Therapists frequently go outside of therapy to consult with supervisors who offer advice on their cases. Therapists' disclosures of patients' confessions to supervisors are considered to be beneficial to patients' well-being, providing further guidance in their quest for redemption.

Today, clear ethical guidelines exist regarding when confession crosses over acceptable limits and thereby becomes betrayal. Let us not forget that Freud, Ferenczi, and Jung were pioneering psychoanalysts, mapping the unchartered terrain of the human psyche. To the extent that the therapist is willing and able to be a supportive, understanding confidant, the patient's confessions can be accepted and worked through. The dangers of betrayal are most likely to occur when unresolved secrets from the therapist's personal life intermingle with the patient's confessions. When Ferenczi's own unprocessed secret anger at his mother transferred over to his patient, she was betrayed as an unwitting pawn in Ferenczi's unwinnable maternal battle. In such instances, the therapy relationship based on trust, constancy, and understanding gives way to one marked by disillusionment and despair. Even in this destructive scenario, however, betrayal can pave the way toward redemption when the therapist confesses to wrongdoing.

Interestingly, it was Ferenczi who fostered the idea that it was the *real* relationship between therapist and patient—one in which the therapist could even disclose his errors—that was vital for healing. Arguably, Ferenczi's awareness of his own foibles, including betrayal, contributed to the therapeutic innovation of fostering a real warm, humane relationship between patient and therapist. Even betrayal can be overcome, according to Ferenczi, if the therapist admits to his error in the service of healing the patient's wounds in part by validating the patient's perceptions.

Freud, perhaps wary of increasing the likelihood of betrayal by loosening the boundaries between patient and therapist, continued to advocate minimal disclosure (if any) on the part of the therapist. Unfortunately, Freud did not always practice what he preached. Indeed, Freud blatantly violated his own recommendations at times. He sometimes asked favors of patients, gave them advice, vacationed with them, played cards with them, once fed a patient, and, at times, addressed correspondence during sessions.

Perhaps the most famous example of betrayal in the annals of psychoanalysis was the case of Dora—a teenager employed by Herr K. and Frau K. Dora's father was having an affair with Frau K. Because of this affair with his friend's wife, it was convenient for Dora's father to ignore the sexual advances Herr K. was making toward his adolescent daughter.

When Dora confided to her father that she was being molested by Herr K., he responded that he did not believe her. Dora knew that her father really did believe her, and thus felt even more betrayed. Frau K., whom Dora loved and trusted, also disbelieved her. In Freud's analysis with Dora, he emphasized her fantasized wish that something would happen with Herr K., blatantly ignoring the possibility of actual sexual abuse and neglecting her feelings of shame. Dora again felt betrayed; the analysis was a failure.

Dora was surrounded by a cadre of betrayers—all of whom she initially loved and trusted. Dora was a teenager used by her father as a pawn in the sexual battle for Herr K.'s wife. She was betrayed by Freud, who exploited Dora to confirm his theories rather than truly listening to her anguish. Freud's interpretations of Dora's unconscious sexual fantasies and impulses toward her father were made to zealously pursue the great man's own agenda—at the expense of Dora's needs. Victimized by her father and her employers, she was then re-victimized at the hands of Freud. Freud unconsciously colluded with Dora's betrayers instead of being his patient's advocate. Having no one to turn to, Dora felt victimized and abandoned.

Because the therapy relationship is so intimate, it can foster betrayal. It can also offer the patient a second chance for healing and redemption from betrayal within a safe haven. In dealing with and working through hidden reactions to trauma—anxiety, anger, despair, and grief—that come to light during therapy, the patient can integrate the pain of the past. Through expressing these hidden feelings, the patient can break the cycle of betrayal.

Sometimes patients' confessions themselves are seen as a betrayal of the hated/loved parent. My patient Mandy's father at times put her in a cage in order to control her. She came to equate this abusive behavior with love. When she finally confided in me, she suddenly experienced guilt for betraying her father, along with rage at me for usurping her secrets and having the power to retaliate against her.

Patients such as Mandy with narcissistic or sadistic parents initially may strongly resist any kind of attachment, since the development of trust is unconsciously equated with parental betrayal. In the early phase of treatment, if the therapist appears too enthusiastic or even supportive, the patient may end therapy prematurely. Such outward gestures may be viewed as ruses to enable the patient to be betrayed again. Since distrust is a fundamental element in betrayal, the therapist may find herself frequently tested to see whether she lives up to the expectations of "good parent."

Patients may, for example, deliberately miss sessions without calling or hand over bad checks to see whether the therapist will abandon them. Patients may identify with their own betraying parents by, for example, falsifying their income in an attempt to dupe the therapist into setting a lower fee. While such patients expect the therapist to discover the deceit and retaliate against them, at this stage they also secretly hope they will be accepted regardless of these external circumstances.

Therapists who prove that they can set limits and interpret such be-
haviors, yet also remain constant in their loyalty to patients throughout the testing period, can monitor gradual changes in their
relationships with patients. In some instances, patients for the first
time feel that they have permission to enter into a relationship in
which they can develop autonomy without fear of repercussions. Patients no longer feel the need to be bound to anyone again in slave-like
submission out of fear of betrayal.

Ethical Dilemmas Revisited:
Betrayal of Privacy versus the Public's Right to Know

I have already mentioned Ferenczi's and Freud's betrayal of patients,
in part knowingly, in part unwittingly. Carl Jung as well was guilty of
professional betrayal as evidenced by his intimate relationship with
his brilliant patient Sabina Spielrein.

Jung fell in love with Sabina, but broke off the relationship when
it threatened to cause a scandal. Sabina confided in Freud, then Jung's
mentor and supervisor, and Freud became a confessor to both of
them.

Sabina wrote to Freud, asking to meet him, and did not tell Jung.
She later moved to Vienna and became Freud's pupil. Jung's wife also
wrote to Freud asking for his advice. Psychoanalyst Aldo Caratenuto
(cited in Rentrop and Karmel) maintains that Jung found himself
twice betrayed: Sabina consulted Freud behind his back; and his wife,
whom Jung himself analyzed, then wrote to Freud about the Spielrein
affair. Because both women had been analyzed by Jung and then
turned to Freud, Jung felt doubly abandoned and betrayed.

Although one could view Jung's indiscretions as the private acts of
a man who happened to become a public figure, what about the larger
ethical picture? Private secrets, sins, and indiscretions shed light on
public theories which, in turn, influence culture, history, and civilization. From this perspective, exposing the private lives of the great can
be an educational or humanizing boon for posterity. Caratenuto observes, "Those who defy conventions and make their minds part of
the public domain lose the right to privacy because their lives throw

light on their thought and give us information that helps us better understand what we have learned." Disclosure of the secret thoughts and deeds of the great, such as Jung, helps us gain insight into how their private lives influenced their public contributions

Yet let us not also overlook the fact that Sabina was shamefully betrayed by Jung and Freud. When Sabina's mother threatened to inform Eugen Bleuler—Jung's superior—Jung and Freud acted with complicity in condemning Sabina for not wanting to give up Jung. Freud even wrote her a letter asking her to examine her conscience, and to desist from taking any public action against Jung.

While we, the public, might applaud this case of betrayal becoming public for our edification, its disclosure raises disturbing issues that speak to us today. In the pioneering days of psychoanalysis, professional boundaries were almost nonexistent. Everybody spoke to everybody—secretly, sometimes openly, sometimes by letter, sometimes in person. Confidentiality was betrayed in every direction. Control—a crucial element in betrayal—was primarily in the hands of Jung and Freud, who acted in unison to protect their professional standing in the community at the expense of Sabina's needs. Today, because therapists are often seen as idealized authority figures, it is especially important for therapists to learn what *not* to do from the lessons of betrayal perpetrated by our analyst ancestors.

For many years, patients were reluctant to disclose wrongdoing by their therapists, either fearing that they would not be believed or that betrayal would ruin the reputation of a famous authority figure. A similar dilemma is faced with famous members in other fields. Do families of famous people have the right to privacy or should all secrets be disclosed? People on both sides of the fence rally to the cry—"betrayal!"—when their positions are assailed. At one extreme, we find James Joyce's grandson Stephen, who, outraged at some of his grandmother Nora's sexual secrets made public in a biography, destroyed many letters written by Joyce's daughter Lucia. For Stephen Joyce, public disclosure of his grandmother's sexual life was an outrageous betrayal—an invasion of privacy with no redeeming value.

At the opposite end of the spectrum is the family of John Cheever.

Soon after he died, his daughter Susan published a memoir in which she wrote frankly and openly about her father's alcoholism and homosexuality. Many families believe they have more control by revealing these confidences themselves rather than reading distortions written by outsiders.

Surviving family members have to weigh what they consider to be the greater betrayal—putting the creator's letters in a library or in a paper shredder. Franz Kafka told his friend and confidant Max Brod to burn all his writings. Fortunately for us, Brod ignored Kafka's request. This personal betrayal arguably was more than offset by Kafka's brilliant written legacy, which would have been consumed in flames. Had Brod followed Kafka's wishes, a horrendous betrayal of humanity—of the universal audience—would have ensued.

Disclosing confidences to a friend, or revealing one's secrets to a therapist, usually takes place in the context of a relationship marked by intimacy, trust, and confidentiality. When details of a private life are revealed to a mass audience through print or other public media, however, guarantees of loyalty and privacy disappear. One always hopes that biographers would treat their subjects as though they were in a relationship built upon love and care, but there are no binding ethical or legal codes to ensure such treatment. It is thus left to the deceased person's intimates to rummage through their consciences to decide how to best serve the memory of the departed.

Trust and the Nature of Relationships in Betrayal

In most instances in our personal lives, we tend to be betrayed by those we truly trust—by friends, parents, siblings, and lovers—rarely by enemies or strangers. Betrayal takes place within the confines of intimacy. Although Iago is technically only Othello's advisor, he has, over time and from a variety of motives, insinuated himself into Othello's very soul, almost becoming a "second self," according to Cicero's definition of friendship.

Trust always contains within it the potential for betrayal. Wherever there is trust, the risk of betrayal is also present. The Jungian psychoanalyst James Hillman clarifies this idea for us: "For we must be clear that to live or love only where one can trust, where there is security and containment, where one cannot be hurt or let down, where what is pledged in words is forever binding, means really to be out of harm's way and so to be out of real life."

Hillman goes on to elucidate the dangers that appear after betrayal, such as seeking revenge in a never-ending "eye for an eye" spiral. Denial or devaluation of the betrayer's qualities force us to focus only on the ugly, dark sides of his nature. A third danger in the aftermath of betrayal is cynicism in all things as well as in all people. A "go it alone," self-sufficient posture sets the stage for never trusting anyone again. Everyone is now seen as a betrayer or potential betrayer.

Yet betrayal need not inevitably result in a massive distrust that cancels out intimacy forever. Hillman points out that betrayal has within it the seeds of forgiveness and reconciliation. However, this can only happen when we allow ourselves to remove the blinders of prejudice, paranoia, and hatred that skew our vision. In *Au Revoir Les Enfants,* as Jean Kippelstein is about to be led away by the Nazi soldier, he forgives Julien by telling him that he would have been discovered sooner or later anyway.

Yet blind trust as a worldview can be just as destructive as blind distrust. In both, a sense of judgment is suspended. Pollyanna-like optimism can result in disillusionment and despair. When we blindly trust others, we set ourselves up to be injured by manipulators who prey on the naïve. We must learn to be self-protective in choosing confidants who are worthy of our trust.

People are not always what they seem to be. Jesus echoed this sentiment when he told his disciples, "One of you will betray me." To counteract betrayal, we must wisely choose confidants who genuinely value us and our welfare.

Virgil wrote that "fortune comes to the aid of the audacious." When you put yourself on the line by risking a secret with a trusted intimate, affirmation for being authentic becomes the reward. Such fortune was not to be the lot of Tess, the tragic heroine of Thomas Hardy's *Tess of the D'Ubervilles.* When Tess confesses to her husband, Angel, that she was raped and had a child who died, Angel is relentlessly unforgiving.

Tess pleads, "I thought, Angel, that you loved me—me, my very self! If it is I you do love, O how can it be that you look and speak so? It frightens me! Having begun to love you, I love you forever—in all changes, in all disgraces, because you are yourself. I ask no more. Then how can you, O my beloved husband, stop loving me?" Tess speaks of the constancy of true love, of love that lasts through trials and tribulations.

None of this constancy attributed to true love holds true for Angel. Ironically, prior to her confession, Angel had revealed to Tess his forty-eight hours of debauchery in London some years before, and Tess had forgiven him. Her unwavering love and forgiveness of Angel's escapades, she believes, will be returned to her in kind. Instead, she is cruelly rejected.

Tess is thus robbed of the spiritual solace she could have gained through her confession. Her secret, once revealed, is her undoing. Abandonment and betrayal follow in the wake of her confession.

Ingmar Bergman's 1966 film *Persona* vividly captures the relational aspects of betrayal in a situation in which two people lose their identities in each other. Elisabeth Vogler, a famous actress, suddenly stops speaking during a performance of *Electra*. Her doctor, who can find nothing physically or mentally wrong with her, puts her in the care of a nurse, Alma. Alma becomes increasingly frank and uninhibited with the silent actress, revealing her insecurity as a nurse, her love affairs, her sexuality, and her guilt over an abortion.

The word *persona* has two meanings relevant to the film. Masks are worn by actors in classical drama, and thus refer to Elisabeth's profession as an actress. In Jung's writings, persona denotes the conscious artificial personality that a person may use as a protection or deception in an attempt to adapt to the world. Both meanings refer to the roles we play in lieu of revealing our authentic natures. It is easier to fool others and deceive them when we are wearing our protective guises.

Because it is Alma who acts "out of character" by escalating her confessions, she is the one who is more likely to be betrayed. Perhaps Alma reveals more of herself than she might wish to in an attempt to draw out the actress. This situation of one-sided intimacy invites betrayal.

When Alma goes to mail a letter from Elisabeth to her doctor, she notices it is not sealed. Alma reads the letter and discovers that Elisabeth enjoys studying Alma and encourages her to talk. Elisabeth thereby objectifies Alma, turning her into an "it" (in Buber's term) by which to be voyeuristically entertained, rather than an "I" to be respected and loved. The tone and substance of the letter underscore the betrayal. Elisabeth writes: "About Alma: it is actually great fun studying her. . . . Anyway I have gained her confidence and she tells me all sorts of things about herself, big and small. As you can see, I'm snapping up everything I can, and as long as she doesn't notice anything it doesn't matter."

This letter is an immense betrayal. Feeling angry and betrayed, Alma takes revenge by leaving a broken glass where Elisabeth will step on it. Elisabeth does not apologize for exploiting her. Yet Alma, in her own way, also betrays Elisabeth. By abandoning her professional persona as a nurse and revealing secrets to Elisabeth as if she were a friend, she betrays her charge by tending to her own needs. Alternatively, perhaps it is also possible that Elisabeth betrays herself by abandoning her humanity as she distances herself through her hysterical silence. The wall of silence she has erected cuts off intimacy. At the same time, it provides a playground for Elisabeth in which the pastimes of manipulation, deception, and betrayal flourish.

Betrayal breeds disillusionment, despair, and distrust. In cases of blinding betrayal, intimates are turned into enemies. No one can ever again be trusted, we cynically maintain.

When we withdraw into self-righteous indignation following betrayal, isolation ensues. All relationships may be seen as hotbeds of betrayal. When we confess a secret to a confidant, we expect to be supported and even guided on the quest toward redemption. Betrayal by the confidant who wrecklessly discloses our secret is a serious setback on our confessional journey.

All is not lost, however. Our faith and trust in others can be resurrected when the betrayer turns around and confesses to us his betrayal of the secret we entrusted to him. When we are willing to hear the betrayer out—to give him a chance to confess and show contrition followed by our forgiveness—this experience can deepen relationships. We can again feel empowered to move from the isolation bred by betrayal to the intimacy of loving relatedness. Reconciliation in which trust is rebuilt and love reborn is truly healing.

8

Healing the Divided Self

OUR SENSE OF SELF—who we are and how we relate to significant others in our lives—is not a simple unity, but a complex mosaic made up of many facets. The healthy self is robust in its ability to adapt to different relationships. For example, we may be open and extroverted with our spouses, while remaining guarded and reserved with our employers. The rigid, one-dimensional person who always seems the same is the one who is more likely to be mentally disturbed. The multifaceted self, in short, is an integrated self bolstered by our awareness of the different ways we relate to others in the social world.

There are times, however, when we sense the self divided. Sometimes the division is so deep that we remain unaware of a part of ourselves too dreaded or repellent for us to disclose—even to ourselves. At other times, we acknowledge parts of ourselves we deem "bad," either attempting to exorcise them from our psyches or simply coming to terms with them as another part of our nature. Confession—to ourselves or to others—is a powerful means to own the splits within ourselves in order to enrich our self-understanding and expand our self-image.

Secrets do not always involve specific events in our lives. They may speak to our very heart—to the core of our being. When we are truly willing to look at *all* of ourselves—including the loathsome, the monstrous, and the evil—we can begin to heal the divided self.

We need not experience the extremes of a Dr. Jekyll and Mr. Hyde existence to realize that we all, at one time or another, can recognize splits in ourselves. Others in our lives—especially friends and lovers—can come to represent parts of ourselves that we disown and split off from awareness. We all have known couples we cannot believe are together. He is obsessive, overly tidy, uptight, and rule-oriented. She is "artsy," rambling in conversation, unfocused, and fun-loving. They snipe at each other and complain about each others' deficiencies. How do they stay together? It soon becomes apparent that each of them embodies secret, disavowed aspects of the other. Instead of running the risk of revealing these hidden aspects of themselves to the world, they instead choose partners who revel in revealing those forbidden split-off parts.

A divided self is not necessarily a negative state in need of healing through integration. A common conscious or unconscious split for many women is the "good girl/bad girl" division. When patients allow the "bad girl" part to emerge, be acknowledged, and even applauded, their self-esteem often soars. This was especially evident with Ida, a twenty-eight-year-old teacher who, in her "good girl" persona, was a compliant, invisible extension of her tyrannical mother, who would not tolerate any displays of emotion or rebellious independence from her daughter. Ida's long split-off "bad girl" side, brimming over with emotions (especially anger and sadness, as well as creativity) was in diametric opposition to her mother's image of who she was. What set Ida on the road to redemption from maternal tyranny was acknowledging and even celebrating her secret "bad girl" side. Healing did not so much involve reconciling or obliterating the split. Rather Ida had to get used to and welcome the "bad girl" part that she only at first felt secure enough revealing to me, as her therapist.

The development of selfhood—establishing who we are and sensing an ongoing identity despite the multiple roles we play—allows us to disclose our thoughts, feelings, and wishes as our own. Only when we move from the darkness of disavowal to the light of acknowledging the secret parts of ourselves can we start to feel comfortable risking self-disclosure. As we come to terms with who we are, the threatening aspects of ourselves gradually seep into our awareness and we come to accept ourselves whole—not just the parts of ourselves that neatly fit into our current self-image.

We enlarge our sense of self when we integrate previously disowned parts of ourselves into our self-image. Simply labeling these hitherto hidden thoughts and feelings lessens the amount of self-deception in our lives. Recognizing our murderous, rageful, envious, or hateful selves means that what was once disowned need no longer exert an effect on us outside of our awareness. By thereby owning our secret selves, we are able to discern and deal with the various aspects that encompass who we are.

It is important for us to feel in control of our emotions, thoughts, actions, and personality. Our sense of self-control is bolstered when we experience ourselves as an integrated personality representing our essential nature. In grossly dissociated states akin to those of the Dr. Jekyll and Mr. Hyde variety, a person may escape from her conflicts by disowning threatening parts of herself. In so doing, she forfeits a vital part of herself in the trade-off.

In disclosing *all* parts of our nature to ourselves or to others, we become integrated beings. Hiding basic parts of ourselves is draining and fragmenting; acknowledging the dreaded, bizarre, or "bad" in us enables us to accept these aspects or transform them into creative expression. The secret murderous rage we might discover during the confessional journey can be transformed into self-assertiveness and productive confrontation. Such self-transformation is healing and redemptive.

For Michel de Montaigne, the father of the essay, confession involved opening himself up to all sides of his nature. In his "Apology for Raymond Sebond," Montaigne explicitly sets forth this theme: "I am glad not to be sick, but if I am, I want to know I am; and if they cauterize or incise me, I want to feel it. In truth, he who would eradicate the knowledge of evil would at the same time extirpate the knowledge of pleasure, and *in fine* would annihilate men." Through awareness of his complete nature, including his seamier side, Montaigne and his readers become the beneficiaries of an unparalleled record of self-experience. In order for us to possess robust selves, we too must not be afraid to risk coming to terms with the secret parts of ourselves that have long been safely tucked away from scrutiny.

In the prologue of *The Inferno*, Dante writes, "I went astray/from the straight road and woke to find myself/alone in a dark wood." Dante experiences the dark world of sin and ignorance in the quest for meaning in his life. Mythology contains many examples of insights gained through the hero's descent into the underworld. Odysseus visits the underworld to acquire the knowledge that will enable him to get safely back to Ithaca; Aeneas also goes there to get instructions from his father on what to do to found the city of Rome. Each receives wisdom that can only be learned from a descent into hell.

We, in turn, must not shy away from entering into our own personal hells. The light of knowledge can emerge only when we are prepared to face the challenge residing within the darkness of our souls. Rollo May observed, "All through history it is true that only by going through hell does one have any chance of reaching heaven." We must confront our own private hells in order to become whole on the confessional journey. Unless we acknowledge our secret selves, we are powerless to make any progress on the road toward self-awareness.

It is the illusion of certainty about who we are that is often the biggest obstacle to self-awareness. Kierkegaard knew that venturing causes anxiety, but he also warned, "Not to venture is to lose oneself." Each of us is called upon to risk recognizing and then living with aspects of ourselves that may change us forever—for better or for worse. When we never take risks, we go through life sensing that some vital part of ourselves is lost or missing.

We may discover the hidden aspects of ourselves through psychotherapy, through living everyday life, or through enduring crises that force us to search our souls. As we encounter these secret parts, we do not inevitably achieve integration or exorcism. Instead, as we face life's paradoxes, we learn to live with contradictions within ourselves.

Living with contradictions can make us more true to ourselves. Instead of opting for simplistic integration that gives our lives an illusory comfort, we come to realize that embracing paradoxes—the differences and even contradictions within ourselves—can help us achieve a fullness to our being. In so doing, we gain relief by not feeling compelled to resort to false resolutions to the divided self.

Becoming aware of secret aspects of ourselves that do not accord with each other or with our conscious self-image helps us live with ambiguity. Welcoming the emergence of these secret parts introduces us to possibilities that would not otherwise be available. For example, many of us disown envious feelings. When we confess to envying our friend's professional success to our spouse or therapist, we free ourselves to own the envy as part of the human condition. Moreover, we can now choose to focus on the positive aspect of envy by aspiring to be professionally successful ourselves.

At first, major secrets that come to light may seem like crises rather than epiphanies. We dread unwanted discoveries that may tear us apart. Yet it is precisely by opening ourselves up to these discoveries and confessing to them that we become whole.

Kierkegaard notes, "He who is educated by dread is educated by possibility." In order to be educated by possibilities, we must have faith. It is especially important, in this age of anxiety, that we continue to forge faith in ourselves—in all aspects of ourselves—so that we have the courage to be truly and more completely known by others. Knowing ourselves, in the Socratic sense, offers possibilities for redemption.

Confession is integral to self-awareness. It is only by making ourselves known to ourselves and to others through risking confession that we can welcome the secret parts of ourselves into our personality. Healing the divided self through confession sets us on the path toward becoming whole.

Ignorance and self-deception condemn us to subterfuge and despair. Keeping things from ourselves puts us in the realm of darkness; allowing secret parts of ourselves to come into clearer focus makes redemption possible.

Psychologist James Bugenthal, in *The Search for Existential Identity*, candidly reveals his own struggles to come to terms with the split within himself. "Now is the time of healing, of hope for a new life. The secret self is hidden no more. I swim in shame and I find I do not drown. With new relationships, I gradually risk letting more and more of me be known, and I find I am welcomed. . . . So is it over, is it healed? Am I 'right' at last? No: no to each of these. It is not over; the split is still there—although so small in comparison to before. I heal and tear open and I heal a bit more. And I am giving up being right in favor of trying to be who I am."

Life is crippling when it is only half-lived. By heightening his self-awareness and "letting himself be," Bugenthal experiences the healing process taking hold. Choosing to be authentic and to "swim" in difficult emotions like shame instead of retreating to shore allows us to integrate the split-off parts of ourselves instead of remaining "a house divided."

Each of us gains strength and resilience when we tend to our internal gardens. Acknowledging and welcoming secret divisions within ourselves enables us to flower rather than become overrun by the weeds of repression and subterfuge. In time, we can transform our obsession with being confessional consumers into a more balanced, harmonious process that also emphasizes self-scrutiny.

Thus far, I have referred to a psychological, subjective self—the self we experience daily as well as the feared, unacceptable parts of ourselves we repress in response to our personal traumas. Donald Winnicott and R. D. Laing speak of divisions between our lost or hidden inner selves that are split off from our outer, compliant, false selves. Most of us resonate with this division which speaks to our experience of ourselves.

The postmodern approach ascribes no single fixed meaning to the self. Instead of a unified self remaining constant over time and situations, this approach views the self as open, flexible, and communal in nature. The focus is on secret selves rather than a secret self. Parts of ourselves are responsive to confession, while other parts are more resistant. Emphasis is placed on the multifaceted social nature of the self that cannot be separated from historical, cultural, economic, and political forces. Psychologist Philip Cushman argues that in the post–World War II era in the United States, the main form the Western self assumes is the isolated consumer self, hungry for food, consumer items, and charismatic leaders.

Some among us hunger to consume "mass-produced" confessions from TV talk shows as a quick-fix approach to fill in a spiritual vacuum and inner emptiness. The consumer self gobbles up these sensational confessions in an illusory quest for self-enlightenment. Instead, the audience receives a kind of confessional junk food for the soul that fails to nourish and heal the divided self. The real nourishment provided by meditation, biofeedback, and other forms of self-monitoring gives us hope that we are beginning to focus more on the inner-directed spiritual life. The secret parts of ourselves—hallmarks of our inner life— present us with the opportunity of dealing with the hidden divisions within ourselves instead of consuming others' confessions.

The social, multileveled self is often divided. In the Western world of the late twentieth century, the narcissistic individual is isolated, having problems with intimacy and inclusion in communal endeavors. Confession is a cogent vehicle for beginning to reestablish a sense of communion with others within as well as outside traditional institutions.

Confessions made to friends and lovers, as well as to hairdressers, bartenders, and co-workers, are ways of allowing our divided, alienated selves to join with the larger community of confidants. This endeavor encourages what psychologist Edward Sampson calls "ensembled individualism" (in which the self always exists in relation to others) rather than "self-contained individualism" (in which the self is pitted against others). We cannot define ourselves apart from the world. According to Sampson, significant others in our lives are integral to who we are, rather than just being outside the boundaries of the self.

When I am with a patient, it soon becomes apparent that there are not two, but tens or even hundreds of people in the room with us with whom the confessional relationship is taking place. Through the transference, I variously appear as parents, grandparents, siblings, and friends, as well as split-off, disavowed parts of the patient's self projected onto me. Psychoanalyst James Grotstein has written extensively about the process of projective identification in which the patient "dumps" unwanted, dreaded, or frightening aspects of himself into the therapist for safekeeping. In this way, I can be seen as the tyrannical, sadistic, withholding mother that may reflect *both* the patient's perception of his mother and a secret part of himself that was disowned and instead attributed to me. The many players internalized by the patient are either attributed to me (through transference or projective identification) or appear through the patient himself, who is speaking in multiple voices to a variety of often undefined others.

The self is social, made up of multiple significant others who have been internalized. How often do we check ourselves, saying, "That's exactly what my mother used to say to me; I'm even speaking to my child in my mother's voice"? Patients with sexual inhibitions often tell me that it is as if they see snapshots of their parents in the bedroom along with parental voices warning them that sex outside of marriage is bad or sinful. If these voices remain unchecked or are not transformed through therapy, they eventually become part of rather than apart from the self. When they are too threatening, they then become part of the person's hidden, disowned self, and thus not available for the confessional journey.

In a related vein, psychologist Hubert Hermans and his associates describe the self as dialogical since many interacting selves engage in dialogue with each other. Even when outwardly silent, we find ourselves communicating with our parents, our friends, our adversaries, and even our reflection in the mirror. These "imaginal others" can also represent secret parts of ourselves split off from our awareness. For many of us, after all, it is easier to deal with malevolent others than with our own secret demonic aspects.

The self is thus forged together with others. The splits arise *in relation to* others—to protect us from others' intrusiveness or to protect others from our destructiveness. We need others as confidants to help us acknowledge and integrate the splits. Opening ourselves up to others can be a daunting experience. Relief is most likely to follow confession when our confidants are soothing presences that guide us on the confessional journey from the moment we reveal our secret until we reach the holy grail of redemption.

Confessions and Roles: The Dramaturgical Perspective

Confession produces a dramatic shift in the *representational world,* which is Joseph Sandler and Bernard Rosenblatt's term for the enduring world "out there" that we internalize made up of the significant others in our lives and the many impressions that enter into our experience. In therapy, the therapist becomes the leading significant other; outside therapy, the confidant takes on this role.

We can compare the representational world to a stage. Characters represent each of us and the significant others in our lives. The confession per se becomes a miniature drama within the larger play, with the self as hero (narcissistic confessions), villain (guilt-ridden confessions), or victim/victimizer (shameful confessions). This drama remains static, however, without an audience. The therapist or other confidant, as both audience and collaborative participant, helps the actor retrieve disavowed parts of the self and delineate or integrate these parts in the process of working them out.

The discloser becomes a character in her own internal play, repeating old roles. Confession helps free the individual from the tyranny of these patterns by breaking the cycle of repetition. In confessing, the discloser severs the unconscious or conscious collusive pact of silence with internalized others, and allies herself with the confidant, who becomes a new pivotal person in the individual's internal cast of characters. Acknowledging and empathizing with the disowned parts of ourselves and redeeming ourselves from the powerful internalized people of the past is a principal part of the confessional experience.

In contrast to Sandler and Rosenblatt's representational world, the world of sociologist Erving Goffman is one of anonymous roles. Here ritualized social interactions allow the actors to "save face" by avoiding honest self-disclosure through impression management. In *Behavior in Public Places,* Goffman elaborates, "Whatever his position in society, the person insulates himself by blindness, half-truths, illusions, and rationalizations."

In Goffman's dramaturgical perspective, our lives are divided into "backstage" and "out front" activities. Goffman notes that most of us are so preoccupied with maintaining a favorable persona that we may actually convince ourselves that the compliant false self is our core identity. The compliant false self is the phony outer shell. It is the inner core identity that most people unfortunately hide, since they fear disapproval or abandonment.

The self has often been described as a performer donning a mask—revealing one image to the world while keeping the essential part of the self hidden. Some have gone so far as to see the mask—the outward appearance—as the essential self. The scholar Desiderius Erasmus said, "What, after all, is human life if not a continuous performance in which all go about wearing different masks?"

The mask is the persona—an outer self from which the term *personality* derives. The persona allow us to protect ourselves, but in some situations, we buy into the mask to such an extent that we "become the mask." People who are constantly "on" to impress others, to further their careers for example, sometimes find that they cannot "turn themselves off" when they are in private. Like a Mr. Hyde who takes over as the dominant personality, the "on" side is in danger of overrunning the authentic hidden self.

In Goffman's world, all the world really is a stage. When we play many roles (e.g., spouse, friend, boss, parent, neighbor) that are appropriate and enhance our lives, we can truly say that we possess a flexible, robust self. But when we don phony roles in our private lives and become a model husband and father while secretly hating our wife and child, then we can no longer get away from our staged performance long enough to take stock of who we really are and how we really feel. Psychiatrist R. D. Laing, in *The Divided Self*, offers a chilling account of a man who had intercourse with his wife two to four times a week, while secretly "being elsewhere." The split he experienced was between his performing body (the embodied self) and his mind (the disembodied self). While playing the outward role of the dutiful husband, his hidden inner self loathed his wife.

The actor Peter Sellers admitted to being so successful at playing a wide array of characters precisely because he was so often unclear about who he really was. Ironically, the more successful we are at role playing, the more danger we are in of not being able to shed the role and "be ourselves" by relating authentically. When this happens, the divided self, as we have hitherto experienced it, no longer exists. The mask wins out; the enfeebled, authentic self retreats even further into hiding.

The public self—what we want others to see—is our censored, staged, "on" self. As long as we do not dare disclose our true selves, we remain prisoners of the false front—masters of the mask. We cannot really know ourselves until we disclose ourselves to others as well as to ourselves.

Rediscovering the True Self

The division between the true self and the false self, though resonating with our experience, is only one slice of the pie we conceptualize as the self. As explained earlier, the postmodernists have emphasized that we are not just a single self, but a collage of selves that includes secret selves or *subselves.* The self is made up of our personal histories and the larger society and historical era in which we live. As such, the self is both personal and social.

Many of us yearn to be our true selves—described by Donald Winnicott as the source of authenticity and psychic aliveness. Too often, though, we instead act compliantly to protect the true self from rejection and exploitation. For example, a thirty-four-year-old banker laments, "Women have their Ph.D.s in emotions and I haven't finished grade school. I project a macho, 'know-it-all' image, but inside I'm a frightened, incompetent little boy." A fine arts graduate student notes how well she manages her many roles: "I have to hand it to myself. I am a conscientious student, a good daughter who speaks to her parents once a week, a fine wife, and a good listener with my friends. Yet sometimes I wonder, 'What happened to me? Where do I fit in on this crowded stage?'" While this patient lauds herself for how well she manages her roles—how well she meets others' expectations of her—she also plaintively alludes to her lost or hidden true self that yearns to emerge and be recognized.

Psychotherapists Carl Rogers and R. D. Laing have also alluded to the true self/false self split. Carl Rogers, founder of humanistic psychology, claimed that the outer self, seduced by "conditional regard" from others (the "if you are compliant and do my bidding, I will love you" script), plays the game to the detriment of the inner self, which becomes more withdrawn and even bizarre. The greater the split between the inner and outer selves, according to Rogers, the greater the possibility for mental disturbance.

Regardless of differences in how the split is perceived, it becomes clear that in order to heal the divided self, the secret true self must emerge and be acknowledged by the individual as well as by significant others in his life. Therapy is a major forum offering an ongoing relationship characterized by trust, empathy, and support, that allows the patient to feel secure enough to "test out" the true self. Therapy is one of the few places on earth where we can "just be." And that means that, in time, we experience enough patience with the process and trust the therapist sufficiently to allow hidden, forbidden parts of ourselves, which are sorely in need of acceptance and affirmation, to emerge.

One of my patients, a man named Harry, referred to therapy as "a coming-out party" in which portions of who he really was came out gradually. "Sometimes I test you," Harry told me. "You know how obnoxious I can be—and how demanding. My mother would never put up with that. She would have slapped me around and used a hundred curses. My mother used to barge into my room and do inspections, like a drill sergeant. If everything wasn't just right, she'd throw all my things on the floor and demand I straighten my room in five minutes or else."

Harry's intrusive mother demanded compliance at all costs. He, in turn, had a rich fantasy life replete with elaborate schemes for torturing and murdering his mother. An outwardly obedient son, Harry believed the only way he could be himself was to do away with his mother. His true self—powerful in fantasy—was helpless in reality. This patient became increasingly convinced he could never risk "being himself"—allowing his true self to emerge. This true self became split off in order to protect himself, in his words, "from being eaten up alive by my mother." At the same time, Harry believed that he needed to protect his mother and others from this "destructive, murderous" hidden self.

At times, we all desire to disclose the hidden true self and be accepted and loved by our confidants. At the same time, we face the dilemma of whether these confessions will serve our needs at the cost of hurting those closest to us. For example, can we risk confessing our long-standing anger at our parents' attempts to strangle our individuality without feeling guilty that this disclosure will emotionally "kill" them, or should the true self remain hidden?

Our need to protect the true self produces a series of defenses and subterfuges that may serve us well in everyday social interactions. Although we may feel drawn to revealing select aspects of our hidden selves to dear friends, lovers, or therapists, we may also be reticent to confess to these confidants. They, too, may be split in our fantasies into benign, loving, accepting others, and malevolent, hate-filled, rejecting others demanding compliance at the expense of the true self.

Each confession brings us closer to the realization that we can be affirmed for being our true selves. Yet since the false self has often served us well in many aspects of living, one can well wonder what motivates us to gradually let go of the false-self facade through confession. Many of us come to realize that a major discrepancy exists between role-related achievement and success in personal relationships. For those who become aware that intimacy cannot be attained by "being on" twenty-four hours a day, therapy provides an opportunity to wrestle with the possibilities of intimacy without risking abandonment and disillusionment. Confession becomes one way to shed the pretenses of the false self and risk bringing the true self "out of cold storage," in Winnicott's words.

For some of us, the true self is so buried by the false self that its belated emergence may be experienced as an event akin to a breakdown. A distraught twenty-seven-year-old patient came into my office beset with fears that she was falling apart. She had decided that her dealings with overly competitive executives in a high-powered industry had corrupted her and that going to graduate school was what she really wanted to do. Because she had grown up in a family that put a premium on status and money, this patient perceived her "identity crisis" as synonymous with a breakdown rather than a breakthrough, in which her true self began to emerge. Having developed a sophisticated false-self defensive system, the shock of recognizing what she really wanted was, at first, perceived as catastrophic when in fact it was liberating.

In *I and Thou*, Buber discusses the essential problem of "being and seeming" within the realm of the false self and relationships. "The widespread tendency to live from the recurrent impression one makes instead of the steadiness of one's being . . . originates in man's dependence upon one another. It is no light thing to be confirmed in one's being by others, and seeming deceptively offers itself as a help in this. To yield to seeming is man's essential cowardice, to resist it is his essential courage. . . . One must at times pay dearly for life lived from the being; but it is never too dear."

Jean Paul Sartre, as a model child, developed multiple means to bolster the false self. Sartre, in *The Words*, writes of himself, "Consider the following: alone in the midst of grownups, I was a miniature adult and read books written for adults. That already sounds false since, at the same time, I remained a child. . . . The fact remains that my hunting and exploration were part of the family play-acting, that the grownups were delighted by it, and that I knew it." By the age of nine, Sartre had developed showmanlike routines, had started to write, and made comments well beyond his years. Sartre sensed the falseness, the lack of authenticity, wherein his conduct was based on pretense.

When we let ourselves be truthful with ourselves and others through confession, we risk narcissistic injuries in the hope of self-transformation. The self-esteem we gain in revealing hidden parts of ourselves is largely a function of being authentic—true to ourselves.

Unification of the Divided Self

Confessions help restore the divided self. We sometimes wonder if something is wrong with us when we discover that we act very differently around different people. On the contrary, an expansive self is open to the many possibilities of existence, including the different roles we assume. Something would be grossly amiss if we acted and reacted in the same way with our parents as we did with our lovers.

Thus, when we speak about uniting the splits in ourselves, we are not aiming toward a bland homogeneity that obliterates threatening or forbidden parts. Instead of possessing a constricted, split-off characteristic, our willingness to acknowledge a part of ourselves we would colloquially refer to as uptight, rigid, or obsessive-compulsive, helps us to expand our personality. We are able to add richness and diversity to who we are. Getting in touch with our evil, malevolent sides is not a signal to bring in the exorcist. These aspects can fuel creativity or simply add new, welcome dimensions to our personalities as the "bad" parts are transformed positively into spunkiness, self-assertion, and the courage to risk new ways of being.

Saint Augustine provides a vivid example of the discordant self. "So these two wills, one old, one new, one carnal, the other spiritual, were in conflict and between them they tore my soul apart." When Saint Augustine confessed to his sins of sexual lust and nonbelief in God, he achieved redemption through his faith in God. In so doing, he achieved self-integration. William James' eighth lecture, part of his *Varieties of Religious Experience,* alludes to the divided self and the process of its unification through secular or religious means. "But to find religion is only one out of many ways of reaching unity; and the process of remedying inner incompleteness and reducing inner discord is a general psychological process, which may take place with any sort of mental material, and need not necessarily assume the religious form." While Saint Augustine resolved his conflict by renouncing the carnal aspects of self, when we confess in everyday life, we generally acknowledge and try to assimilate split-off aspects of ourselves in order to achieve an integrated self.

Profound religious conversions and rites of passage frequently involve decisions to give up a part of the self as a means of achieving self-integration. Saint Augustine's renunciation of carnality, as well as the addict's repudiation of her addiction, represent attempts to rid the self of harmful aspects on the journey toward self-transformation and redemption. Our everyday confessions generally involve less dramatic, all-encompassing life changes. Confession helps us to accept the formerly hidden petty, disagreeable, and flawed aspects of our natures as part of the human condition.

Self-Deception

When essential parts of ourselves remain hidden, our basic potential remains locked up. We experience what the ancients termed a "sickness of soul" when our defenses ensure that we will be ruled by self-deception as a protection against reality.

Freud believed that by making the unconscious conscious through psychoanalysis, split-off, repressed aspects of ourselves could come to light, be accepted, and ultimately integrated. The major defense Freud suggested we use in keeping secrets from ourselves is repression. In this view, any secret or secret part of ourselves that evokes anxiety, guilt, shame, trauma, and so on is thus split off from consciousness.

Defenses, used in moderation, often serve us well. They protect us from unpleasant emotions and situations, and help preserve our sense of self-esteem. By keeping repellent or forbidden parts of ourselves underground—especially forbidden aggressive or sexual sides, according to Freud—the defenses help us preserve a favorable self image. Daniel Goleman, in *Vital Lies, Simple Truths,* offers neurophysiological evidence to show how defenses are ways to keep secrets from ourselves by skewing attention and thereby protecting ourselves against anxiety by creating blind spots—areas of self-deception.

Defense mechanisms, or any other attention-deflecting device, block confession. The self-deception thereby created not only enables aspects of ourselves to remain hidden, but also allows an illusory self-esteem to be maintained at the expense of reality.

An unforgettable example of the dangers wrought by self-deception as a life theme is evidenced by Willy Loman in Arthur Miller's *Death of a Salesman.* After Willy's death, his oldest son, Biff, remarks, "He never knew who he was." Biff is one of the few characters who does not collude with Willy in his self-deception, knowing that his father's grandiose schemes and simplistic notions of being liked as the key to success are far from the grim realities of their lives. Willy's lonely funeral underscores the falseness of his self-perceptions. He had lived his life unable to reveal who he was to himself. If Willy had had the opportunity to unburden and scrutinize himself in such a way as to gain self-acceptance concurrently with lessening his unrealizable grandiosity, his suicide might well have been prevented. Confession could literally have redeemed his life.

Body Confessions

There are times when our "body's confessions" in the form of physical symptoms—what Freud and Breuer referred to as *conversion reactions*—clue us in that the body is ready to reveal a hidden part of ourselves even before the psyche is. My patient Lynn, the patient previously discussed in chapter 4 who had been continually raped by her father, told me after several months of therapy that about once a month she experienced "something like an anxiety attack, although I'm not sure what it is."

I asked her to describe what happened. She said, "I'm lying in bed and I feel myself beginning to sweat. My heart starts beating faster and I cannot move—I'm very still. I'm waiting for something to happen, but I don't know what it is."

"Were you still," I asked, "when you anticipated that your father might enter the room and rape you?" Lynn started to hyperventilate. "Yes. When it was happening, all I could do was focus on my breathing—something that happens in these once-a-month states now. I'd lie very still and wait for it to be over."

"Sometimes the body registers secret trauma before we become mentally aware of what happened," I noted. "Your body now becomes frozen into the position of terror you assumed earlier on. This frozen memory is your body's confession that enables this split-off experience to be integrated into your consciousness."

Lynn's split-off, terrified childhood self was converted into the frozen bodily posture, symbolic of her state during the incestuous experiences. Through her bodily symptoms, she was able to regain access to the trauma and begin to heal the previously hidden terrified child part of herself through the ongoing therapy experience.

Lynn's split-off self concerned a specific childhood trauma of repeated rape. The splits between the true self and false self experienced by people with schizophrenia are much more global and diffuse, sometimes consisting of an elaborately constructed secret inner world peopled by imaginary others and the dreaded or deadening outer world we all live in.

R. D. Laing transfers this split between the true self and the false self to an existential plane in describing the basic division between the inner self and the body and external world in schizophrenia. The schizophrenic's secret true self is often experienced as futile or murdered, though the body and the false self live on. In Hannah Green's best-selling book *I Never Promised You a Rose Garden,* a series of confessions takes place when a therapist becomes willing to enter into her schizophrenic patient's world. The therapist's action enables the patient to risk revealing the splits between her constructed inner world of characters and her deadened outer world. The patient, Hannah Green, first acknowledges the transformation in her split-off bodily self when she burns herself with a cigarette and actually feels the pain.

Reparation

The psychoanalyst Melanie Klein conjectured that *all of us,* not just people with schizophrenia, possess a rich, complex inner world made up of monstrous, aggressive fantasies as well as loving, nurturing images of the significant others in our actual lives "out there." She observed that splitting could be either adaptive or defensive.

We sometimes need to keep separate good and bad internal images of important others in our lives. The same holds true for ourselves as our "bad" parents become split off from our conscious favorable image. When splitting is adaptive, it helps us order our lives by discriminating between good and bad.

Yet it is usually important for us to experience ourselves as whole people who perceive ourselves and others with ambivalence—good *and* bad; loving *and* hateful. When splitting gives way to ambivalence, we no longer need to suppress or split off undesirable parts of ourselves and others. We instead exist in the fullness of our being.

Klein also maintained that we can resolve splits through making reparation to others. I believe it is equally important for us to engage in self-reparation. The disclosure of art—writing, painting, composing, and performing—is one way we repair damage done to the self through owning secret parts of ourselves that find expression through the chosen art medium.

In my work with patients, I have observed how powerful art can be as a means to repair a damaged self. As we begin to integrate previously split-off, disowned parts of ourselves—demonic, degraded, resigned, or grandiose—we come to experience ourselves as whole people with enhanced self-esteem and a greater zest for life.

When secret parts of ourselves are restored to us, we may not only achieve integration, but also sense ourselves transformed. Neil was one such patient who brought his creative potential to bear on the art symbols he referred to in therapy. His attempts to heal his damaged self he kept locked up inside was evident from the "show-and-tell" stage he went through in therapy. An accomplished amateur oboist, Neil would bring in tapes of his performances in order to elicit from me the "gleam in the eye," in Kohut's words, he never received from his critical parents. During another session, Neil assembled his oboe for me.

It soon became evident that the symbolic aspect of Neil's behavior primarily indicated his need to exhibit his secret grandiosity to me. In effect, Neil, like the Humpty Dumpty of nursery rhyme fame, was reparatively putting together his damaged self for me.

In time, as Neil felt more and more comfortable exhibiting this secret grandiose self to me through his oboe performances, he was able to transform some of his grandiosity into living more creatively on a daily basis. My empathic reception of his split-off grandiosity enabled Neil to integrate it into his personality as well as carry it over creatively to other nonmusical areas of his life.

This patient's disclosure of his secret grandiose self through his oboe performances was essential in his self-transformation. He felt safest and most comfortable disclosing his secret grandiosity through the medium of his art.

In my threefold description of the confessional journey, the *risk* inherent in confession concerns the person's acknowledgment of a split or multiple splits in the self. The first step in confession occurs with the discloser owning each part of the divided self. The second step, *relief,* is afforded by the discloser's learning to empathize with split-off parts of the self. This can happen when the therapist, for example, encourages the opposing parts of the self to have dialogues with each other enlivened by her presence. In so doing, the different subselves can begin to bridge the dissociative gap between them. What were formerly secret selves at odds with each other now become emergent selves acknowledging, listening to, and responding to each other. Relief is gained both by unburdening aspects of the split-off secret self to the accepting confidant and by becoming familiar with these splits by literally "giving them a voice." If the discloser succeeds in integrating the now acknowledged split-off subselves instead of retreating or withdrawing back to the old splits, *redemption* can ensue.

Coming to terms with the splits in ourselves is redemptive; keeping the self split with the two or more parts warring against each other or, worse still, the demonic part gaining ascendancy, can result in destruction. People who are psychotic murder the self existentially; people who commit suicide kill the self biologically. Because psychotics are convinced that it is dangerous to disclose their true selves to significant others, they shut down, withdrawing into themselves. Since suicide destroys the entire self, it is sometimes seen as an easier solution to the pain and torment of "living a lie"—adopting a phony persona. The more difficult path, often chosen by psychotics, is to split the self—preventing the true self from authentically relating to others by forcing it to remain underground.

Narcissistic Splits

The parts of our personality that we hide from ourselves and the world are usually those we view as shameful, dreaded, or repugnant. Sometimes, though, the divided self contains positive, growth-promoting aspects that we may simultaneously fear and secretly wish to reveal. Narcissistic splits involve this kind of conflict.

We all have grandiose selves that long to shine; selves that yearn to bask in their accomplishments, to be appreciated—even to be "oohed and aahed" over—for their competence and creativity. Even though we live in a culture of narcissism which values grandiosity, many people split off or repress this aspect of themselves. Deprived of narcissistic enrichment, they appear to be vaguely depressed, lacking in self-confidence and in zest for work—a state of being Kohut terms a "horizontal split."

We all know people who fold at the slightest sign of rejection or discouragement, yet may harbor secret fantasies of being able to write "the great American novel." When this fantasy becomes too threatening—too out-of-synch with their conscious image of themselves as procrastinators or failures, the grandiose self again goes into hiding.

For other people, the grandiose self is always out there in their awareness; however, they constantly vacillate between almost megalomaniacal "highs" and self-deprecation—a state of being Kohut terms a "vertical split." A thirty-eight-year-old professional who entered into long relationships with women but could never ultimately commit himself to marriage was the embodiment of this kind of narcissistic split. When he felt terrific about himself, he would summarily devalue his current love, citing everything from the shape of her nose to her parental pedigree to justify ending the relationship. Each of these women, in turn, would undergo the fate of assuming the aura of his own negative, devalued aspects. When he was not feeling so positive about himself, these women were idealized as their numerous virtues were extolled to me in rapturous detail. This patient's grandiosity was now attributed to them—as he was now only aware of the negative, devalued part of his own nature.

The problem for people with severe narcissistic splits is that they cannot regulate and maintain fairly evenly balanced self-esteem. We all experience highs and lows; we all feel "down in the dumps" when rejected or terminated from a job, but we bounce back after a time. This is so because we do not feel that our entire self is on the line every time adverse conditions beset us. If I am reprimanded by my boss, for example, this does not mean that I become, as a totality, a stupid, incompetent nincompoop. People with severe narcissistic splits, on the other hand, would see themselves precisely this way.

The greater the discrepancy between how I see my ideal self and how I perceive myself in reality, the greater the likelihood that my secret grandiosity will not be acknowledged. Alternatively, when I am aware of my grandiosity, I may suffer even more because I perceive myself as lagging far behind my expectations of where I should be or who I should be.

For people with severe narcissistic splits, any confession that emphasizes perceived defects meets with internal resistance. On the other hand, when therapists or friends are seen as safe and accepting "containers" for confessions, these same people are able to risk confession without dreading the danger of diminished self-esteem. With such affirming confidants, secret grandiosity is more likely to emerge and become integrated into the personality.

Affirming Confidants as the Lost-and-Found

Many of us have had the experience of feeling lost—disoriented, "out of sorts," hopeless, or helpless. This sense of alienation, of self-alienation, occurs when we feel divided. We can reclaim the lost, disowned parts of ourselves when we use our capacity to be self-reflective with the right confidants in our lives.

Robert Frost, in his great 1947 poem "Directive" wrote, "And if you're lost enough to find yourself/By now, pull in your ladder road behind you/And put a sign up CLOSED to all but me." In this poem, Frost sets forth the crucial paradox of finding-in-losing. The paradox presents itself in many areas of our lives. Before we are able to "find ourselves," we often initially experience ourselves as feeling lost—cut off, alienated, demoralized, or divided. We sense ourselves as "a house divided"; rifts exist between ourselves and the world as well as within ourselves.

As I reread "Directive" late one night, I realized how important it is for us to fully acknowledge and experience the splits within ourselves in order to become whole. The *lost and found* metaphor, encompassing separation and relatedness, speaks to different aspects of ourselves simultaneously. For some people, the phrase "lost and found" is associated with secret, disowned parts of themselves retrieved during therapy or during the course of a romantic relationship in which their guard is down. Others see possibilities for reparation in finding lost loves or cherished earlier relationships, evoking feelings of comfort and security. In our fantasies, "found" is sometimes equated with being rescued and "lost" with feeling demoralized.

The sense of being found is universal as well as idiosyncratic to each of our experiences. We hide aspects of ourselves from our awareness out of dread, shame, guilt, or even security to protect the sound aspects of ourselves from those we view as crazy, bizarre, traumatized, or demonic. When we split off these feared parts, we can temporarily live with the illusion that all is well and we are safe.

Yet all is not well. As long as fundamental aspects of our being remain lost—cut off from our awareness—we are truncated and constricted. By risking opening ourselves up to the full range of our being, secret, disavowed parts of ourselves can enter consciousness as forces to be reckoned with rather than cast asunder.

When we confess, we allow ourselves to own the secret parts of ourselves. We thereby widen the horizon of our self-awareness. The habitually "nice, good-natured" person, through confession, adds hostility, envy, and hatred as selectively acceptable feelings in an expanded self-image.

Self-deception gives way to enlightenment as we come to realize that the naughty, evil, disgusting, and ridiculous are also part of ourselves. Becoming acquainted with these hidden parts of ourselves and exposing them to the light of scrutiny reverses the destructive tide of self-deception. In coming to terms with all parts of ourselves, we are no longer a house divided.

9

Toward Enhanced Relationships

WE ARE social beings through and through. The need to connect with each other is as basic to our well-being as the air we breathe and the food we eat.

In a letter to his friend Thomas Ward dated January 1868, William James discusses the absolute importance of connection in each of our lives. "Every thought you now have and every act and intention owes its complexion to the acts of your dead and living brothers. *Everything* we know and are is through men. We have no revelation but through man."

Even when we are left to our own devices, we are rarely really alone. Stereotypical religious hermits sit on mountaintops communing with God. When we read, listen to the radio, or watch television, we are relating to our favorite hero, surrogate family, or idealized team.

Further, our world is comprised not only of significant relationships "out there," but also of myriad internalized relationships, including ones with our parents, our childhood friends, our teachers and mentors, and so on. These relationships, which influence our lives on an ongoing basis, are taken in and assimilated, becoming part of our being. We carry around with us these significant others' "scripts"—sayings, precepts, beliefs, and values—that continue to affect us even after these individuals are no longer physically present in our lives.

The Scottish psychoanalyst Ronald Fairbairn elaborated on the richness of our internal world of relationships—relationships comprised of both positive and negative presences. Psychoanalysis was seen by Fairbairn as a medium to help rid individuals of the powerful influence of negative relationships. He compared psychoanalysis to an exorcism in which the devils of our unconscious world are cast out. He viewed these devils as internalized bad presences that must be abolished and substituted for actual positive relationships with others in the external world.

Fairbairn maintained that we often cling to bad relationships, convincing ourselves that they are better than no relationships. We all have known people who continuously get into manipulative or sadistic relationships in order to be acknowledged by others, no matter how critical or humiliating the response. Confessions of abuse, sadism, or other manipulations on the part of parents, friends, and lovers not only involve the risk of revealing "forbidden" material but also involve the fantasy of totally losing these internalized others by expelling them through confession. In other words, for some people such confessions carry the cataclysmic consequences of "throwing the baby out with the bathwater." Just as bad habits are hard to break, these individuals discover that it is equally hard—or harder—to break free of bad internalized relationships.

In the all too familiar example of abused children who do not want to be taken away from their abusive parents, love or attention is equated with abuse. To confess to the authorities, or later to disclose the abuse to a therapist or lover, seems to be a betrayal of the external or internal parent. These ties, no matter how abusive, still provide the person with a vital human connection. So strong are these internalized relationships that sometimes patently abusive parents continue to exert an influence, it would seem, from the grave.

The good news is that lovers, friends, or therapists can become positive, reliable confidants who provide alternatives to the world of internalized relationships. These confidants offer the love, support, and appreciation that was missing from the original rigidly scripted world of childhood. To confess in the presence of empathic confidants is to undergo a new experience offsetting the burdensome hold of the internalized albatrosses.

Throughout our lives, we are faced with our need for others on the one hand and our desire to be autonomous on the other. We want to connect deeply with confidants through confession. Should we have positive early confessional experiences, our relationships grow even stronger and more loving as we continue to share confidences. When confidants disappoint us, we may lose trust in others and even retreat into a cocoon of imagined self-sufficiency.

If we were given one wish in life concerning confession, most people would wish to be able to reveal themselves entirely to another human being who would love and accept them unconditionally. Intimate relationships have the power to comfort us, making us feel secure in the confidant's emotional embrace. Trust among intimates is a prerequisite, yet many lovers, even within the bounds of marriage, feel shaky about disclosing secrets precisely because the institution of marriage itself is no longer perceived as the Rock of Gibraltar it once was. With one out of two new marriages ending in divorce, many married people feel less free about sharing secrets with their spouses.

A friend once confided in me, "Thank God for our friendship. If I told my husband half my sexual fantasies, not to mention my hidden shopping compulsions, I think he'd divorce me on the spot." Friendships, as will be explained more fully later, can be alternative safe havens for intimacy outside the confines of marriage.

We feel more alive and vital when we share our secrets with others. When a child or adult feels secure with a confidant, genuine spontaneity can take place in lieu of false compliance to the demands of others. John Bowlby's work on attachment shows that when children have strong, reliable attachment figures in childhood, these confidants promote a sense of security and confidence in adult life. In this fortunate climate, others are sought out and welcomed as confidants and guides on the confessional journey.

The human need to seek relationships is conducive to our well-being, and sharing secrets is one of the most cogent ways to cement relationships. Best friends have secrets that they share with no one else. Mutual confidences bind together spouses against the world.

The ancient Greek philosopher Heraclitus said, "I searched out myself." Heraclitus believed that self-reflection in the absence of others was a vain pursuit. Others were there to provide a dialogue integral to self-awareness. He came to understand himself through such encounters with others. In our times, psychologist Sidney Jourard's writings on self-disclosure revolve around the premise that we can only know ourselves by disclosing ourselves to others. Authentic self-disclosure becomes a major criterion for growth and health.

Confession is capable of cutting through or destroying games based on control and manipulation. At its best, confession is a "game-free" communication that enhances intimacy and authenticity. We need others to help us reveal ourselves to ourselves in full. Secrets left unsaid fester as they become increasingly bizarre in the black hole that encapsulates them. Confidants provide a forum for our secrets to unfold as we literally educate ourselves—lead ourselves out of our former secrecy.

In *Existentialism,* Sartre notes, "In order to get any truth about myself, I must have contact with another person. The other is indispensable to my own existence, as well as to my knowledge about myself." Secrets emerge in the context of relating to others. Even as I am learning about myself *vis-à-vis* my confidants, it is equally true that I am, at the same time, learning more about the confidants. My relationship changes in the direction of greater intimacy and often greater mutuality, since self-disclosure in turn promotes self-disclosure.

Suppose a friend confesses an infidelity to another friend. The confidant listens empathetically, thereby making the discloser feel understood, mirrored, and supported. The confidant then reveals a similar secret from her past. While the discloser feels good and more confident about herself, she also realizes that she likes her friend even more for being accepting and sharing the secret. Thus, both the friendship—and the discloser's self-esteem—are strengthened through the mutual confession.

Intimate companions become closer when the secret binds them together in a more exclusive relationship. Both friends' sense of self-worth is heightened through such mutual disclosures which, in turn, enhance the friendship's value.

Confessions thus help us grow in the relationship as well as individually. Growth requires relatedness, which is one reason why we marry and have friends. Yet the paradox remains: Those we are closest to are often the ones we most fear confiding in, since possible repercussions are greater in these crucial relationships.

Growth rarely takes place in a straight line. As we wend our way along the confessional journey, we sometimes choose to either approach those closest to us as confidants or avoid them. We may choose alternative confidants such as therapists and friends who may, at times, accept and appreciate us more than our mates.

Relationships can grow and develop in the fertile soil of self-disclosure. We cannot always expect blanket acceptance or agreement from our confidants, but we can hope and expect that disagreements can become productive as partners learn to respect each other, despite divergences of opinion following confession.

One common sore spot for disclosure in many marriages is one partner's desire to reveal with relish her former sexual exploits, which conflicts with the other partner's wish to have her keep her "sex-capades" to herself. When each partner respects the wishes of the other—agreeing to disagree—the marriage continues to grow in a congenial atmosphere marked by respect for differences. Should the eager-to-reveal spouse need an ear, she can turn to her friends, therapist, or acquaintances as confidants.

On the other hand, the same spouse may be the ideal confidant for many other secrets. In earthy intimate relationships, each person is free to temporarily lose himself with the other and go wherever the experience takes him. For this reason, the bedroom is sometimes the place *par excellence* for the revelation of secrets. After sex, some partners feel safe enough to confide in each other. Having just lost themselves in each other, they are often less guarded and more receptive to each other's concerns.

In these situations, each partner feels freer to "go with the flow." Psychologist Mihaly Csikszentmihalyi, in his book *Flow: The Psychology of Optimal Experience*, defines *flow* as "the state in which people are so involved in an activity that nothing else seems to matter." Confession can sometimes be a by-product of a loving, intimate relationship in

which part of the flow—the spontaneous, joyful process of being together—is the revealing that becomes part of the ongoing stream of
intimacy.

According to Csikszentmihalyi, flow helps us achieve happiness
through exercising control over our inner lives. When we risk sharing
a vital part of our inner selves—our secrets—with cherished others
who welcome them as part of us, we start to gain greater control over
these secrets. This happens when we start to summon the courage to
acknowledge our secrets in the presence of confidants as an integral
and necessary part of our relationships with them.

The Therapy Relationship

The decision about whether or not to confess depends not only upon
how we see ourselves, but also upon our relationships with current
and past significant others, internal and external. We encounter a host
of significant others whose enduring presences continue to influence
the outcome of revealing ourselves. Thus when we opt for concealment, we may be consciously or unconsciously protecting not only
ourselves, but also parents or siblings whose collective presence operates to undermine confession. The ghosts of the past are thus often
strongly present as they operate to damage or strengthen our relationships with the others.

In our culture, many people who feel cut off from others seek a
therapist as an alternative confidant, since fears revolving around betraying a family secret or destroying a parent through "ruthless" confession are common resistances to disclosure to other confidants.
Throughout our lives, we try to separate from others to strive toward
autonomy, even as we rely on them for empathy and support. Confession underscores the dilemma of patients who find themselves pitted
against past and present relationships in a drama in which release
from oppressive past relationships simultaneously connotes attachment to the therapist.

Patients become particularly attached to the therapist when they
feel that they have been truly understood. In accepting the patient's
confession, the therapist becomes transformed in the patient's psyche

from a strict parental figure to a benign and loving parent. Patients can thereby assimilate the therapist as an accepting confidant and become correspondingly less harsh on themselves.

Confessions become reparative to the extent that patients re-create a situation in which the benign and valued parents now accept them unconditionally. In this scenario, past relationships are literally re-created rather than statically repeated. Parental and other significant relationships are given the opportunity to be transformed and redeemed in the context of an ongoing therapeutic relationship.

The Nature of the Confidant

Confidants come in many stripes and sizes. While at one time the confessor was synonymous with the priest or minister, today the friend or lover, not to mention the therapist, is more likely to be confided in for a broad range of secrets.

Confidants range from totally passive listeners providing no feedback to active advisors. We often intuitively sense which confidants would most sensitively respond to which secrets.

Let us start with the passive listener. The hairdresser or bartender lends a welcoming ear to clients who want to pour their hearts out to a sympathetic background presence. To the extent that regulars can count on these confidants to always be there for them as empathetic recipients of secrets, the relationship becomes even more valued by customers over time. Friends and therapists often also function simply as ears for the insecure secret sharer who wants to be silently appreciated.

Depressed disclosers seek out friends, lovers, and therapists who will support them through their ordeals. Secrets concerning job failure or social rejection due to perceived ineptitude are hesitatingly revealed and often accompanied by guilt or shame. The confidant's words of encouragement or advice here become crucial as nutrients to fill disclosers up—a source of fulfillment—as well as tide them over crises. Bartenders and hairdressers I interviewed told me that simple clichés such as "things will get better" or "keep trying" temporarily lifted depressions. Clients seemed to feel better about themselves and experienced a surge of gratitude and well-being from these associations.

The more active confidant gives advice or guidance in an ongoing, intimate relationship. A discloser is often able to tolerate friends' or lovers' reactions, especially when she appears to be confiding in them with that very purpose in mind. A spouse who is told that his wife's former lover is pestering her to get together for dinner is directly enlisted in a problem-solving venture. While the wife initially may have been hesitant about confiding in her husband, fearing reproval, her need to find a quick solution to get rid of the intruder overrides her hesitation. Friends with problematic in-laws confide in each other rather than their spouses who do not share their enmities or frustrations. Sharing secrets they are reticent to share with spouses, friends actively support each other in trying to resolve these in-law dilemmas. Such friendships grow in a supportive atmosphere of shared confidences.

Lillian Rubin, in her book *Just Friends,* noted that most people found it easier to confide in friends than family, because friends were perceived as less judgmental and more accepting. On the other hand, these same people found it easier to acknowledge their secret "shadow side," such as a nasty temper, to family, knowing that their family was "stuck" with them.

Friends represent a link to the larger world—the world beyond kinship and marriage. Friends help us see that there is life and ways of being outside the confines of family convention. The aforementioned in-law secrets confided to friends get us out of the sometimes stifling symbiosis of marital intimacy. Moreover, the overlap between family and historical friends—friends you know from "way back when"—means that these friends can truly appreciate a family secret since they know the family firsthand.

The therapists, hairdressers, friends, and spouses I interviewed surprisingly agreed on the basic qualities in a confidant that facilitate confession. According to those interviewed, the best confidant is

1. *Nonjudgmental:* The confidant neither adopts a religious confessional posture in branding the confession sinful nor repeats the critical, evaluative stand assumed by the discloser's past significant relationships.

2. *Safe and trustworthy:* Disclosers feel free to confess anything, knowing the confidant will not betray them.
3. *Soothing:* The confidant's empathic presence contributes to relief and a feeling of calm following confession.
4. *Nonintrusive and empathic:* The confidant is able to hear the confession without interpreting it.
5. *Understanding:* The confidant is empathic and makes attuned interpretations. The interpretation that "hits home" both facilitates the truth-gaining function of confessions and strengthens the relationship between discloser and confidant.
6. *"Nonphony":* The confidant is genuinely concerned and interested in the confession, rather than simply doing a job by rote. The perception of a confidant as authentic and caring strengthens a discloser's conviction that she will be taken seriously and that confessions will be followed through to completion.

The confiding relationships regular clients form with bartenders, hairdressers, and other service providers have been unjustly underestimated or even trivialized. True, many of these relationships are one-sided, "coming with the territory," as one hairdresser put it, and sometimes downright manipulative, since earning tips may be as much a function of the confidant's role as providing professional expertise. Yet there are times when these "familiar strangers" who get to know regulars over time really do care. Mutuality of disclosure sometimes even fosters friendships outside the bar and salon.

Bartenders and hairdressers I spoke with told me that regulars confided in them about occurrences that they believed would be greeted with disbelief or ridicule by their families. One client whose music teacher and mentor had been tragically killed disclosed to her hairdresser that whenever she rehearsed songs she had studied with her teacher on the piano, her lamp would flicker on and off. Figuring it was a defect in the lamp, she would then attempt to "trick" the lamp by playing new songs. The lamp would operate normally until she returned to her teachers' songs, at which time the lamp again began to flicker on and off.

For our purposes, what is most relevant about this confession is that the client felt enough trust and constancy in her relationship with her hairdresser to disclose this happening. As a confidant, the hairdresser was viewed midway between a friend and a "professional ear." Moreover, from previous lighthearted conversations, the client knew her hairdresser was fascinated by and positively disposed toward psychic phenomena. Her family's skeptical attitude made her feel ill at ease risking this secret with them. Her need to feel accepted rendered her hairdresser the ideal confidant. The two eventually became friends outside the shop.

The relaxed, informal salon, "coffee klatch," or bar invites confession. A hairdresser observed: "Customers relax once they know you for a while. But they still feel safe because you're separated from the rest of their lives. When they establish an ongoing relationship with you, they can relax since they see you as a friend in a limited capacity."

Moreover, the discloser often also sees the community of regulars as confidants who become quasi-friends bound by an away-from-home ambiance that invites confession. As such, a common turf is established for sharing secrets outside the riskier domain of lovers, friends, and family.

Trust and Connectedness

The ability to trust is the bedrock of confession. Erik Erikson viewed the development of basic trust, which he placed developmentally in the first year of life, as "the cornerstone of a healthy personality." Trust naturally grows out of nurturing experiences with caretakers who give the baby a sense of security that forms the foundation of later identity.

As adults, most of us experience the essence of trust as emotional security. When we can place our deepest secrets in another's trust, knowing they will be handled with care, we sense the power of connectedness.

Yet even in the best relationships, we have to realize that trust is something to be earned—not an inevitable outgrowth of the human condition. We have all had hurtful experiences of placing our trust in others, only to be betrayed or let down in some fashion. When we

have experienced rejection, betrayal, and other assorted disillusion-
ments, we cannot immediately trust others, even if we did experience
a blissful first year of life.

It is the task of the lover, friend, or therapist to provide an atmosphere of safety and constancy where we can gradually develop or
rediscover a sense of trust. In this milieu, we feel freer revealing ourselves despite disappointing experiences with significant others in the
past. Psychoanalyst Ethel Person, in her book *Dreams of Love and Fateful Encounters*, points out that falling in love is predicated on risk taking. She writes, "In order to achieve mutual love, we must gamble on
opening up psychically to achieve real intimacy and mutuality. But by
revealing oneself to the other, one becomes vulnerable." Trust in the
beloved is the cement that attaches us to the partner, giving us the
courage to risk confession in an atmosphere of love and acceptance.

Playing builds trust. When as children or adults we play with others, we become exhilarated by spontaneity, excitement, and freedom.
Teammates are more likely to share confidences with each other as
they get to know each other better. United by the physical challenge
of the sport, shared uniforms, practice time, and time spent together
on the road, they often develop a camaraderie evolving from "playing
together." It is easier to bare our souls in play with confidants whom
we know and have grown to trust over time. Successful confessions
become "win-win" situations in which the bond with the confidant is
strengthened.

We learn to be close to each other and trusting as we exercise our
imaginations through play or in being playful. Divulging a secret can
be introduced as part of play. Secrets make us feel special in the context of play, especially when the confidant shows anticipatory appreciation or excitement.

Trust is also heightened when therapists, lovers, or special friends
provide missing relational experiences at the point when the world of
significant relationships has failed us. For example, allowing ourselves
to "benignly regress" in a trusting, love relationship—acting silly,
showing neediness—means that we have the opportunity to act childlike without repercussions emanating from authoritarian parents. In
trusting love relationships or in therapy, disclosure of our secret child-

like selves that are now allowed to flower facilitates what psychoanalyst Michael Balint terms a "new beginning."

Forbidden Thoughts and Feelings in Relation to the Other

Relationships are strengthened by fully experiencing our hatred, rage,
and destructiveness, along with love, gratitude, and joy. Hatred, rage,
and destructiveness are often purposefully suppressed "secret" feelings that we believe must remain underground if we are to keep our
parents, friends, and lovers. The idea of separation or abandonment is
so fraught with dread that we may repress or disavow these feelings in
childhood. The secrets we start out hiding from others thereby also
become hidden from ourselves.

One reason why we hold back is that we fear our own destructive
impulses. People who confess have voiced the fear that if they expressed their sadness fully, they would never stop crying, and confidants would leave them en masse. Others dread that expressing their
hidden rage would result in murder. They see themselves as seething
cauldrons ready to explode. They believe that getting too close and revealing their rage would result in an explosion of their pent-up hostility
at the price of severe repercussions from the recipients of their feelings.

People with a history of suppressed rage or hatred sometimes work
very hard not to expose these feelings, believing that something is in-
herently wrong with them and that others will find them out. When
they tentatively drop hints to a friend or guardedly reveal a small dose
of these feelings to test a spouse, they usually experience immediate
minor relief. But it is the discussion that ensues regarding why they
are reticent to reveal these feelings, along with what happened to
them in past relationships when they tried to confess, that slowly results in change. The confidant's respectful, attentive, inquiring presence soothes and encourages individuals to further confess. They no
longer feel crazy and sick. What were once taboo feelings now make
these same people feel soothed and cradled within the calm of the
trusted relationship.

Getting out forbidden thoughts and feelings is not simply a matter
of biological release, as discussed in chapter 2. Confessions are rela-

tional acts—forms of communication that tie us to others for better or for worse. How we view the confidant is vital in decoding the meaning of these disclosures. Some may venomously spew out a secret, e.g., "I had an affair," to hurt another or themselves. Here confessions become destructive, divisive, adversarial acts where the discloser is pitted against the confidant. When forbidden secrets emerge collaboratively with confidants rather than in spite of them or expressly to spite them, these relationships are likely not only to survive but also to thrive. Here confession becomes a participatory, ongoing process where the discloser and confidant work together to better serve each other and the relationship.

Heightened Intimacy, Heightened Individual Identity

Self-disclosure grows in the soil of intimate relationships. Failures in early intimacy are not fatal when later relationships foster trust and support as preludes to confession.

When two people with strong selves are bound together by love and respect, either can encounter the other with a confession without fearing a loss of self. True intimacy is the climate for secret sharing when we sense that we are maintaining or enhancing our self-integrity. Judith Wallerstein, in her book *The Good Marriage*, writes that an important marital task is building togetherness by creating intimacy while, at the same time, recognizing each person's autonomy. Confession involves both tracks: expanding togetherness (marital we-ness) while also heightening individuality. Those with fragile selves, in turn, feel more vulnerable experiencing the intimacy of confession—as if pieces of an already shaky self were being wrested away from them.

The word *intimacy* derives from the Latin *intimus*, meaning "innermost." Through confession, the other becomes aware of our innermost thoughts and feelings. Lillian Rubin, in *Intimate Strangers*, observes that genuine intimacy involves putting aside our public persona and believing "we can be loved for who we really are, that we can show our shadow side without fear, that our vulnerabilities will not be counted against us." Here the confidant becomes privy to the discloser's inner-most self in the sanctuary of interpersonal relation.

Intimacy is the basis for self-disclosure. In enhancing intimacy through confessing, the desire for closeness exists together with the need to be an autonomous person who can stand back and examine the nuances of the confession. To this end, psychologist Warren Wilner remarks, "In all intimate relationships the presence of simulta-neous connectedness and separateness is established in the require-ment that individuals move beyond their own inner contradictions and differences with others in order to grasp the other's full presence through their own."

Relating to others is a crucial dimension in establishing intimacy. We confess when we sense that we truly have found a reliable friend or lover who respects us and cares enough about us to warrant the risk involved.

Erik Erikson sees intimacy as the capacity to commit oneself to others and maintain such commitments, even though they may call for sacri-fices and compromises. Identity precedes intimacy, according to Erik-son; we must have a firm sense of who we are before we are willing or able to surrender ourselves in openness and love to another. Feelings of intimacy often give us the courage to confess in the first place. Con-fession, in turn, helps us retrieve disowned parts of our identity and further consolidate a sense of who we are.

In other words, intimacy may precede identity and provide a foun-dation on which an identity can be built. When intimacy is seen as re-vealing one's inner self as a way to enhance closeness, it becomes clear why children as young as three confide in each other. The feel-ings of mutual intimacy experienced in these earliest relationships provide a blueprint for further strengthening of identity.

Intimacy is thus not always or inevitably the next step after identity. Intimacy actually piggy-backs onto identity—especially since our iden-tities are affected, strengthened, and transformed through intimacy. When I share a secret with my mate who affirms me, I not only feel good about myself for taking the risk, but now also feel strengthened in my conviction that it is okay to share secret parts of myself, such as my feelings of murderous rage, which were not acceptable in my family of origin. As a result, I gradually get in touch with a host of further "forbidden" secrets that I start to acknowledge and express. My sense of who I am, thereby, is expanded and enriched through the newfound intimacy and freedom I find in my marriage or special friendships.

When confession to the beloved is successful, it can change the "I, you, and we" elements that enter into being a couple. A healthy love relationship thrives when all three parts work together harmoniously. Each partner is an "I" with independent interests and aspirations. In order for the relationship to work, each partner engages in independent activities in tandem with acknowledging and appreciating the other—the "you" element. As a couple, the partners function as a "we." They appreciate their time together engaged in shared activities and feel good about their collective identity as a couple.

Let us return to Erikson's dictum: "identity precedes intimacy." When we have a firm sense of ourselves, we are less afraid to change the boundaries of a self as we form new identifications, especially the sense of ourselves as part of a "we."

When we share a secret with our beloved, we have the sense that "we are in this together." Together we can tackle the most difficult dilemmas, ranging from unplanned pregnancies to harassment on the job. Confession forms a soul-to-soul bridge that takes us out of our aloneness into the heart of relatedness.

At the same time, confession makes us feel affirmed as individuals who have the courage to take risks. Love renders us less fearful as we abandon the dread of disclosure surrounding constricting past relationships. Disclosure to the beloved enhances self-realization and, at the same time, takes the relationship to new levels of intimacy.

Love can flourish in the mutuality of shared secrets when there is deep understanding and acceptance. When the relationship itself is valued and cherished, partners are less afraid to risk disclosure knowing they are dedicated to the preservation of the marriage. Willingness to reveal secrets—to share what is inside—becomes an act of faith in the partner.

Psychoanalyst James Hillman equates "reveal thyself" with the commandment to love, since in fulfilling intimate relationships we can be especially disclosing through our mutual love for each other. He continues: "We can be known to ourselves through another, but we cannot go it alone. . . . The opus of the soul needs intimate connection, not only to individuate, but simply to live. For this we need relationships of the profoundest kind through which we can realize ourselves, where self-revelation is possible . . . and where eros may move more freely—whether it be in analyses, in marriage and family, or between lovers or friends."

When we sense our own individuality, we can allow ourselves to get profoundly close to others. In a good marriage or friendship, partners mostly accept themselves and each other for who they are. Disclosures to intimates are not about "fixing" each other, but about being there for the other in loving acceptance. When we share confidences with each other in intimate relationships, we are receptive and open with each other. Power gives way to relatedness as we seek to surrender ourselves to each other rather than dominate through control. Partners care deeply about each other and are comfortable being in close proximity. Gazing at one another, standing close to each other, and perhaps touching—all are nonverbal inducements to reveal oneself in a harmonious atmosphere of mutuality and equality.

Respect and Recognition

Respect (from *respicere*—to look back at or examine) means seeing each other for who we are, rather than who we would ideally like each other to be. In disclosure, respect encompasses recognition of the confidant's uniqueness.

Partners who have not developed autonomy have a hard time grasping the concept of each other as individuals. When we serve as extensions of narcissistic parents, lovers, or friends, we are not viewed as separate beings worthy of love and esteem in our own right.

While idealization connotes looking up to others positioned on the Olympian heights, respect involves looking at others with all their foibles, idiosyncrasies, and imperfections in a less illusory, more direct way. In so doing, we can begin to acknowledge others' authenticity and accept their uniqueness.

Confession calls for respect. Relationships are enhanced when the confidant neither looks down on nor up to the discloser. Rather we look directly at the discloser in all her transparency and see her one-to-one.

Psychoanalyst Jessica Benjamin has written extensively about our need to be recognized and our need, in turn, to recognize others. Both discloser and confidant need to be attuned to each other and, at the same time, be able to tolerate differences in perspective.

In recognition, we both acknowledge the other and assert ourselves. Disclosure to others enables us to gain greater self-awareness — a greater sense of our own individuality — by recognizing the confidant and the confidant's input in helping us work out the confession. We can recognize the confidant's viewpoint as a contribution, even when it differs from our own. When the teller and listener can appreciate each other as collaborators, despite different "takes" on the meaning and proposed outcome of sharing the secret, the relationship is strengthened. Each can feel respected and cherished without the need to reach a joint consensus. It is only when one partner tries to dominate the other that intimates turn into adversaries.

Transparency, Mutuality, Complementarity, and Mirroring

James Hillman speaks of confessions as "love becoming clarified. We are working at transparency. Impossible dark spots of the interior person get lit up . . . all the shames and embarrassments regarding the concealed personal tied-up self." We become transparent — clear and cleansed — through confessing. The burden of hiding ourselves is lifted when we courageously reveal ourselves to each other.

Transparency is rarely automatic. Love may sometimes take place at first sight, but transparency requires protracted effort. The astute scholar of perception, Gustav Ichheiser, noted that the rule of perception is that we always misperceive. Yet when a foundation of caring exists, partners try to correct their own misperceptions about the other in order to move the relationship forward. Confession is the means for that correction.

Nowhere are the lessons of transparency better related than in

Jane Austen's novel *Pride and Prejudice*. The story revolves around the
Bennet family's five daughters who enter the marriage mart, goaded
on by their strident, often silly mother. The duo we become most fascinated with early on is Mr. Darcy, a gentleman of wealth and breed-
ing, and Elizabeth Bennet, a spirited woman with sparkling eyes.

A major portion of the plot turns on Elizabeth's wrongful perception of Mr. Darcy based on a false confession made by a mutual ac-
quaintance, Mr. Wickham—a dashing officer Elizabeth meets and
takes a fancy to. Wickham confirms Elizabeth's disgust with Darcy's
pride, which becomes manifest at a neighborhood ball where Darcy
does nothing to conceal his apparent sense of superiority and contempt for the company present. Wickham reveals to her that Darcy's
father (who had been Wickham's godfather) had bequeathed a parish
to Wickham, as he was destined to enter the church. Wickham then
falsely discloses that Darcy, out of pride and jealousy, rescinded his father's promise, thereby forcing Wickham to enter the military.

In many ways, Darcy and Elizabeth are equals—both vastly superior in intellect and wit to their friends and kin. In the scene where
Darcy first proposes to Elizabeth and she turns him down, a reversal of
their usual pattern takes place. Elizabeth is prideful and Darcy preju-
diced. In perhaps the most disagreeably obnoxious proposal in literature, Darcy asks Elizabeth for her hand in marriage, despite her social
inferiority. She refuses, accusing him of breaking up the relationship
between Mr. Bingley and her sister Jane, and charging him with in-
justice to Mr. Wickham.

Note here the similarities in character that presage the inevitability
that the two will get together. Elizabeth matches Darcy's pride when
he tells her of the great sacrifice he is making in proposing. She has the
self-esteem to reject him, despite his advantages of wealth and family.

He accuses her of pride, telling her she would not be so adamant
"had not your pride been hurt by my honest confession." She accuses
him of prejudice when he divulges the obstacles he had to overcome
in proposing because of her degrading family. Both are guilty of pride
and prejudice—sometimes mirroring each other in a "birds of a
feather" pattern—usually appearing as opposites who supposedly do
not complement each other.

Can these characters who are constantly locking horns and misperceiving each other find true happiness? Just as Wickham's false confession helped spin the web of deceit that keep the two apart, Darcy's true confession is a catalyst in clarifying his character, paving the way toward transparency and intimacy.

The next morning following Elizabeth's refusal, Darcy hands her a letter as she is out walking. He reveals how Wickham never intended to enter the church, squandering money that Darcy gave him in idleness and dissipation, and even trying to elope with Darcy's sister to get her fortune and take revenge on him. Elizabeth realizes how willing she was to accept Wickham's story—not taking into account the social inappropriateness in Regency manners of a stranger revealing such intimacies to another. She progresses on her voyage of self-discovery when she acknowledges her own pride. She realizes it is important to look beyond appearances. This lesson is further brought home when she visits the gorgeous estate of Pemberley House, Darcy's home. Elizabeth hears the extravagant praise heaped on Darcy by Mrs. Reynolds, the housekeeper, who comments on his gentleness, generosity, and devotion to his sister.

Each incident—the letter, the housekeeper's evaluation of Darcy's character, and finally Darcy's rescue into respectability of Elizabeth's capricious sister, Lydia, who has run away with Wickham—corrects Elizabeth's misperceptions of Darcy. When Elizabeth tells Darcy that Lydia has run off with Wickham, he is very sympathetic. She can no longer hide the truth from herself—she loves him. And when she discovers that Darcy paid Wickham's debts and bought him a commission in the army in return for his agreement to marry Lydia (who would otherwise be "ruined"), Elizabeth's admiration of Darcy and her gratitude to him grow ever stronger.

Misunderstandings give way to transparency as confessions clarify character. Yet more than transparency takes place. True, we see Darcy's kind, caring, generous side emerge, and we see Elizabeth's contrition and remorse regarding her pride and prejudice. *Pride and Prejudice*, however, is also a novel about transformation. Darcy becomes outwardly humble and agreeable through his love for Elizabeth. Elizabeth is also humbled as she is forced to admit to herself that she is not as insightful as she thought she was and that her pride could have been her downfall.

One way to display our love is to allow our partners to know us. Because Elizabeth and Darcy are similar to each other in intellect and outlook—soulmates in today's parlance—disclosure is more likely to develop and flourish in such an atmosphere of mirrored appreciation.

Lovers need each other to take on particular roles as confidants— sometimes mutual ("we are in this together, we'll support each other and solve this problem"), sometimes complementary ("you are more vulnerable right now, I will help get you out of the dilemma wrought by the confession"). Acceptance of each lover's right to have problems or a secret life apart from the beloved enhances the closeness between partners following confession. When rigid rules (e.g., never allow vulnerability; never burden me with your problems) take the place of flexibility, confessions can become risky business that threatens the relationship.

Confessions strictly cast in stereotyped roles diminish the relationship. For example, when it is understood that the vulnerable partner always confesses to the strong partner who arrives at a solution, mutual resentments tend to build up over time, eroding the relationship. Another unsatisfying match is the philandering, alcoholic husband confessing to the long-suffering wife who submits to her fate in a never-changing sadistic-masochistic duet. In such confessions, the partners cannot break the yoke of rigid past relationships and move beyond them.

Confession can add newness to the relationship and demystify it. Confession to a romantic partner offers hope that the beloved will heal a wound inflicted by unempathic or downright cruel parents, for example. This is one reason why lovers are low-risk confidants when the secret is shrouded in the mists of the past. It is the secrets *directly* concerned with the beloved that involve the greatest danger of repercussion.

Transformation and Transcendence

When we fall in love, we risk opening ourselves up and becoming more vulnerable to our lovers. The beloved, like a therapist, at times represents a new edition of past relationships—what Freud viewed as a "refinding." At the same time, the sheer newness of the relationship provides healing possibilities enabling us to transcend past resistances to disclosure in an atmosphere of openness and transformation.

Psychoanalyst Christopher Bollas speaks of the "transformational object" that we seek to surrender to as a medium that alters us. We search for others who can revitalize us, who can guide us in new ways of experiencing the world. We may optimize confession in the presence of a new, less judgmental, more insightful confidant.

The film *Casablanca* addresses the transformational qualities of relationships that are tested and then enhanced through disclosure. Casablanca in December 1941 is swarming with refugees desperate for exit visas. The petty crook Ugarte has murdered two German couriers and stolen the letters of transit they carried. He asks Rick, owner of Rick's Café Américain, to keep them until he can sell them.

Rick is upset by the entrance of Victor Laszlo and his beautiful companion, Ilsa Lund. A flashback reveals that Ilsa and Rick had been lovers in Paris and had planned to leave together when the Germans invaded. However, Ilsa stayed in Paris, sending Rick a mysterious note saying they could never see each other again.

When Ilsa runs into Rick in Casablanca, she confesses that she still loves him, explaining that she was married to Victor during the Parisian affair but thought that he was dead. The day they were to leave she learned he was alive. She had to abandon Rick to help her husband—a leader of the French Resistance.

Ilsa's sacrifice for the greater good of humankind is, of course, paralleled in Rick's sacrifice of his relationship with her—a sign of true intimacy and caring—at the end of the film. In that closing scene, Rick tells Captain Renault to arrest Victor when he gives him the letters. But when Captain Renault tries to do so, Rick at gunpoint tells him to take them all to the airport. Rick puts a teary-eyed Ilsa on the plane with Victor, who has the letters of transit.

When Ilsa confesses her love for Rick, the two are again drawn closer together. Rick observes to Ilsa, "The problems of three little people don't amount to a hill of beans in this crazy world." The "hill of beans" speech appeals to our noblest principles and aspirations. Rick's sacrifice—letting go of the person he loves the most for the wartime effort—ennobles him. Further, Rick's love for Ilsa, renewed and strengthened through her confession, results in a profound self-transformation. He moves from bitter self-pity marked primarily by self-interest ("I'm the only cause I'm interested in") to commitment to the fight against fascism.

We are forever attempting to strike a balance between seeking after confidants and deriving autonomy from them. Confession dramatizes this conflict. If we share our secrets with another, we wonder whether we will feel closer to the confidant or be ridiculed and abandoned. *Consuming Confessions* presents us with many examples of how the need to take someone into our confidence is an antidote to loneliness and isolation. In risking making ourselves known, confession creates a bond between the discloser and the confessor joining each to the other in a remarkably close union. Through mutuality and caring, each partner can be revitalized and transformed on the confessional journey.

Epilogue

The Power of Confessions

CONFESSIONS have consumed me for the past fifteen years. My initial fascination with the proliferation of confidants in our society—from priests and therapists to the strangers on our travels—turned to an exploration of the effect confession has upon each of us, almost daily.

Confessions concern spiritual, psychological, and social aspects of our being. When Charles Borromeo instituted the confessional in the Roman Catholic Church in the sixteenth century, the life history and individual psychology of each believer suddenly took on new importance. Today, many people yearn to go beyond ritual to achieve connection and redemption through confession.

How we develop a sense of intimate connection varies enormously from person to person. This is especially true in our contemporary world where there is a compulsion to confess through multiple channels. In the past, confession almost always involved talking to one another or revealing oneself through diaries or letters. As our sense of community and opportunities for face-to-face contact with friends and family diminishes, new confessional modes, like e-mail, are gaining in popularity. Relationships formed over computers can be remarkably stable, ongoing, and sometimes permanent, evidenced by the first crop of "computer-generated" marriages.

Leonardo da Vinci went to great lengths to make his notes illegible or cryptic, inventing his own shorthand and spelling, and combining and

dividing words according to his own system. To further ensure secrecy, he wrote characters backwards, requiring a mirror to decipher
them.

We can only surmise why this genius felt the need to hide so
much, especially material that could greatly benefit humankind. Perhaps Leonardo went overboard in his need for secrecy, but there is
much to be gained by not disclosing everything. It is healthy and fit-
ting to maintain a zone of privacy—a part of ourselves known only to
ourselves.

In *Consuming Confessions*, I neither glorify nor advocate indiscriminate disclosure—just the opposite. I contend that journalistic snoop-
ing and media exposés have cheapened and trivialized confession.
Confession, sincerely offered and lovingly received, is one of the few
routes we possess to attain authenticity and achieve intimacy. As a
voyage of self-discovery, confession can lead to nothing less than what
the ancients called "cure of the soul."

Confessions give us a chance to tell our story—to make ourselves
known. Too often we feel at sea, overwhelmed with too many stories
that clash, collide with, or contradict each other. Confessions give us a
rare opportunity to stay with the disclosure of a particular secret or secret part of ourselves over time. When we choose a special
confidant—therapist, lover, or friend—for certain secrets, we ideally
find a kindred spirit who can help us gain more meaning and coher-
ence in our lives.

For most people, the word *confessor* is synonymous with priest. In our
time, however, many people have moved away from confidants who
are institutionalized authority figures to those who are more mutually
disclosing. These latter confidants are not afraid to show their own
vulnerabilities and are, thereby, often perceived as more empathic and
human than stereotypical dispassionate clerics. For many, the ideal
confidant is one who is a mutual partner in dialogue—someone who
is there with us and for us throughout the confessional journey.

We were not meant to be loners. Confession is a soul-to-soul
communion that breaks through the barriers of fear to reveal our
authentic selves. We can "come clean," laying bare vital parts of our-

selves, freed from our tyrannical pasts and the armor of our habitual personas.

People will always use quick-fix confessors—cab drivers, strangers on their travels—to get a troublesome secret off their chests and find a measure of relief. Yet confessions which are truly meaningful and long-lasting are psychological and spiritual journeys that touch some of the deepest aspects of our being, while connecting us to our fellow humans.

Confession is a journey, always beginning with risk and often ending in redemption, that can change the entire course of our lives. The risks involved in revealing ourselves are real: abandonment, loss of love, censure, and blackmail. Yet the rewards are great—understanding and acceptance of us as whole people with all our foibles, vices, and weak spots. The journey may take place within ourselves or can catapult us into a riveting external adventure. We only know our point of departure. We do not clearly see our destination.

When we embark on an inner journey, we enter into the underworld of our own dark natures. Forbidden as well as transcendent aspects of ourselves emerge in the process. Such confessions are self-reflective journeys of discovery. In coming to terms with the confession, we arrive at an expanded view of ourselves which is now seen as not so dreadful or catastrophic after all.

Outer confessional journeys encourage us to present ourselves to the world as we really are. These are heroic travels in which we risk seemingly everything to be authentic. For contemporary gay men and lesbians, "coming out" is one such journey. Disclosing one's addiction to the world is another. Our engagement with confidants who offer love, acceptance, and guidance fuels us to risk disclosures that enable us to transform rather than relive the past.

Albert Camus said that travel brings us back to ourselves. We often rediscover lost or disowned parts of ourselves on the confessional journey. When we welcome *all* parts of our psyche in a mindful, receptive way, we can flow with the confession and see where it takes us, instead of trying to fit it into a prepackaged, rule-bound itinerary.

There are travelers who assiduously visit the sites listed in their guidebooks, packing in as much as possible within the narrowest time parameters. They frenetically see everything, but do not take the time to make the experience part of their being. Other travelers meander here and there, discovering delights not mentioned in the guidebooks and enjoying every moment.

The confessional journey lends itself more readily to the nonprogrammed style of travel. The more we let ourselves be with the confidant in a free-flowing way, the more we can take in the experience as part of our mental terrain. The therapist's office, the confessional, and even the beauty salon all have their props and rituals that ground us, lending safety and familiarity to the confessional journey.

Guideposts are useful, yet they only go so far. When we have faith in ourselves and in our confidants, we can explore our inner lives in a more spontaneous, relaxed way.

Confessions enable us to become time travelers, bringing ourselves into the past through memory and then sweeping those secrets into the present through disclosure. We can heal the secret wounds of the past by opening ourselves up to confidants who value and appreciate us—all of us. When heart and mind work together as we confess, we can truly seek to become whole people instead of divided, alienated selves.

Emily Dickinson, in her 1876 poem, put it this way:

> The Heart is the Capital of the Mind——
> The Mind is a single State——
> The Heart and the Mind together make
> A single Continent——
>
> One——is the Population——
> Numerous enough——
> This ecstatic Nation
> Seek——it is Yourself.

Pascal believed that it is the heart that finds its reason in revelation. If confession is to be a healing experience, both the heart and the mind must be involved. Our past secrets are remembered in a new way in the presence of loving others; meaning, hitherto hidden, is unveiled.

Think for a moment of the inspirational mythic heroine Penelope, the wife of Ulysses, who waited twenty years for her husband's return from the Trojan War. After a while, suitors gathered from far and near to pursue her in matrimony. When it became doubtful, even to Penelope herself, that Ulysses could still be alive, let alone that he would return, she promised to choose one suitor from among the many when she had completed the robe she was weaving. As a faithful wife, she adopted the following strategy: during the day, she worked on the robe; at night, she unraveled what she had woven by day.

Penelope never lost her hope or faith that her husband would return, no matter how many doubters sought to "set her straight." Like Penelope, we must not abandon the hope that when we are feeling most lost, hidden, and disowned secrets or secret parts of ourselves will return to us if we have the courage to risk revealing ourselves.

Penelope perpetually weaves her robe, but it is never done. So are our lives works in progress in which the process—the journey itself—is as important as the destination.

We have come to our journey's end. Yet our ends are also our beginnings. May each of your confessional journeys be marked by growth, enlightenment, and love.

References

Aeschylus. (1953). *Oresteia*. (R. Lattimore, Trans.). Chicago: University of Chicago Press.

Ainsworth, M. D. S. (1969). Object relations, dependency and attachment: A theoretical review of child developmental issues. *Child Development, 40*, 969–1026.

Albee, E. (1973). *Who's afraid of Virginia Woolf?* New York: Pocket Books. (Original work published 1962)

American Psychological Association. (1992). *Ethical principles of psychologists and code of conduct*. Washington, DC: Author.

Anthelme, P. (Author), Talori, G., & Archibald, W. (Screenwriters), & Hitchcock, A. (Director). (1952). *I confess* [Film]. Hollywood, CA: Warners.

Anzieu, D. (1979). The sound image of the self. *International Review of Psychoanalysis, 6* (1), 23–36.

Argyle, M. (1969). *Social interaction*. New York: Aldine-Atherton.

Aristotle. (1938). *The poetics*. (W. H. Fyte, Trans.). New York: Putnam.

Aristotle. (1955). *The ethics of Aristotle*. (J. Thomson, Trans.). New York: Penguin.

Artaud, A. (1976). *Antonin Artaud. Selected writings*. (S. Sontag, Ed.). New York: Farrar, Straus & Giroux.

Atwood, G. (1978). On the origins and dynamics of messianic salvation fantasies. *International Review of Psychoanalysis, 5*, 85–96.

Austen, J. (1956). *Pride and prejudice*. Boston: Riverside. (Original work published 1813)

Azar, B. (1994, November). Research plumbs why the 'talking cure' works. *APA Monitor, 25* (11), 24.

Bachelard, G. (1964). *The poetics of space*. (M. Jolas, Trans.). Boston: Beacon Press. (Original work published 1958)

Balint, M. (1979). *The basic fault.* New York: Brunner-Mazel.

Becker, E. (1973). *The denial of death.* New York: The Free Press.

Benedict, R. (1977). *The chrysanthemum and the sword.* London: Routledge & Kegan.

Benjamin, J. (1988). *The bonds of love: Psychoanalysis, feminism and the problem of domination.* New York: Pantheon.

Bergman, I. (Screenwriter & Director). (1961). *Through a glass darkly* [Film].

Bergman, I. (Screenwriter & Director). (1966). *Persona* [Film].

Bergman, I. (Screenwriter & Director). (1973). *Scenes from a marriage* [Film adaptation].

Blake, W. (1974). The marriage of heaven and hell. In A. Kazin (Ed.), *The portable Blake* (pp. 249–266). New York: Penguin Books. (Original work published 1903)

Bollas, C. (1987). The transformational object. In *The shadow of the object: Psychoanalysis of the unthought known* (pp. 13–29). London: Free Association Books.

Bonhoeffer, D. (1981). Confession and communion. In N. O'Gorman (Ed.), *Perfected steel/Terrible crystal* (pp. 201–207). New York: Seabury Press. (Original work published 1954)

Bowlby, J. (1969). *Attachment and loss: Vol. 1. Attachment.* New York: Basic Books.

Brandon, S. G. F. (1970). Redemption in ancient Egypt and early Christianity. In R. J. Werblowsky & C. J. Bleeker (Eds.), *Types of redemption* (pp. 36–45). Leiden: E. J. Brill.

Brown, R. M. (1973). *Rubyfruit jungle.* New York: Bantam Books.

Buber, M. (1937). *I and thou.* Edinburgh: T. & T. Clark.

Budge, E. A. W. (Ed.). (1965). *The Egyptian book of the dead.* New York: Dover Publications.

Bugenthal, J. (1976). *The search for existential identity.* San Francisco: Jossey-Bass.

Buhrmester, D., & Furman, W. (1987). The development of companionship and intimacy. *Child Development, 58* (4), 1101–1113.

Bulfinch, T. (1978). *Bulfinch's mythology.* New York: Avenel.

Byron, G. (1990). *Byron. A self-portrait in his own words. Letter and diaries 1788 to 1824.* (P. Quennel, Ed.). Oxford: Oxford University Press.

Campbell, J. (1973). *The hero with a thousand faces.* Princeton, NJ: Princeton University Press. (Original work published 1949)

Campbell, J. (1988). *The power of myth.* New York: Doubleday.

Camus, A. (1963). *Notebooks, 1935–1942.* New York: Knopf.

Camus, A. (1956). *The fall.* New York: Vintage Books.

Cicero. (1982). *On the good life.* (M. Grant, Trans.). New York: Penguin Books.

Clark, R. T. (1959). *Myth and symbol in ancient Egypt.* London: Thames & Hudson.

Coles, R. (1986). *The moral life of children.* Boston: Atlantic Monthly Press.

Cottle, T. (1980). *Children's secrets.* Reading, MA: Addison-Wesley.

Csikszentmihalyi, M. (1990). *Flow: The psychology of optimal experience.* New York: Harper & Row.

Cushman, P. (1990). Why the self is empty: Toward a historically situated psychology. *American Psychologist, 15,* 599–611.

Dali, S. (1942). *The secret life of Salvador Dali.* New York: Dial Press.

Dante, A. (1954). *The inferno.* (J. Ciardi, Trans.). New York: Mentor Books. (Original work written 1306)

Descartes, R. (1969). *The essential Descartes.* (L. Bair, Trans.). New York: American Library. (Original work published 1628)

Dewey, J. (1977). Human beings are not machines. In N. Capaldi & L. Navia (Eds.), *Journeys through philosophy* (pp. 455–462). Buffalo: Prometheu. (Original work published 1896)

Dickens, C. (1950). *Great expectations.* New York: Dutton. (Original work published 1861)

Dickinson, E. (1961). The heart is the capital of the mind. In T. Johnson (Ed.), *Final harvest: Emily Dickinson's poems.* Boston: Little, Brown & Company. (Original work written 1876)

Dore, J. (1975). Holophrases, speech acts and language universals. *Journal of Child Language, 2,* 21–40.

Dostoyevsky, F. (1927). *Crime and punishment.* (C. Garnett, Trans.). New York: Grosset & Dunlap. (Original work published 1866)

Dostoyevsky, F. (1957). *The brothers Karamazov.* (C. Garnett, Trans.). New York: Signet. (Original work published 1881)

Dumas, A. (1961). *The three musketeers.* New York: Washington Square Press. (Original work published 1844)

Du Maurier, D. (1938). *Rebecca.* London: V. Gollancz.

Eagle, M. (1987). *Recent developments in psychoanalysis. A critical evaluation.* Cambridge, MA: Harvard University Press.

Eliade, M. (1958). *Rites and symbols of initiatiation. The mysteries of birth and rebirth.* (W. Trask, Trans.). New York: Harper Torchbooks.

Eliot, G. (1981). *Adam Bede.* New York: Signet Classics. (Original work published 1859)

Eliot, G. (1965). *The mill on the floss.* New York: Signet. (Original work published 1860)

Eliot, T. S. (1971). *Four quartets.* New York: Harvest/HBJ Books. (Original work published 1943)

Emerson, R. W. (1965). Illusion. In W. H. Gilman (Ed.), *Selected writings of Ralph Waldo Emerson* (pp. 402–412). New York: Signet Classics. (Original work published 1857)

Epstein, J., Epstein, P., & Koch, H. (Screenwriters) & Curtis, M. (Director). (1942). *Casablanca* [Film]. Hollywood, CA: Turner Entertainment Company.

Erikson, E. (1959). Identity and the life cycle. *Psychological Issues, 1* (1). (Monograph no. 1).

Erikson, E. (1962). *Young man Luther: A study in psychoanalysis and history.* New York: Norton.

Euripides (1972). *Orestes and other plays.* (P. Vellacott, Trans.). New York: Penguin.

Fairbairn, R. (1954). *An object relations theory of the personality.* New York: Basic Books.

Favazzo, A. (1989, March/April). Little murders. *The Sciences,* 5–7.

Ferenczi, S. (1955). The principles of relaxation and neocatharsis. In *Final contributions to the problems and methods of psycho-analysis* (pp. 108–125). New York: Basic Books. (Original work published 1930)

Ferenczi, S., & Rank, O. (1925). *The development of psychoanalysis.* New York: Nervous and Mental Disease Publishing Company.

Flaubert, G. (1957). *Madame Bovary.* (F. Steegmuller, Trans.). New York: Modern Library. (Original work published 1856)

Foucault, M. (1980). *History of sexuality* (Vol. 1). New York: Vintage Books.

Frank, A. (1952). *Anne Frank: The diary of a young girl.* New York: Doubleday.

Freud, S. (1953). Fragment of an analysis of a case of hysteria. In J. Strachey (Ed. and Trans.), *The standard edition of the complete psychological works of Sigmund Freud* (Vol. 7, pp. 3–122). London: Hogarth Press. (Original work published 1905)

Freud, S. (1959). Family romances. In J. Strachey (Ed. and Trans.), *op. cit.* (Vol. 9, pp. 237–241). London: Hogarth Press. (Original work published 1908)

Freud, S. (1953). Recommendations to physicians practicing psychoanalysis. In J. Strachey (Ed. and Trans.), *op. cit.* (Vol. 12, pp. 109–120). London: Hogarth Press. (Original work published 1912)

Freud, S. (1958). Observations of transference-love. (Further recommendations on the technique of psycho-analysis III). In J. Strachey

(Ed. and Trans.), *op. cit.* (Vol. 12, pp. 157–173). (Original work published 1915)

Freud, S. (1961). The ego and the id. In J. Strachey (Ed. and Trans.), *op. cit.* (Vol. 19, pp. 3–66). (Original work published 1923)

Freud, S. (1985).*The complete letters of Sigmund Freud to Wilhelm Fliess, 1877–1904.* (J. Masson, Trans.) Cambridge, MA: Belknap Press/ Harvard University Press.

Freud, S., & Breuer, J. (1966). *Studies on hysteria.* New York: Avon. (Original work published 1895)

Freud, S., & Ferenczi, S. (1993). *The correspondence of Sigmund Freud and Sandor Ferenczi* (Vol. 1). (P. Hoffer, Trans.). Cambridge, MA: Belknap Press/Harvard University Press. (Original work written 1908–1915)

Frost, R. (1947). Directive. In O. Williams (Ed.), *Master poems of the English language.* New York: Washington Square Press.

Gilligan, C. (1982). *In a different voice.* Cambridge, MA: Harvard University Press.

Goffman, E. (1959). *The presentation of self in everyday life.* New York: Anchor Books.

Goffman, E. (1963). *Behavior in public places; notes on the social organization of gatherings.* New York: Free Press of Glencoe.

Goleman, D. (1985). *Vital lies, simple truths.* New York: Simon & Shuster.

Goleman, D. (1995). *Emotional intelligence.* New York: Bantam Books.

Greeley, A. (1989). *Myths of religion.* New York: Warner Books.

Green, H. (1964). *I never promised you a rose garden.* New York: Rinehart & Winston.

Greenberg, I. (1988). *The Jewish way.* New York: Summit Books.

Greene, G. (1980). *Ways of escape.* Toronto: Lester & Orpen Dennys Limited.

Grotstein, J. (1981). *Splitting and projective identification.* New York: Jason Aronson.

Hardy, T. (1992). *Tess of the d'Urbervilles.* New York: Bantam Classic. (Original work published 1891)

Havens, L. (1993). Is there a psychological real? *Contemporary Psychoanalysis, 29* (4), 613–627.

Hawthorne, N. (1962). *The scarlet letter.* Columbus, OH: Ohio State University Press. (Original work published 1850)

Hermans, H., Kempen, H., & van Loon, R. (1992). The dialogical self: Beyond individualism and rationalism. *American Psychologist, 47* (1), 23–33.

Herrera, H. (1983). *Frida: A biography of Frida Kahlo.* New York: Perennial Library.

Hesse, H. (1966). *Demian.* (M. Roloff & M. Lebeck, Trans.). New York: Bantam Books. (Original work published 1925)

Hillman, J. (1989). *A blue fire.* (T. Moore, Ed.). New York: Harper & Row.

Horner, M. (1972). Toward an understanding of achievement-related conflicts in women. *Journal of Social Issues, 28* (2), 157–175.

Ibsen, H. (1970). Ghosts. (R. Fjelde, Trans.). In *Four major plays* (Vol. 2, pp. 41–114). New York: Signet Classics. (Original work published 1881)

Ichheiser, G. (1970). *Appearances and realities.* San Francisco: Jossey Bass.

James, W. (1963). *The varieties of religious experience.* New Hyde Park, NY: University Books. (Original work published 1902)

James, W. (1961). *The selected letters of William James.* (E. Hardwick, Ed.). New York: Anchor Books.

James, W. (1975). *The will to believe and other essays in popular philosophy.* Cambridge, MA: Harvard University Press.

Jourard, S. (1964). *The transparent self.* Princeton, NJ: Van Nostrand.

Jung, C. G. (1933). *Modern man in search of a soul.* New York: Harvest Books.

Jung, C. G. (1963). *Memories, dreams, reflections.* London: Kegan Paul.

Kafka, F. (1979). Letter to his father. In M. Kowal (Ed.), *The basic Kafka* (pp. 186–236). (Original work published 1919)

Kant, I. (1927). *The critique of practical reason and other works in the theory of ethics.* (T. Abbott, Trans.). London: Longmans, Green.

Karr, M. (1995). *The liars' club.* New York: Viking.

Kierkegaard, S. (1959). *Journals.* (A. Dru, Ed.). New York: Harper Torchbooks. (Original work published 1839)

Kierkegaard, S. (1944). *The concept of dread.* (W. Lowrie, Trans.). Princeton, NJ: Princeton University Press. (Original work published 1844)

Klein, M. (1975). *Envy and gratitude.* New York: Delta.

Kohlberg, L. (1969). Stage and sequence: The cognitive-developmental approach to socialization. In D. Goslin (Ed.), *Handbook of socialization theory and research* (pp. 347–489). Chicago: Rand McNally.

Kohut, H. (1984) *How does analysis cure?* Chicago: University of Chicago Press.

La Barre, W. (1964). Confession as cathartic therapy in American Indian tribes. In A. Kiev (Ed.), *Magic, faith and healing* (pp. 36–49). New York: The Free Press.

Laing, R. D. (1990). *The divided self.* New York: Penguin. (Original work published 1960)

Lawrence, D. H. (1993). Healing. In F. W. Roberts & V. de Sola Pinto (Eds.), *The complete poems of D. H. Lawrence* (p. 826). New York: Penguin.

Lazarus, R. (1991). *Emotion and adaptation.* New York: Oxford University Press.

Lichtenstein, H. (1977). *The dilemma of human identity.* New York: Jason Aronson.

Lifton, R. J. (1986). *The Nazi doctors.* New York: Basic Books.

Lucretius. (1924). *On the nature of things.* (A. Bailey, Trans.). Oxford: Clarendon Press.

Mahler, M. (1968). *On human symbiosis and the vicissitudes of individuation.* New York: International Universities Press.

Malle, L. (Screenwriter & Director). (1987). *Au revoir les enfants* [Film].

May, R. (1973). *Love and will.* New York: Delta. (Original work published 1969)

McCarthy, M. (1957). *Memories of a Catholic girlhood.* New York: Harcourt, Brace, Jovanovich.

McGovern, J. (Screenwriter) & Bird, A. (Director). (1995). *Priest* [Film]. Hollywood, CA: Miramax.

McLuhan, M. (1964). *Understanding media.* New York: McGraw-Hill.

Meares, R. (1976). The secret. *Psychiatry, 39,* 258–265.

Meares, R., & Orlay, W. (1988). On self-boundary: A study of the development of the concept of secrecy. *British Journal of Medical Psychology, 61* (4), 305–316.

Miller, Alice. (1981). *Prisoners of childhood.* New York: Basic Books.

Miller, Alice. (1983). *For your own good.* New York: Farrar, Straus & Giroux.

Miller, Arthur. (1957). Death of a salesman. In *Collected plays* (pp. 130–222). New York: Viking Press.

Modell, A. (1992). The private self and private space. *Annual of Psychoanalysis, 20,* 1–14.

Montaigne, M. (1965). *The complete works of Montaigne.* (D. M. Frame, Trans.). London: Hamish Hamilton.

Moore, B. (1983). *The lonely passion of Judith Hearne.* Boston: Atlantic-Little, Brown.

Mowrer, O. H. (1961). *The crisis in psychiatry and religion.* Princeton, NJ: Van Nostrand Company.

Murdoch, I. (1975). *A word child.* New York: Penguin Books.

Nietzsche, F. (1967). *Thus spake Zarathustra.* New York: Heritage. (Original work published 1885)

Nietzsche, F. (1956). *The genealogy of morals.* (F. Golffing, Trans.). Garden

City, New York: Doubleday & Company. (Original work published 1887)

Nietzsche, F. (1971). *Nietzsche. A self portrait from his letters.* (P. Fuss & H. Shapiro, Eds. and Trans.). Cambridge, MA: Harvard University Press.

O'Brien, E. (1987). *Johnny I hardly knew you.* New York: Penguin Books. (Original work published 1977)

Okano, K. (1994). Shame and social phobia: A transcultural viewpoint. *Bulletin of the Menninger Clinic, 58* (3), 323–328.

Oldenburg, R. (1989). *The great good place.* New York: Paragon House.

O'Neill, E. (1940). *The iceman cometh.* New York: Random House.

O'Neill, E. (1955). *Long day's journey into night.* New Haven: Yale University Press.

Pennebaker, J. (1990). *Opening up. The healing power of confiding in others.* New York: William Morrow & Company.

Person, E. (1988). *Dreams of love and fateful encounters.* New York: Penguin Books.

Piaget, J. (1932). *The moral judgment of the child.* New York: The Free Press.

Piaget, J. (1952). *The origins of intelligence in children.* New York: International Universities Press.

Pinter, H. (1978). *Betrayal.* New York: Grove Press.

Plato. (1932). *The republic.* (B. Jowett, Trans.). New York: Random House.

Plato. (1932). *The symposium.* (B. Jowett, Trans.). New York: Random House.

Plato. (1952). *The Phaedrus.* (R. Hackforth, Trans.). Cambridge: Cambridge University Press.

Proust, M. (1981). *Remembrance of things past.* New York: Random House. (Original work written 1913–1927)

Racine, J. (1986). *Phaedra.* (R. Wilbur, Trans.). New York: Harcourt, Brace, Jovanovich. (Original work published 1677)

Rank, O. (1973). *The trauma of birth.* New York: Harper Torchbooks. (Original work published 1929)

Rank, O. (1932). *Art and artist; creative urge and personality development.* (C. F. Atkinson, Trans.). New York: Knopf.

Reich, W. (1972). *Character analysis.* New York: Farrar, Straus & Cudahy. (Original work published 1949)

Reik, T. (1959). *The compulsion to confess.* New York: Farrar, Straus & Cudahy.

Rentrop, C., & Karmel, R. (1993, Summer). Vicissitudes of transference love and sublimation: Sabina Spielrein, Carl Jung, and Sigmund Freud. *Psychologist Psychoanalyst, 13* (3), p. 30.

Rich, A. (1979). *On lies, secrets and silence. Selected prose 1966–1978.* New York: Norton.

Rogers, C. (1961). *On becoming a person.* Boston: Houghton Mifflin.

Rubin, L. (1983). *Intimate strangers: Men and women together.* New York: Harper & Row.

Rubin, L. (1985). *Just friends.* New York: Perennial Library.

Saint Augustine. (1961). *Confessions.* (R. S. Pine-Coffin, Trans.). New York: Penguin.

Sampson, E. E. (1988). The debate on individualism: Indigenous psychologies of the individual and their role in personal and societal functioning. *American Psychologist, 43,* 15–22.

Sandler, J., & Rosenblatt, B. (1962). The concept of the representational world. *Psychoanalytic Study of the Child, 17,* 128–145.

Sartre, J. P. (1949). *Existentialism.* New York: Philosophical Library.

Sartre, J. P. (1966). *The words.* New York: Fawcett Crest.

Schafer, R. (1976). *A new language for psychoanalysis.* New Haven: Yale University Press.

Schafer, R. (1983). *The analytic attitude.* New York: Basic Books.

Scheibe, K. (1979). *Mirrors, masks, lies, and secrets.* New York: Praeger.

Schneider, K., & May, R. (1995). *The psychology of existence. An integrative, clinical perspective.* New York: McGraw-Hill.

Schulberg, B. (Screenwriter), & Kazan, E. (Director). (1954). *On the waterfront* [Film]. Hollywood, CA: Columbia Pictures.

Searles, H. (1979). *Countertransference and related subjects. Selected papers.* New York: International Universities Press.

Shakespeare, W. (1975). The life and death of King Richard lll. In *The complete works of William Shakespeare* (pp. 627–669). New York: Avenel. (Original work published 1597)

Shakespeare, W. (1958). *Hamlet.* New York: Washington Square Press. (Original work published 1603)

Shakespeare, W. (1966). *Othello.* Waltham, MA: Blaisdell. (Original work published 1622)

Shakespeare, W. (1959). *Macbeth.* New York: Pocket Books. (Original work published 1623)

Shaw, G. B. (1919). *Mrs. Warren's profession.* In *Plays pleasant and unpleasant* (Vol. 1, pp 165–245). New York: Brentano. (Original work published 1894)

Shengold, L. (1989). *Soul murder. The effects of childhood abuse and deprivation.* New York: Fawcett Columbine.

Simmel, G. (1950). Secrecy. In K. Wolff (Ed.), *The sociology of Georg Simmel* (pp. 330–344). New York: The Free Press.

Soderbergh, S. (Screenwriter and Director). (1989). *Sex, lies, and videotape* [Film].

Soderbergh, S. (1990). *Sex, lies, and videotape.* New York: Perennial Library.

Sophocles. (1982). *Oedipus the king.* In M. Hadras (Ed.), *Greek drama.* New York: Bantam Books.

Steiner, J. (1985). Turning a blind eye: The cover for Oedipus. *International Review of Psychoanalysis, 12* (2), 161–172.

Stern, D. (1985). *The interpersonal world of the infant.* New York: Basic Books.

Stolorow, R., & Atwood, G. (1979). *Faces in a cloud.* New York: Jason Aronson.

Sullivan, H. S. (1953). *The interpersonal world of psychiatry.* New York: Norton.

Suzuki, D. S. (1956). *Zen Buddhism.* New York: Doubleday.

Tavris, C. (1984). *Anger: The misunderstood emotion.* New York: Touchstone Press.

Tillich, P. (1952). *The courage to be.* New Haven: Yale University Press.

Tolstoy, L. (1983). *Confession.* (D. Patterson, Trans.). New York: Norton. (Original work published 1882)

Tolstoy, L. (1975). The death of Ivan Ilyich. In *Leo Tolstoy. Short stories* (pp. 136–198). Moscow: Progress Publishers. (Original work published 1886)

Topper, M. (1987). The traditional Navajo medicine man: Therapist, counselor, and community leader. *Journal of Psychoanalytic Anthropology, 10* (3), 217–249.

Trevarthan, C. (1993). The self born in intersubjectivity: The psychology of an infant communicating. In U. Neisser (Ed.), *The perceived self: Ecological and interpersonal sources of self-knowledge* (pp. 121–173). New York: Cambridge University Press.

Twain, M. (1940). *The adventures of Huckleberry Finn.* New York: Heritage Press. (Original work published 1885)

Tyler, A. (1985). *The accidental tourist.* New York: Knopf.

Tyler, A. (1991). *Saint maybe.* New York: Ivy Books.

Updike, J. (1985, September 2). Personal history: At war with my skin. *New Yorker,* 39–57.

Wallerstein, J., & Blakeslee, S. (1995). *The good marriage.* Boston: Houghton Mifflin.

Waring, E. M., & Chelune, G. (1983). Marital intimacy and self-disclosure. *Journal of Clinical Psychology, 39,* 183–190.

Wilkes, M., & Shuchman, M. (1988, October 2). Holy secrets. *The New York Times Magazine,* 57–58.

Wilner, W. (1982). Philosophical approaches to interpersonal intimacy. In M. Fisher & G. Stricker (Eds.), *Intimacy* (pp. 21–38). New York: Plenum.

Wilson, E. (1941). *The wound and the bow; seven studies in literature.* Boston: Houghton Mifflin.

Winnicott, D. (1964). *The child, the family, and the outside world.* New York: Penguin Books.

Winnicott, D. (1965). *The maturational processes and the facilitating environment.* New York: International Universities Press.

Woodward, K., & King, P. (1989, August 28). When a pastor turns seducer. *Newsweek,* 48–49.

Woolf, V. (1977). *The diary of Virginia Woolf: Volume 1, 1915–1919.* A. O. Bell (Ed.). New York: Harcourt, Brace, Jovanovich.

Woolf, V. (1985). *Moments of being.* (J. Schulkind, Ed.). New York: Harvest/HBJ Books.

About the author

SHARON HYMER, Ph.D., published her first work on the therapeutic nature of confession in 1982. She has appeared on national
television and radio programs, and has written articles for consumer
magazines. Dr. Hymer has published widely in the areas of victimol-
ogy, narcissism, art, the creative process, sex roles, and social change.
As a psychologist, she works extensively with couples and with survivors of child abuse. Dr. Hymer is also a psychology professor at New
York University. She lives in New York City.